SAME-SEX MARRIAGE

Selected Titles in ABC-CLIO's
CONTEMPORARY WORLD ISSUES
Series

American Families in Crisis, Jeffrey S. Turner
Animal Rights, Clifford J. Sherry
Climate Change, David L. Downie, Kate Brash, and
     Catherine Vaughan
Corporate Crime, Richard D. Hartley
DNA Technology, David E. Newton
Domestic Violence, Margi Laird McCue
Education in Crisis, Judith A. Gouwens
Energy Use Worldwide, Jaina L. Moan and Zachary A. Smith
Environmental Justice, David E. Newton
Gangs, Karen L. Kinnear
Gay and Lesbian Rights, David E. Newton
Global Organized Crime, Mitchel P. Roth
Globalization, Justin Ervin and Zachary A. Smith
Identity Theft, Sandra K. Hoffman and Tracy G. McGinley
Lobbying in America, Ronald J. Hrebenar and Bryson B. Morgan
Mainline Christians and U.S. Public Policy, Glenn H. Utter
Modern Sports Ethics, Angela Lumpkin
Nuclear Weapons and Nonproliferation, Sarah J. Diehl and
     James Clay Moltz
Obesity, Judith Stern and Alexandra Kazaks
Policing in America, Leonard A. Steverson
Renewable and Alternative Energy Resources, Zachary A. Smith and
     Katrina D. Taylor
Sentencing, Dean John Champion
Sexual Crime, Caryn E. Neumann
Sexual Health, David E. Newton
U.S. Border Security, Judith A. Warner
U.S. National Security, Cynthia A. Watson
U.S. Trade Issues, Alfred E. Eckes, Jr.
Waste Management, Jacqueline Vaughn

For a complete list of titles in this series, please visit
www.abc-clio.com.

Books in the Contemporary World Issues series address vital issues in today's society, such as genetic engineering, pollution, and biodiversity. Written by professional writers, scholars, and nonacademic experts, these books are authoritative, clearly written, up-to-date, and objective. They provide a good starting point for research by high school and college students, scholars, and general readers as well as by legislators, businesspeople, activists, and others.

Each book, carefully organized and easy to use, contains an overview of the subject, a detailed chronology, biographical sketches, facts and data and/or documents and other primary-source material, a directory of organizations and agencies, annotated lists of print and nonprint resources, and an index.

Readers of books in the Contemporary World Issues series will find the information they need to have a better understanding of the social, political, environmental, and economic issues facing the world today.

SAME-SEX MARRIAGE

A Reference Handbook

David E. Newton

**CONTEMPORARY
WORLD ISSUES**

ABC-CLIO

Santa Barbara, California • Denver, Colorado • Oxford, England

Copyright 2010 by ABC-CLIO, LLC

Library of Congress Cataloging-in-Publication Data

Newton, David E.
    Same-sex marriage : a reference handbook / David E. Newton.
        p. cm. — (Contemporary world issues)
    Includes bibliographical references and index.
    ISBN 978–1–59884–707–9 (hard copy : alk. paper) — ISBN 978–1–59884–708–6 (ebook)
    1. Same-sex marriage—Handbooks, manuals, etc. I. Title.
HQ1033.N494   2010
306.84′8—dc22   2010021774

ISBN: 978–1–59884–707–9
EISBN: 978–1–59884–708–6

14 13 12 11 10   1 2 3 4 5

This book is also available on the World Wide Web as an eBook.
Visit www.abc-clio.com for details.

ABC-CLIO, LLC
130 Cremona Drive, P.O. Box 1911
Santa Barbara, California 93116-1911

This book is printed on acid-free paper ∞

Manufactured in the United States of America

For Raliegh, Julie, and Roxanne
For all that has been in the past and all that is yet to come.

Contents

Preface, xiii

1   **Background and History**, 1
    Introduction: The Early Days, 1
    Same-Sex Relationships in History, 3
       Early Civilizations, 4
       China, 5
       Islam, 5
       American Indians, 6
       Greece and Rome, 7
       Some Cautions, 9
    Attitudes Toward Same-Sex Relationships
       in Western Culture, 11
    Sodomy Laws in the United States, 14
    The Gay and Lesbian Civil Rights Movement, 16
       Early Organizations, 17
       The Storm Breaks, 18
    Same-Sex Marriage in the United States, 22

2   **Problems, Controversies, and Solutions**, 31
    Introduction, 31
    Same-Sex Marriage in Judeo-Christian History, 33
    Rome and the Middle Ages, 36
    "Traditional Marriage," 42
    Nontraditional Marriage in Western Culture, 45
    Same-Sex Marriage: Arguments Pro and Con, 49
       Arguments in Opposition to Same-Sex Marriage, 49
       Arguments in Favor of Same-Sex Marriage, 61
    The Status of Same-Sex Marriage in the United States, 67
    Alternatives to Same-Sex Marriage, 70
    The Future of Same-Sex Marriage in the United States, 71

3 **Worldwide Perspective**, 81
Introduction, 81
Same-Sex Marriage in History, 82
Same-Sex Marriage: Recent Developments: Opposition, 84
Same-Sex Marriage: Recent Developments: Support, 87
 Western Europe, 87
 Other Regions of the World, 93
 Actions by Subnational Entities, 96
 Argentina, 98
 Mexico, 99
 Court Decisions on Same-Sex Unions, 100
Public Opinion about Same-Sex Marriage, 100
The Future of Same-Sex Marriage, 102

4 **Chronology, 111**

5 **Biographical Sketches, 133**
Barry T. Albin, 133
Jack Baker, 134
Bob Barr, 135
David Boies, 136
Mary Bonauto, 137
John E. Boswell, 138
Chris Bryant, 139
Charles J. Cooper, 140
Irwin Cotler, 141
Dennis Damon, 142
James Dobson, 142
William N. Eskridge, Jr., 144
Maggie Gallagher, 144
Julie Goodridge, 145
Phyllis Lyon, 146
Richard Malone, 147
Del Martin, 148
Michael McConnell, 149
Thomas S. Monson, 150
Marilyn Musgrave, 151
Jerry Nadler, 152
Theodore Olson, 153
David Paterson, 154
Jason West, 155

6　**Documents and Data**, 157
　　Legislation, 157
　　　　Federal Defense of Marriage Act (1996), 157
　　　　Alabama Marriage Protection Act (1998/2006), 158
　　　　Federal Marriage Amendment (2003), 159
　　　　Oregon Family Fairness Act (2007), 160
　　House Bill 2007, 160
　　　　Summary, 160
　　A Bill for an Act, 160
　　　　Arkansas Same-Sex Adoption Law (2008), 162
　　　　Uniting American Families Act (2009), 164
　　　　An Act to End Discrimination in Civil Marriage and Affirm
　　　　　　Religious Freedom (2009), 166
　　Reports, 168
　　　　United States General Accounting Office (2003), 168
　　　　Adoption by Same-Sex Couples (2009), 169
　　　　European Parliament Resolution of 14 January 2009 on the
　　　　　　Situation of Fundamental Rights in the European
　　　　　　Union 2004–8 (2009), 172
　　Court Cases, 174
　　　　E. B. v. France, Application No. 43546/02 (2008), 174
　　　　Goodridge v. Department of Public Health, 440 Mass. 309
　　　　　　(2003), 176
　　　　Lewis v. Harris, 908 A.2d 196 (2006), 180
　　　　In re: Gill (2006), 185
　　　　Varnum v. Brien, 763 N.W.2D 862 (IOWA 2009), 188
　　　　Kutil and Hess v. Blake, WL 1579493 (2009), 190
　　　　Order on Intervenor's Plea to the Jurisdiction (2009), 192
　　Data and Statistics, 194
　　　　Table 6.1: Same-Sex Marriages in Massachusetts (2009), 194
　　　　Table 6.2: Number of Same-Sex Couples in Legally
　　　　　　Recognized Relationships (2009), 195
　　　　Table 6.3: Same-Sex and Opposite-Sex Marriage Data from
　　　　　　the Netherlands (2009), 195
　　　　Table 6.4: Same-Sex and Opposite-Sex Marriage Data from
　　　　　　Belgium (2009), 196
　　　　Table 6.5: Divorce Rates by States, 2004–2007 (2009), 197

7　**Organizations**, 199
　　Organizations in Favor of Same-Sex Marriage, 199
　　Organizations Opposed to Same-Sex Marriage, 215

Organizations with an Interest in Marriage, but Who Are
   Neutral about Same-Sex Marriage, 224

8 **Resources, 227**
   Print, 227
      History, 227
      Gay and Lesbian Civil Rights Issues, 230
      Arguments in Favor of Same-Sex Marriage, 237
      Arguments Opposed to Same-Sex Marriage, 241
      General Reviews of Same-Sex Marriage and Adoption, 245
   Nonprint, 254
      History, 254
      Gay and Lesbian Civil Rights Issues, 256
      Arguments in Favor of Same-Sex Marriage, 259
      Arguments Opposed to Same-Sex Marriage, 262
      General Reviews of Same-Sex Marriage, 265

Glossary, 269
Index, 273
About the Author, 297

Preface

Same-sex marriage? What an absurd idea! Marriage has always been between one man and one woman. How can anyone imagine any kind of legal union called "marriage" between two women or two men?

Well, perhaps so. But also, perhaps not. Anyone who has studied American history knows that it is not quite true that "marriage has always been between one man and one woman." In fact, one of the largest religious denominations in the United States, the Church of Jesus Christ of Latter-day Saints (the Mormon church), not only endorsed but also encouraged polygamous marriages of its members for more than half a century. Church leaders made it a requirement of their faith that men take multiple wives in order for both men and women to ensure their entry into heaven after their deaths. Reflecting the importance of such marriages, the church referred to them as "celestial marriages."

And a careful study of human civilization shows that many other types of marriage are possible and, often, have been the norm among various societies. In some cultures, a one-man, one-woman marriage is often augmented by the addition of additional wives or husbands who may or may not live with the primary family all or part of the time. And same-sex marriages, while certainly not common in most societies, have existed in many cultures.

So perhaps the idea of same-sex marriage in the twenty-first century is not such a revolutionary idea as it first seems. Perhaps the question really is whether the United States and other nations of the world are now ready to acknowledge the right of two women or two men to join together in a social institution that bears the name of marriage. Or whether they should, at the very least, be entitled to some type of legal union that bestows all or most of the rights associated with opposite-sex marriage.

Various nations have taken different stands on this question. In the Muslim world, for example, same-sex relationships of any kind are regarded as sinful and, in some countries, are punishable by death. The concept of same-sex marriage is, therefore, unthinkable in such cultures. Christianity has long taken a similar stand on same-sex relationships, and in countries that were part of colonial empires established by Christian nations such as England, Belgium, and the Netherlands, same-sex relationships and same-sex marriage are simply not a possibility in today's world.

But a number of other nations have taken a different view. Same-sex marriage has actually become legal in eight nations: Belgium, Canada, the Netherlands, Norway, South Africa, Spain, Portugal and Sweden. Twenty other nations have adopted civil unions, domestic partnerships, or other marriage-like arrangements that extend to same-sex couples nearly all of the same rights available to opposite-sex couples in a legal marriage. The most striking fact about these data may be that all eight nations that have legalized same-sex marriage (and many political subdivisions that have taken the same action) have done so within the last decade. Is the world witnessing a revolution in the way nations think about the meaning of marriage as a social institution?

Certainly, the issue of same-sex marriage has become a topic of vigorous debate in many parts of the world. In the United States, for example, every state of the union, as well as the federal legislature, has held often acrimonious discussions as to what rights, if any, same-sex couples have in forming marriage-like unions. In the vast majority of cases, states have taken legislative and/or constitutional actions that specifically prohibit same-sex marriage and, in many cases, any comparable type of union. But a number of states have resisted this overall trend. Five states, the District of Columbia, and one Indian nation (the Coquille tribe) currently recognize same-sex marriage. Three other states recognize same-sex marriages conducted in other states, and nine states have adopted marriage-like arrangements called civil unions or domestic partnerships that provide same-sex couples with many rights available in an opposite-sex marriage.

The purpose of this book is to review the current status of same-sex marriage and similar institutions in the United States and other parts of the world. Chapter 1 provides a general background on social attitudes about same-sex relationships in general, in both the United States and other nations of the world, going back as far as historical records are available. This review explains how same-sex marriage has grown to be an issue of significance in many parts of the world. Chapter 2 focuses on some of the most fundamental aspects of the same-sex marriage debate. An important feature of the chapter is a review of the arguments offered both in favor of and against such legal arrangements. Chapter 3 expands this discussion to the worldwide stage, explaining how the issue of same-sex marriage is similar to and different from the debate in the United States and how other nations have resolved the conflict.

The remaining chapters of the book provide background information to assist readers in pursuing their research on this topic in greater detail. Chapter 4 provides a chronology of important events in the history of the debate over same-sex marriage. Chapter 5 includes brief biographical sketches of some important individuals in the history of this controversy. Chapter 6 contains a number of important documents and some useful data about same-sex unions in the United States and other parts of the world. Chapter 7 provides a list of organizations who support or oppose same-sex marriages and unions, while Chapter 8 contains a list of print and electronic resources on the topic. A brief glossary of important terms used in discussions of same-sex marriage is also provided.

1

Background and History

Introduction: The Early Days

On May 18, 1970, two men, Jack Baker and Michael McConnell, applied for a marriage license at the office of the county clerk for Hennepin County, Minnesota. The county clerk, Gerald R. Nelson, declined to issue a license, basing his decision on the fact that the applicants were of the same sex. Baker and McConnell then filed suit against Nelson, claiming that there was no specific prohibition of same-sex marriage in the Minnesota constitution or law. They further claimed that withholding a marriage license was unconstitutional under Articles 1, 8, 9, and 14 of the U.S. Constitution (freedom of speech; cruel and unusual punishment; right to privacy; and due process and equal protection clauses). When the trial court ruled against them, Baker and McConnell appealed to the state supreme court, which affirmed the lower court's decision, and then to the U.S. Supreme Court, which declined to hear the case "for want of a substantial federal question" (*Baker v. Nelson* 1972). As their case was working its way through the courts, Baker and McConnell continued to pursue other avenues of formalizing their relationship. In August 1971, McConnell legally adopted Baker, and they began to enjoy a few of the rights afforded legally married opposite-sex couples. At about the same time, they applied for a marriage license in Blue Earth County, Minnesota, were granted the license, and were married by a Methodist minister in Mankato, county seat of Blue Earth County. In 1974, Baker and McConnell applied to adopt a child, but their application was rejected by the

Children's Home Society of Minnesota, largely because of strong objections raised by "militant Christians" (Bronson 2004).

Baker and McConnell are generally regarded as pioneers of the same-sex marriage movement in the United States. In the decade that followed their first attempts to receive a marriage license, a number of other gay and lesbian couples made similar efforts. Also in 1970, for example, two Kentucky women, Tracy Knight and Marjorie Jones, applied for a marriage license from the Jefferson County clerk. On the advice of the district attorney, the clerk denied the license because the applicants were of the same sex. When Knight and Jones sued to force the clerk to issue a license, the district court rejected their claim, relying almost exclusively on definitions of marriage found in standard dictionaries of the time. The court noted that state statutes were essentially silent on the issue of same-sex marriage, so it had no statutory or case law precedent on which to base its decision (*Marjorie Jones et al., Appellants v. James Hallahan, Clerk of the Jefferson County Court, Appellee* 1973). Jones and Knight did not pursue their case beyond the court of appeals.

A somewhat different situation arose in Colorado in 1975, when two men, David McCord and David Zamora, approached the county clerk in Colorado Springs seeking a marriage license. The clerk responded that "[w]e do not do that here in El Paso County, but if you want to, go to Boulder County, they might do it there" (elephantjournal.com 2009). The Boulder County clerk, Clela Rorex, consulted the assistant district attorney for Boulder County, who said that there appeared to be no state law that prevented the clerk from issuing a marriage license to two individuals of the same sex, which she proceeded to do. In succeeding months, she issued five more marriage licenses to same-sex couples. The practice came to a halt, however, when state attorney general J. D. McFarlane issued an opinion on May 7, 1975, that Rorex's actions were illegal under state law. Just to clarify the situation, the Colorado state legislature passed a law in 1977 defining marriage as an act that can take place only between one man and one woman.

The move by lesbian and gay couples for equality in marriage did not go unnoticed by religious groups and legislators opposed to the practice, who began to work for legislation limiting marriage to one man and one woman. By 1980, half of the states had passed laws or constitutional amendments specifically defining marriage as a legal entity involving a single opposite-sex couple.

A decade later, that number had risen to 40 out of 50 states, and by 1994, 45 of the 50 states had adopted some form of opposite-sex limitation for marriage through statute or constitutional amendment. In 1996, the U.S. Congress passed and President Bill Clinton signed the Defense of Marriage Act (DOMA), banning the federal government from recognizing same-sex marriages performed in any of the states ("Same Sex Marriage, Civil Unions and Domestic Partnerships" 2009).

Same-Sex Relationships in History

As is the case with almost any current social issue, it is impossible to understand the dispute over same-sex marriage without appreciating the historical context of that debate. Individuals have engaged in same-sex behaviors from the dawn of civilization. One authority on the topic has opined that "there seems to be little doubt that homosexual behavior would have been widespread among . . . Neolithic tribes, as well as among their Paleolithic forebears . . . (Neill 2009, 82). A host of studies have now shown that various cultures at various times in history have held varying views about the morality and validity of same-sex relationships. One classic study that has cast light on this variability of attitudes was conducted by anthropologist Clellan S. Ford and psychologist Frank A. Beach in 1950. Ford and Beach used data from the Yale Human Relations Files to study attitudes about same-sex relationships in 76 societies for which sufficient data were available. They found that 49 (64%) of those societies approved of some form of same-sex behavior among men and/or women in the culture (Ford and Beach 1951, 130).

It is of no surprise to a modern reader that many cultures have held strongly negative views about same-sex relationships. Even today, a number of nations assign their most severe condemnation for such practices, as in Iran, Mauritania, Nigeria, Saudi Arabia, Sudan, United Arab Emirates, and Yemen, where a single same-sex act is punishable by the death penalty (Kennedy 2007). Studies show that about 80 nations worldwide still have laws that prohibit sexual behavior between two men (although the number is much smaller for such behavior between two women) ("Homosexual Rights around the World" 2006). Such views are not restricted to developing nations. A recent candidate for the

U.S. Senate, for example, suggested that homosexual behavior should be listed as a felony, punishable by death (U.S. Senate Candidate Wants Death Penalty for Homosexuals 2006). A nonscientific poll conducted by the Web page about.com found that one out of five Americans agreed with that position (Poll Results 2007).

Early Civilizations

What might be more surprising to the modern reader is that many societies at many times in history have either exalted same-sex relationships or, at the least, held them to be roughly comparable to opposite-sex relationships. One finds examples of such attitudes reflected in pictorial and written records from the very earliest civilizations. Considerable research suggests, for example, that homosexual practices were not uncommon in Mesopotamia, dating from about 1700 BCE. Among the art objects found by archaeologists, for example, are clay statuettes showing two men engaged in anal intercourse. A society's attitudes about such behaviors may well be reflected in the lack of legal prohibitions against such acts. The Code of Hammurabi, which deals with a vast array of very detailed prohibited behaviors, nowhere mentions same-sex behavior as being prohibited. Some authorities also point to the strongly homoerotic themes in the Gilgamesh, the region's creation myth similar to the creation story in the Christian Bible. In that myth, Gilgamesh speaks of awaiting the arrival of his companion, Enkidu, in terms that would be similar for an opposite-sex relationship:

> At the gate of my marital chamber there lay an axe,
> . . .
>
> I laid it down at your feet,
> I loved it and embraced it as a wife,
> and you made it compete with me.

When Gilgamesh asks his mother about the dream's meaning, she explains,

> The axe that you saw [is] a man.
> [that] you love him and embrace as a wife . . .

("The Epic of Gilgamesh" 2009, Tablet 1;
for more on this topic, see Bullough 1976, 17–36).

China

Another of the world's oldest civilizations, that of China, is also thought to have a long tradition of same-sex loving relationships. This information is relatively new and contrary to traditional Chinese beliefs that same-sex relationships were essentially absent from Chinese cultures until the very recent past (if even then). The work that significantly altered scholarly view on this subject was Bret Hinsch's 1990 book, *Passion of the Cut Sleeve*. The title of the book comes from a classic Chinese tale of the Han emperor Ai and his male companion Dong Xian. When called to an important meeting, the emperor cut the sleeve from his elaborate gown, on which Dong was lying, rather than having to awake and disturb him (Hay 2009). Hinsch has found that long-term same-sex loving relationships were common during certain periods of early Chinese history, with at least 10 emperors between the period 206 BCE and 1 CE known to have been involved in such relationships (Hinsch 1990, 35–36).

One of the most comprehensive studies of the place of same-sex relationships in Chinese society is *Their World: A Study of Homosexuality in China*, by Dr. Li Yinhe of the Institute of Sociology at the Chinese Academy of Social Sciences. Li has concluded that "historical traces of male homosexuality persist through dynasty to dynasty from ancient times and never disappear." In fact, she writes that "a calm and dispassionate attitude to the homosexual phenomenon was always prevalent in ancient China. There was neither eulogy, nor criticism. It seemed to do no harm in maintaining traditional family ethics" ("History of Chinese Homosexuality" 2004).

Islam

Given the strong condemnations of same-sex behavior in modern Islam, it may be something of a surprise that homosexual relations were probably not uncommon in the religion's earliest history. Apparently Mohammed adopted the prohibition of same-sex relationships that he learned from the Christian story of Sodom and Gomorrah, but he assigned no specific penalty for the practice (Greenberg 1988, 173). As in Christianity, the strongest criticisms of and penalties for same-sex behavior came not from the religion's founder, but from later disciples and commentators. In any case, there is strong evidence that, whatever the caliphate's official position on the topic, same-sex behavior was common throughout early Islam. One early writer, the Dominican priest William of Adam, wrote about his trip to Egypt, noting that "[t]hese Saracens, forgetting human dignity, go so far that men live with each other in the same way that men and women live together in our own land" (Daniel 1994, as cited in Greenberg 1988, 176). Later in history, as Westerners became better acquainted with Islamic culture, such comments were much more frequent. Writer after writer, from Lord Byron to Gustave Flaubert, noted that young Muslim men in particular were readily available for sexual contact, not only with visiting foreigners, but apparently with each other (Neill 2009, 299–301).

The argument has long been that same-sex relationships are so common in Islamic cultures because opposite-sex opportunities outside of marriage are essentially unavailable to men, as is the case with women who have no access to men. In such a case, the only sexual outlet for unmarried men is with other men (see, for example, Dunne 2010). While that argument may be true to some extent, it does not fully explain the apparent widespread same-sex behavior discernible in Islamic cultures throughout almost all of its history. Some commentators have observed, for example, that same-sex behavior has apparently always been essentially absent from Islamic bedouins, who often live in a single-sex (male) society for months at time, without their being same-sex contacts (Bianquis 1986, as quoted in Greenberg 1988, 175).

American Indians

Same-sex relationships were common in American Indian cultures and were often revered. In his classic study, *Gay American History*, Jonathan Katz offers a number of documents from early explorers about the same-sex practices they observed, always with the greatest disgust. Among the earliest of these documents was a note by the Spanish explorer Alvar Nuñez Cabeza de Vaca, who reported a "devilish thing" that he observed, a marriage between two men. Reports of similar events came from other explorers, including Hernando de Alarcón in 1540, René Goulaine de Laudonniére in about 1562, Jacques le Moyne de Morgues in 1564, Francisco de Pareja in the period 1593–1613, Jacques Marquette in the period 1673–1677, Pierre Liette in 1702, Joseph François Lafitau in the period 1711–1717, and an increasing number of observers in the eighteenth century (Katz 1976, 281–334). A report from 1819 reflects the general view of Westerners who first encountered many Indian cultures, acknowledging both how common the practice was and how little concern it seemed to raise. "Sodomy is a crime not uncommonly committed"; two explorers write, "[M]any of the subjects of it are publicly known and do not appear to be despised, or to excite disgust" (Katz 1976, 299). A modern confirmation of the practice of same-sex relationships came from Jack D. Forbes, professor emeritus of Native American Studies at the University of California at Davis. In 2004, he wrote that "[c]ouples of the same sex also were recognized as legitimate in many or perhaps most tribes. This style of marriage may not have been overly common, but it is certainly noted for a number of American Nations" (Forbes 2004).

Part of the confusion apparent among Western explorers about the nature of same-sex couples in Native American tribes was their lack of understanding as to Indian views on the nature of human sexuality. In contrast to the opinions held by most people today, Indians believed that there were more than two genders. A third gender, the berdache, consisted of individuals who melded both male and female characteristics within one body, so-called two-spirited people. Berdache were commonly (but not always) morphological males who were raised to carry out many of the responsibilities usually assigned to women. In many Indian cultures, they were highly revered, chosen to settle disputes between tribe members, and responsible for religious ceremonies. In addition, they often married other males (as did female berdache with other females), forming a family unit virtually identical to those of opposite-sex couples (Williams 1986). Interestingly enough, many young male Native Americans who might have grown into the role of a berdache in another era now appear to be most comfortable in the gay male culture of urban environments to which they have moved (Williams, 1986, 207–29).

Greece and Rome

The history of same-sex relationships in ancient Greece and Rome is so well known as hardly to be worthy of extended discussion here, which, in any case and given the length of this book, is not possible. Suffice it to say that such relationships were common and generally accepted both in Greece and in pre-Christian Rome. In Greece, the most common pattern was for an older man to adopt a younger man as his close partner, during which he educated his younger companion into the traditions of the society. The older/younger relationship closely mirrored that of opposite-sex formal marriages, in which older men most commonly chose younger women as their brides.

Such age differences in same-sex relationships were, however, by no means the only type of such relationships. In fact, one of the earliest and most famous same-sex relationships between men was that of Achilles and Patroclus, described in the *Iliad*. Although the sexual component of this relationship has long been the subject of debate among scholars, it seems difficult to ignore that aspect of their relationship. When Patroclus dies, Homer describes Achilles' grief to some extent:

> Once the funeral gathering broke up, the men dispersed, each one going to his own ship, concerned to eat and then enjoy sweet sleep. But Achilles kept on weeping, remembering his dear companion. All-conquering Sleep could not overcome him, as he tossed and turned, longing for manly, courageous, strong Patroclus, thinking of all he'd done with him, all the pain they'd suffered, as they'd gone through wars with other men and with the perilous sea. As he kept remembering, he cried heavy tears, sometimes lying on his side, sometimes on his back or on his face. Then he'd get up, to wander in distress, back and forth along the shore. (Homer 2004, Book 24)

Such expressions of grief may be no more than the sorrow of two "good buddies," as some scholars suggest, but it may also represent somewhat deeper feelings between two men who are perhaps more than just close friends (for one of the most complete bibliographies of documents dealing with this topic, see "Homosexuality in Greece and Rome: A Sourcebook of Basic Documents in Translation" 2010).

Same-sex relationships in pre-Christian Rome were apparently also common, and many have been carefully studied. Among the most frequent examples mentioned is that of the emperor Nero, who apparently participated in two same-sex "marriages," once as a bride with a wine steward named Pythagoras, and once as a groom with the castrated actor Sporus (see, for example, Frier 2004). Nero, however, was apparently anything but an exception. Edward Gibbon, perhaps the greatest historian of ancient Rome, wrote that "of the first fifteen emperors Claudius was the only one whose taste in love was entirely correct" (Gibbon 1880, 118–19, note 40; this note appears in Gibbon's discussion of the same-sex relationship between the emperor Hadrian and his partner Antinous, perhaps the most famous long-term relationship of its kind in ancient Rome, thus removing any doubt as to what Gibbon thought of as an "entirely correct" relationship. For more details on the relationships between Hadrian and Antinous, see Henderson 1923, 130–34).

Considerably less is known about same-sex relationships (or almost any other topic) among ordinary citizens of Rome. There is some evidence, however, that such relationships were not uncommon nor were they particularly despised by society in general. In his review of the role of same-sex relationships in early Rome, John Boswell concludes that the broad appeal of the relationship between Hadrian and Antinous may have been due at least in part to the popularity of same-sex themes in literature of the time. He observes that "[e]verywhere in the fiction of the Empire—from lyric poetry to popular novels—gay couples and their love appear on a completely equal footing with their heterosexual counterparts" (Boswell 1980, 85–86).

Some Cautions

Boswell's interpretation of the place of same-sex relationships in ancient Rome—as is true for much of what has been written for other cultures discussed so far in this chapter—has been the subject of considerable (often contentious) dispute among academic scholars. Indeed, almost any report of the nature of human sexual activities (or any other kind of activity) in ancient civilizations is likely to be criticized by someone for being inaccurate. There are at least three reasons that such vigorous debates occur about the "facts" of history, especially those relating to sexual activity. First, it is impossible and misleading to think about same-sex relationships in Mesopotamia, China, Islam, Greece, Rome, or other early civilizations in the same terms with which one views same-sex relationships today. In fact, until recently it was probably rare, if not unheard of, to define a person in terms of his or her sexual orientation—as "gay" or "lesbian"—as many people do today. Instead, people were statesmen, warriors, or workers who may have been physically, socially, intellectually, or otherwise attracted to someone of the same sex all of the time, some of the time, never, or "it depends." A society's response to such a situation might have ranged anywhere from "how terrible! He or she must die!" to "ho-hum" to "he/she must be a deity."

Second, historians often have only the dimmest notions as to what common attitudes toward same-sex behavior were in any given culture. Unfortunately, history is usually the record of the lives of king and queens, of other royalty, of military leaders, or of other great figures. Historians often know next to nothing directly about the lives of ordinary people. So the fact that Nero legally and formally married two other men tells us nothing at all about the nature of same-sex relationships among ordinary Roman citizens.

Third, historians often disagree about the way people in any given culture loved, thought, and believed. Trying to make sense out of glyphs on an Egyptian temple, a poem on a 2,000-year-old scroll, or an ancient Chinese law is often profoundly difficult, with different scholars arguing vehemently over the meaning of some obscure word or phrase from a long-dead language.

Finally, no matter how hard they try, scholars tend to bring their own training, history, feelings, and prejudices to the analyses they make of historical works. One might understand, for example, how a man in the tenth century who was erotically attracted to other men might join a single-sex group of other men (as in a monastery) rather than try to survive in a strongly heterosexual culture for the rest of his life. But a Roman Catholic historian might find it difficult to acknowledge that the church has historically been a refuge for men attracted to other men, when church teachings today so strongly condemn every aspect of same-sex behavior and feelings. That person might find it difficult to acknowledge that same-sex relationships may once have been common and even sanctioned by the early church.

Similarly, modern scholars who personally support same-sex relationships may treat the historical record with their own gloss. A lesbian or gay historian today might very much "want" to find meanings in ancient records that support her or his views, especially when the record is unclear. After all, many classical texts have been routinely mistranslated (with change of pronouns, for example) or left untranslated to avoid exposing same-sex relationships (see Boswell 1980, 19–21). Still, the temptation may be to go beyond uncovering the falsification of history and finding (conceivably unwarranted) support for one's own position on this contentious issue.

These cautions are not entirely an exercise in scholarly ethics. People who argue today about the legitimacy of same-sex marriage frequently refer to "tradition," calling upon customs that have apparently existed in civilization for thousands of years. Yet some of the claims made for and against same-sex marriage may not always be based on the best scholarship available. For example, critics of same-sex marriage frequently point to biblical references (the Sodom and Gomorrah story and passages from Leviticus) that supposedly condemn same-sex relationships between adults. Yet the earliest modern scholarly analysis of the biblical meaning of these passages raised very serious questions as to whether the passages actually have the condemnatory meaning about same-sex relationships that virtually all Christians today believe they have (Bailey 1955).

All these cautions suggest is that ancient records, while fascinating clues about the lives and thoughts of long-dead people, are only clues and not absolute guidelines as to the way modern people should live their lives.

Attitudes Toward Same-Sex Relationships in Western Culture

For the modern debate over same-sex marriage, probably the most important historical story is that which begins in the lands inhabited by and surrounding the early Israelites. A common position is that the early Israelites may very well have held attitudes about same-sex behavior similar to those of surrounding cultures. One observer has characterized those attitudes by observing that "homosexuality in many forms pervaded the ancient Near East, and with more openness beyond Egypt. As long as persons got married and had families, homoerotic activity was generally accepted as part and parcel of life (Gerig 2010). It seems likely that the early Israelites held generally similar views. One historian of the period has written that "sodomy is not prohibited in the pre-exilic section of Scripture" and, in fact, "there is a distinct lack of preaching on sexual matters among the Hebrews" during this period (Epstein 1948, 3–4).

Perhaps the best-known examples of same-sex relationships found in the Bible are those between David and Jonathan and Ruth and Naomi. The former relationship is described and discussed at some length in the first book of Samuel, chapter 20, and the first chapter of 2 Samuel. In those passages, the love between the two men is described when Jonathan attempts to save David from the wrath of his father, Saul:

> And Jonathan had David reaffirm his oath out of love for him, because he loved him as he loved himself. . . .
>
> Then they kissed each other and wept together—but David wept the most.
>
> Jonathan said to David, "Go in peace, for we have sworn friendship with each other in the name of the LORD, saying, 'The LORD is witness between you and me, and between your descendants and my descendants forever.' " (1 Samuel 20: 16, 41–42)

Later, when David learns of Jonathan's death (along with his father, Saul), he responds by saying

> I grieve for you, Jonathan my brother;
> you were very dear to me.
> Your love for me was wonderful,
> more wonderful than that of women. (2 Samuel 1: 26)

The relationship between Ruth and her daughter-in-law, Naomi, is described in the first chapter of Ruth in the Bible. When Ruth decides to return to Bethlehem after her two sons die, her daughter-in-law, Naomi, vows to go with her. She says:

> Intreat me not to leave thee, or to return from following after thee: for whither thou goest, I will go; and where thou lodgest, I will lodge: thy people shall be my people, and thy God my God:
>
> Where thou diest, will I die, and there will I be buried: the LORD do so to me, and more also, if ought but death part thee and me. (Ruth 1: 1–2)

While these two passages would appear to affirm same-sex relationships, in at least two specific instances, critics of such relationships point to two other sections of the Bible as condemning such practices. The first of these passages, dealing with the classic story of Sodom and Gomorrah, is found in the 19th chapter of Genesis. According to that story, two angels visit the city of Sodom and are lodged in the home of one of its residents, Lot. When the citizens of Sodom hear about the visitors, they go to Lot's home and call for him to send the angels out "so that we may know them," according to the passage in the King James version of the Bible. Lot refuses to do so and, instead, offers his two daughters, both of whom are virgins. The crowd refuses the offer, and the angel's "save the day" for Lot by telling him to leave the city, because they are about to destroy it. In the end, the angels do just that, raining fire and brimstone down upon Sodom and its sister city of Gomorrah.

The second selection from the Bible used to condemn same-sex relationships consists of two verses from the book of Leviticus—chapter 18, verse 22, and chapter 20, verse 13. They read as follows:

> Thou shalt not lie with mankind, as with womankind: it is abomination. (Leviticus 18: 22)

> If a man also lie with mankind, as he lieth with a woman, both of them have committed an abomination: they shall surely be put to death; their blood shall be upon them. (Leviticus 20: 13)

Both of these verses, along with the story of Sodom and Gomorrah, have traditionally formed the basis for opposition to same-sex relationships in the Christian religion in particular, and Judeo-Christian culture in general. As with most ancient texts, these biblical references have been the subject of much scholarly scrutiny, with dramatically different interpretations as to their meaning. This feature of the scriptural references will be discussed in greater detail in Chapter 2 of this book.

Suffice it to say, the more conservative interpretation, that is, that same-sex relationships are forbidden and that those who engage in them must be put to death, has been the basis of most of the legal prohibitions against such relationships in Western culture. Probably the first expression of this legal theory can be found in the Theodosian Code, issued by the emperor Valentinian III in 430 CE. That code, whose name is derived from the emperor Theodosius II, who initiated its compilation, summarizes all

Roman laws issued under the Christian emperors beginning with Constantine in 312. Among the laws included are prohibitions on same-sex activity, such as the provision that

> All persons who have the shameful custom of condemning a man's body, acting the part of a woman's to the sufferance of alien sex (for they appear not to be different from women), shall expiate a crime of this kind in avenging flames in the sight of the people. (Theodosian Code 9.7:6 as cited in DeYoung 2000, 273)

Through most of the Middle Ages, prohibitions against same-sex behavior were common in canonical law, although such restrictions did not become part of secular law until the early thirteenth century (Johansson and Percy 2009 169). The extent to which the most severe provisions of these laws were imposed is not clear, since records of executions are relatively rare. Apparently the first person killed under a secular law against same-sex behavior was one Lord Haspisperch, who was burned to death by order of King Rudolph I in 1277 in Basel. Similar punishments for same-sex activities have been reported throughout Western Europe in the following century (see, for example, Crompton 2003, 201–2).

The first law in England prohibiting same-sex behavior was the Buggery Law of 1533, issued by King Henry VIII. The law provided that anyone convicted of "the detestable and abominable Vice of Buggery committed with mankind or beast" be put to death by hanging, without benefit of clergy ("The Law in England, 1290–1885" 2010). That act was revoked when Mary became queen of England in 1553, but was reinstated when Mary was succeeded by her half-sister Elizabeth in 1558 (Fone 2000, 215–18). The Buggery Law remained in effect in England until it was repealed by the Sexual Offences Act of 1967. The capital punishment feature of the law had been repealed in 1861, however, by the Offences Against the Person Act and replaced by a maximum penalty of penal servitude for life (Barrett 1979, 1024–25).

Sodomy Laws in the United States

Early laws about same-sex behavior in the United States were very similar to those of England. This pattern has long held true for most, if not all, ex-British colonies ("This Alien Legacy:

The Origins of 'Sodomy' Laws in British Colonialism" 2008). The first American law dealing with sodomy, the term most commonly used for same-sex acts, was passed in Virginia on May 24, 1610. It stated that "[n]o man shal [sic] commit the horrible, and detestable sinnes of Sodomie upon pain of death" (Painter 2004). The first man sentenced under this law, one Richard Cornish, was hanged for his acts in 1625 ("Sodomy Laws: Virginia" 2004). Other colonies soon followed suit, sometimes simply adopting existing English law on the topic, and sometimes adopting legislation very similar in spirit, if not in text. In 1641, for example, the Massachusetts Bay Colony adopted its now-famous Body of Laws and Liberties, designed to highlight the greater freedom available to colonists, compared to the situation in the mother country. Those freedoms did not extend to those who engaged in same-sex activities, which the Body prohibited, quite remarkably, simply by restating the biblical prohibition from Leviticus, namely: "If any man lyeth with mankinde as he lyeth with a woman, both of them have committed abhomination, they both shall surely be put to death" (Whitmore 1887, 15). Such a practice, in which direct quotations from the Bible were used as civil laws, was hardly unusual in the early colonies. Connecticut, for example, had a similar law that remained in effect in precisely the same words until 1687 (Crompton 1976, 279).

Over time, every state in the union adopted some type of legislation prohibiting sodomy and/or other types of same-sex behavior. It was not until the 1950s that public attitudes slowly began to change on the topic. In 1955, the American Law Institute published its Model Penal Code, a recommended guideline for state legislatures in adopting laws dealing with criminal behavior. The model code made no recommendations for "criminal penalties for consensual sexual relations conducted in private," essentially suggesting that such relationships did not belong under the purview of civil law in the United States ("*Lawrence v. Texas*" 2003).

Individual states gradually began to adopt that principle and to repeal their sodomy laws. Illinois was the first such state to do so in a revision of its criminal code in 1961. Idaho was the second state to take such an action, omitting sodomy laws from its revised criminal code adopted in 1971. (When legislators realized what they had done, they acted a year later to reinstate the sodomy prohibition, becoming the first and only state to reinstate a sodomy statute; "History of Sodomy Laws" 2004). By 1986, 24 states and the District of Columbia still retained sodomy laws on their books, at a time when the U.S. Supreme Court first decided a case dealing with the issue (*"Lawrence v. Texas"* 2003). In the case of *Bowers v. Hardwick*, the court ruled five-to-four that individuals had no right to privacy when they were engaged in consensual same-sex acts in the privacy of their own homes.

That decision stood until 2003, when the court reconsidered its 1986 stand on sodomy. By that time, 13 more states had repealed their sodomy laws or had them declared invalid by judicial decisions. Only Alabama, Florida, Idaho, Kansas, Louisiana, Michigan, Mississippi, Missouri, North Carolina, Oklahoma, South Carolina, Texas, Utah, and Virginia still have sodomy laws on their books. Those laws were also invalidated when the court announced its decision in the case of *Lawrence v. Texas*, in which it decided by a six-to-three vote that its 1986 decision was incorrect and that, in fact, private consensual sexual behavior is constitutionally protected (*"Lawrence v. Texas"* 2003). As of early 2010, only three states still had sodomy laws on the books—Kansas, Oklahoma, and Texas—although those laws are unenforceable under provisions of the *Lawrence v. Texas* decision.

The Gay and Lesbian Civil Rights Movement

The move by states to begin repealing their sodomy laws in the 1960s and 1970s coincided with another sea change in U.S. social policy, the rise of the gay and lesbian rights movement and the legal changes that movement initiated. Historically, lesbians and gay men in the United States were not looked upon favorably. As Jonathan Katz has summarized in his documentary history of gays and lesbians in the United States, such individuals were, for most of America's history, "condemned to death by choking, burning, and drowning; they were executed, jailed, pilloried, fined, court-martialed, prostituted, fired, framed, blackmailed, disinherited, entrapped, stereotyped, mocked, insulted, isolated, pitied, castigated, and despised." In the more "enlightened" decades of the first seven decades of the twentieth century, they were also "castrated, lobotomized, shock-treated, and psychoanalyzed" (Katz 1976, 11; although many good histories of same-sex behavior in the United States are available, Katz's documentary text provides some of the starkest and most dramatic illustrations of what life was like for lesbians and gay men prior to the modern era beginning in the 1970s).

Early Organizations

That situation changed only very slowly. The first attempt of which we know by gay men to work for a greater acceptance of same-sex relationships in the United States dates to 1924. In that year, a very small group of gay men formed the Society for Human Rights, whose purpose it was to provide a social and educational club for other gay men and to educate public officials about the nature of homosexuality (Gerber 1962). That organization lasted only a few weeks, as one of the member's wives reported the group to the police. One of the founders, Henry Gerber, was fired from his job and lost his home when his employers learned of his actions.

It was to be more than three decades before other gay men and lesbians would feel safe enough to repeat Gerber's efforts. In 1951, gay pioneer Harry Hays and a small group of his friends formed the Mattachine Foundation (later called the Mattachine Society), a group named after a medieval French society of unmarried men who performed dances and plays during the Feast of Fools. The goals of the Mattachine group were to provide a safe and comfortable social setting in which gay men could meet, to educate public officials and the general public about the nature of homosexuality, to develop a program of "political action" against "discriminatory and oppressive legislation," and to assist "our people who are victimized daily as a result of our oppression," and who constitute "one of the largest minorities in America today" (Cutler 1956, 13–14).

A year after the Mattachine Society was legally incorporated (1954), a group of lesbians in the Los Angeles area met to form a similar organization of women. They called the organization the Daughters of Bilitis (DOB), after a fictional lesbian character in *The Songs of Bilitis*, an 1894 work by the French poet Pierre Louÿs. Interestingly enough, both the Mattachine and DOB groups selected these abstruse names at least partly because they were obscure enough to have little meaning to nongays and nonlesbians, providing the security that lesbians and gay men so desperately needed at the time.

Both Mattachine and DOB had somewhat checkered and relatively short histories. Mattachine had splintered and dwindled to a collection of local groups within a half dozen years, while DOB hung on for 14 years, albeit in an increasingly diminished form. Other groups with regional and national ambitions also developed. In January 1963, a group of local lesbian and gay groups met in Philadelphia for a conference under the auspices of the newly created East Coast Homophile Organizations (ECHO). The theme of that conference was "Homosexuality—Time for Reappraisal." The group met twice more, in Washington in 1964 ("Homosexuality—Civil Liberties and Social Rights") and in New York City in 1965 ("The Homosexual Citizen in the Great Society"). The success of the ECHO conferences encouraged activists to aim even higher, resulting in a conference of yet another new organization, the National Planning Conference of Homophile Organizations (NPCHO), later to become the North American Conference of Homophile Organizations (NACHO). In addition to representatives from the five ECHO organizations, there were attendees from the Midwest, South, and West, resulting in the first truly national organization of gay men and lesbians to form in the United States. As with other gay and lesbian groups, NACHO had a relatively brief, but also quite successful, existence. It held a total of four national conferences after the Kansas City meeting, conducted and reported on research on the legal status of gay men and lesbian and on discrimination in housing and employment, organized demonstrations in a variety of cities over injustices based on sexual orientation, and established a legal defense fund to be used in court cases involving gay men and lesbians.

The Storm Breaks

By the mid-1960s, American society was in turmoil, at least partly because of the ongoing conflict in Vietnam, but more generally as a variety of minority groups began to press for equal rights under the law. For society in general, the defining moment of that movement was passage of the Civil Rights Act of 1964, an act that prohibited discrimination in the areas of housing, employment, and public accommodations on the basis of race, color, religion, sex, or national origin (but not sexual orientation). Thus, the events that occurred on the evening of June 27, 1969, at a gay bar in New York City were to have a significance that they might not otherwise have had at a different time and under different circumstances. The event unfolded as follows:

On the evening of June 27, 1969, a group of plainclothes New York City police officers raided the Stonewall Inn, a popular gay bar in the city's Greenwich Village neighborhood. Such raids were not uncommon in New York, nor in almost any other large city in the United States at the time. During such a raid, law enforcement officers routinely removed some patrons of the bar to a local police station, where they often spent the night. Names, addresses, and occupations of the bar customers were routinely taken and often released to the local newspapers. Occasionally the police physically assaulted patrons. Most gay men and lesbians accepted this practice as just one of the hazards of having a somewhat open social life. For reasons that will probably never be completely clear, the night of June 27, 1969, was an aberration in this pattern. As police began to remove patrons from the bar for transfer to a police paddy wagon, other customers began to fight back. They used whatever weapons they could find, including an uprooted parking meter, to resist police activities, to the point that some police officers were eventually trapped inside the bar. Customers then set fire to the bar. (No lives were lost nor were there any serious injuries as a result of this action.) (A number of excellent histories of the Stonewall riots and their consequences are available. See especially Carter 2004, Duberman 1993, and Teal 1995.) For many lesbians and gay men in America, the riots that took place at the Stonewall on the night of June 27 and following evenings were historic; some historians have even called them the beginning of the modern gay and lesbian civil rights movement.

At the time of the Stonewall riot, only one state (Illinois) had repealed its sodomy laws, making same-sex acts illegal in every other state of the union, the District of Columbia, and all U.S. possessions. No state, city, or other political entity had as yet enacted legislation extending to lesbians and gay men the same general civil rights enjoyed by heterosexuals, such as protection against loss of one's job, loss or refusal of housing opportunities, or right of access to places of public accommodation, on the basis of one's sexual orientation. It was the attainment of these civil rights that became an important focus of the so-called gay liberation movement that developed after the Stonewall riots. (The movement was actually more diverse than this, with the goal of achieving sexual freedom an important element for many members of the movement. For reviews of the complex character of the movement, see Cruikshank 1992 and Rimmerman 2008). Over the next decade, those engaged in the gay liberation movement and its offshoots and successors developed and implemented a relatively sophisticated program for achieving their goal of gaining equality under U.S. laws with their heterosexual counterparts, an equality similar to that guaranteed to blacks,

Hispanics, Italians, Catholics, Lutherans, and virtually every other special-interest group covered by the Civil Rights Act of 1964. That program included lobbying local, state, and federal officials, writing books and articles, appearing on radio and television, supporting and opposing candidates for public office, finding gay and nongay candidates to run for office, writing and supporting legislation for civil rights, and creating new organizations to meet the special needs of lesbians and gay men.

The accomplishments of one of the most successful gay and lesbians organizations illustrate these efforts. The National Gay Task Force (now the National Gay and Lesbian Task Force [NGLTF]) was founded in 1973 by a small group of women and men from an earlier organization, the Gay Activists Alliance (GAA), who felt that that organization was not sufficiently committed to political action to achieve the goals in which they believed. Over the first 15 years of its existence, the Task Force led or was involved in almost every social and political issue of interest to lesbians and gay men in the United States. It convinced the American Psychiatric Association to remove homosexuality from its list of mental disorders in 1973; persuaded the U.S. Civil Service Commission to remove its ban on employing lesbians and gay men in federal positions; worked with members of the U.S. Congress to introduce the first federal antidiscrimination legislation in 1975; led a 1981 campaign to defeat an anti-gay/ lesbian bill called the Family Protection Act; formed the Privacy Project in 1986 to work for revocation of state sodomy laws; and established the Military Freedom Project in 1988 to work against bans on gay men and lesbians in the military. Today, along with the Human Rights Campaign (founded in 1980), the Task Force is still one of the largest, best funded, most highly respected, and most effective national agencies working for the civil rights of lesbians and gay men.

Slowly—sometimes very slowly—the efforts of the Task Force and other gay and lesbian organizations began to bear fruit. In 1972, two cities in Michigan became the first governmental entities to grant civil rights to lesbians and gay men. East Lansing passed an ordinance banning discrimination against lesbians and gay men in employment, while Ann Arbor followed a few months later with a comprehensive ban against discrimination in all areas, including employment, housing, and public accommodation. Two years later, Elaine Nobel became the first (self-acknowledged) lesbian to be elected to a major political office, when she was chosen to be representative to the Massachusetts state assembly from the state's sixth district (Boston). Adoption of antidiscrimination legislation in the states proceeded very slowly. Wisconsin was the first state to ban discrimination based on sexual orientation in housing, employment, and public accommodation. It did so in 1981, but it took another eight years before another state—Massachusetts—followed suit. Wisconsin and Massachusetts were followed by Connecticut and Hawaii in 1991 and by California, Vermont, and New Jersey in 1992, although some states limited protection to only one of these areas, usually employment. As of early 2010, 21 states and the District of Columbia ban some form of discrimination based on sexual orientation. Table 1.1 summarizes those laws for employment

TABLE 1.1
State Antidiscrimination Laws

State	Law(s) Passed[a]
California	1992, 2003
Colorado	2007
Connecticut	1991
District of Columbia	1997, 2006
Delaware	2009
Hawaii	1991
Illinois	2006
Iowa	2007
Maine	2005
Maryland	2001
Massachusetts	1989
Minnesota	1993
Nevada	1999
New Hampshire	1998
New Jersey	1992, 2007
New Mexico	2003
New York	2003
Oregon	2008
Rhode Island	1995, 2001
Vermont	1991, 2007
Washington	2006
Wisconsin	1981

[a]Inclusion of a second date refers to laws being extended to transgendered individuals.
Sources: Human Rights Campaign, "Statewide Employment Laws and Policies," http://www.hrc.org/documents/Employment_Laws_and_Policies.pdf; Institute of Real Estate Management, "Laws Prohibiting Discrimination Based on Sexual Orientation and Gender Identity," http://www.irem.org/pdfs/publicpolicy/Antidiscrimination.pdf.

discrimination. In the remaining 29 states, a person can still be fired from a job, and, in most cases, also be removed from housing or prevented from owning or renting a home or be expelled from a place of public accommodation based on her or his sexual orientation (Human Rights Campaign 2010).

National legislation to prohibit discrimination in employment on the basis of sexual orientation has been introduced in the U.S. Congress in every session since 1994, with the exception of the 109th (2005–2007). That legislation came closest to passing in 2009, but failed once again. As of early 2010, it was still under consideration by the 110th Congress (The Task Force 2009).

Same-Sex Marriage in the United States

If one reads the history of the battle for lesbian and gay civil rights up to about 1985, there is very little about same-sex marriage or same-sex adoption as a priority among movement leaders. Individual efforts to get a marriage license, like those of Jack Baker and Michael McConnell, Tracy Knight and Marjorie Jones, and David McCord and David Zamora, described at the beginning of this chapter, were extraordinarily rare. By far, the greatest emphasis by gay and lesbian organizations was on achieving fundamental civil rights, such as nondiscrimination in employment, housing, and public accommodation, as outlined previously. By 1985, even that goal became secondary to other concerns of lesbian and gay leaders in the United States. The reason for this change was the rise of the HIV/AIDS epidemic. For about a decade, from the mid-1980s to the mid-1990s, no subject came anywhere near the importance of that epidemic for the nation's gay and lesbian political community. Tens of thousands of men and women were dying every year, many of them founders and/or leaders of the gay and lesbian civil rights movement, and finding a cure for the disease and providing aid and comfort for the hundreds of thousands of individuals with the disease drained the movement of the energy and opportunity to maintain its drive for civil rights. (The classic history of the early years of the HIV/AIDS epidemic is Shilts 2007; also see Holleran 2008.)

(Interestingly enough, the HIV/AIDS epidemic had little effect on efforts by those opposed to granting civil rights to lesbians and gay men. In fact, individuals and organizations who had long opposed equal rights for gay men and lesbians simply added the epidemic to its list of reasons to oppose granting civil rights to homosexuals. In fact, some observers continue to use the epidemic as one of the reasons to oppose same-sex marriage, arguing that same-sex behavior is "unhealthy," and for that reason those who engage in such practices should not have the right to marry [see, for example, Camenker 2008]. This point is discussed in greater detail in Chapter 2.)

As the HIV/AIDS epidemic began to moderate in the mid-1990s, efforts by gay men and lesbians to achieve the rights of marriage and adoption that opposite-sex couples traditionally enjoyed reappeared, albeit once more in rare and isolated circumstances. Undoubtedly, the most significant of these efforts occurred in the state of Hawaii in December 1990, when three same-sex couples, Ninia Baehr and Genora Dancel, Tammy Rodrigues and Antoinette Pregil, and Pat Lagon and Joseph Melillo, applied for a marriage license in Honolulu. When their applications were denied, the three couples filed suit against Lawrence Miike, Director of the Department of Health for the state of Hawaii. They contended that they qualified for a marriage on every criterion required by the state, except for being of the same sex. Further, they pointed out that the Hawaii constitution prohibits discrimination on the basis of a number of criteria, including gender. The clerk's decision to withhold a marriage license, they argued, was therefore unconstitutional under the state constitution.

A trial court found in favor of the defendant on October 1, 1991, a decision the plaintiffs appealed to the Hawaii Supreme Court. In 1993, the supreme court vacated the trial court's decision and sent the case back to that court with the instructions "that the burden will rest on [the defendant] to overcome the presumption that HRS 572-1 [the state's marriage law] is unconstitutional by demonstrating that it furthers compelling state interests and is narrowly drawn to avoid unnecessary abridgments of constitutional rights" (*Baehr v. Miike* 1996).

The case was then reheard before the First Circuit Court for the state of Hawaii in late 1996. On December 3 of that year, Judge Kevin S. C. Chang issued his decision in the case. He concluded that

The evidentiary record presented in this case does not justify the sex-based classification of HRS 572-1.

Therefore, the court specifically finds and concludes, as a matter of law, that Defendant has failed to sustain his burden to overcome the presumption that HRS 572-1 is unconstitutional by demonstrating or proving that the statute furthers a compelling state interest.

On that basis, Judge Change ruled that

The sex-based classification in HRS 572-1, on its face and as applied, is unconstitutional and in violation of the equal protection clause of Article I, Section 5 of the Hawaii Constitution. (*Baher v. Miike* 1996)

A day after issuing his ruling, Judge Chang issued a stay on the decision, allowing time for an appeal of the decision. Thus for a period of 24 hours, marriages between same-sex couples were legal in Hawaii.

Chang's ruling motivated the state legislature to take action in order to preserve the intent of the existing marriage law, that is, to restrict the practice to one man and one woman. In March 1997, the legislature adopted legislation calling for a statewide vote on a constitutional amendment restricting marriage in the state to one man and one woman. Two months later, the state also passed legislation creating an entity called reciprocal beneficiaries, which provided benefits on about 60 matters for same-sex couples equivalent to those for opposite-sex couples. In November of 1998, voters ratified the proposed constitutional amendment, permitting (but not requiring) the state legislature to limit marriage to opposite-sex couples.

At the time of that vote, the status of the original *Baehr* lawsuit was still in limbo because of Judge Chang's ruling and the vote on the constitutional amendment. In December 1999, the state supreme court resolved that ambiguity by ruling that the legislature's action in limiting the scope of marriage in the state made the *Baehr* case moot (for a detailed chronology of the *Baehr* case, see Partners Task Force for Gay and Lesbian Couples 2002; for the supreme court's ruling, see No. 20371 2006).

Baehr and the possibility it created that same-sex marriage might be ruled a constitutional right in Hawaii caused a wave of panic through most of the United States. During 1996, legislation banning same-sex marriages was introduced in 32 states (Alabama, Alaska, Arizona, California, Colorado, Delaware, Florida, Georgia, Hawaii, Idaho, Illinois, Indiana, Iowa, Kansas, Louisiana, Maine, Maryland, Michigan, Missouri, Nebraska,

New Jersey, New Mexico, New York, North Carolina, Oklahoma, Pennsylvania, Rhode Island, South Carolina, South Dakota, Tennessee, Virginia, and Washington), and the governors of Alabama and Mississippi issued (probably illegal) executive orders banning the practice (United Church of Christ 1998, 8). (Utah had already banned same-sex marriage in 1995, the first state in the union to do so.) At the same time, state legislatures also became concerned about the possibility of having to recognize same-sex marriages conducted in other states. Under the so-called full faith and credit clause of the U.S. Constitution (Article 4, Section 1), states are generally expected to respect the "public acts, records, and judicial proceedings" of other states. Passing legislation renouncing that practice is very unusual, but the *Baehr* case inspired legislators in nearly every state to introduce bills taking just that action. Eventually, all but about a half dozen states have passed laws of this kind, now known as "defense of marriage" acts. And in September 1996, the U.S. Congress passed (by a vote of 85 to 14 in the Senate and 342 to 67 in the House) and President Bill Clinton signed a National Defense of Marriage Act, allowing the U.S. government to ignore any acts of marriage between individuals of the same sex conducted in any individual state.

References

Baehr v. Miike. 1996. http://archives.starbulletin.com/96/12/03/news/ssruling.txt. Accessed on January 17, 2010.

Bailey, Derrick Sherwin. 1955. *Homosexuality and the Western Christian Tradition*. New York: Longmans, Green.

Baker v. Nelson. 1972. http://www.scribd.com/doc/21017674/Baker-v-Nelson-409-U-S-810-1972. Accessed on January 6, 2010.

Barrett, Ellen M. 1979. "Legal Homophobia and the Christian Church." *Hastings Law Journal* 30 (4): 1019–27.

Bianquis, Thierry. 1986. "La Famille en Islam Arabe." In Andre Burguière et al., eds., *Histoire de la Famille*. Vol. 2. Paris: Armand Colin, , 389–449.

Boswell, John E. 1980. *Christianity, Social Tolerance, and Homosexuality*. Chicago: University of Chicago Press.

Bronson, Ken. 2004. "Children's Home Society Waffles," http://www.may-18-1970.org/Quest-40.html. Accessed on January 5, 2010.

Bullough, Vern L. 1976. *Sex, Society, and History*. New York: Science History Publications.

Camenker, Brian. 2008. "What Same-Sex 'Marriage' Has Done to Massachusetts. It's Far Worse than Most People Realize." http://www .massresistance.org/docs/marriage/effects_of_ssm.html. Accessed on January 17, 2010.

Carter, David. 2004. *Stonewall: The Riots That Sparked the Gay Revolution*. New York: St. Martin's Press.

Crompton, Louis. 1976. "Homosexuals and the Death Penalty in Colonial America." *Journal of Homosexuality*. 1 (3): 277–93.

Crompton, Louis. 2003. *Homosexuality and Civilization*. Cambridge, MA: The Belknap Press of Harvard University Press.

Cruikshank, Margaret. 1992. *The Gay and Lesbian Liberation Movement*. London: Routledge.

Cutler, Marvin, ed. 1956. *Homosexuals Today: A Handbook of Organizations and Publications*. Los Angeles: ONE, Inc.

Daniel, Marc. 1994. "Arab Civilization and Male Love." Translated by Winston Leyland. In Jonathan Goldberg, ed., *Reclaiming Sodom*. New York: Routledge., 59–65

DeYoung, James B. 2000. *Homosexuality: Contemporary Claims Examined in Light of the Bible and Other Ancient Literature and Law*. Grand Rapids, MI: Kregel Publications.

Duberman, Martin. 1993. *Stonewall*. New York: Penguin Books.

Dunne, Bruce. 2010. "Power and Sexuality in the Middle East." http:// www.merip.org/mer/mer206/bruce.htm. Accessed on January 12, 2010.

elephantjournal.com. 2009. http://www.elephantjournal.com/2009/02/ gregory-hinton-for-daily-camera-march-26-1975-the-first-same-sex -marriage-licenses-in-the-united-states-were-heroically-issued-in -boulder-by-county-clerk-clela-rorex/. Accessed on January 5, 2010.

"The Epic of Gilgamesh." 2009. http://www.ancienttexts.org/library/ mesopotamian/gilgamesh/. Accessed on January 12, 2010.

Epstein, Louis M. 1948. *Sex Laws and Customs in Judaism*. New York: D. D. Bloch Publishing Company.

Fone, Byrne. 2000. *Homophobia: A History*. New York: Metropolitan Press

Forbes, Jack D. 2004. "What Is Marriage? A Native American View." http://nas.ucdavis.edu/Forbes/what_is%20Marriage.pdf. Accessed on January 13, 2010.

Ford, Clellan S., and Frank A. Beach. 1951. *Patterns of Sexual Behavior*. New York: Harper & Brothers.

Frier, Bruce W. 2004. "Roman Same-Sex Weddings from the Legal Perspective." *Classic Studies Newsletter* 10 (Winter 2004). ~http://www.umich.edu/~classics/news/newsletter/winter2004/weddings.html. Accessed on January 13, 2010.

Gerber, Henry. 1962. "The Society for Human Rights—1925." *One*. September. http://www.glapn.org/sodomylaws/usa/illinois/ilnews02.htm. Accessed on January 15, 2010.

Gerig, Bruce L. 2010. "Homosexuality in the Ancient Near East, Beyond Egypt." http://epistle.us/hbarticles/neareast.html. Accessed on January 13, 2010.

Gibbon, Edward. 1880. *History of the Decline and Fall of the Roman Empire.* 6 vols. Edited by Dean Milman, François-Pierre-Guillaume Guizot, and William Smith. New York: Harpers.

Greenberg, David F. 1988. *The Construction of Homosexuality.* Chicago: University of Chicago Press.

Hay, Bob. "Comrades of the Cut Sleeve: Homosexuality in China." 2009. http://bobhay.org/_downloads/_homo/11%20Comrades%20of%20%20the%20Cut%20Sleeve.pdf. Accessed on January 12, 2010.

Henderson, Bernard W. 1923. *The Life and Principate of the Emperor Hadrian, A.D. 76–138.* London: Methuen & Company.

Hinsch, Bret. 1990. *Passion of the Cut Sleep.* Berkeley: University of California Press.

"History of Chinese Homosexuality." 2004. http://www.chinadaily.com.cn/english/doc/2004-04/01/content_319807.htm. Accessed on January 12, 2010.

"History of Sodomy Laws." 2004. http://www.glapn.org/sodomylaws/history/history.htm. Accessed on January 14, 2010.

Holleran, Andrew. 2008. *Chronicle of a Plague, Revisited: AIDS and Its Aftermath* . Philadelphia: Da Capo Press.

Homer. 2004. *The Iliad.* Translated by Ian Johnston. http://www.mlahanas.de/Greeks/Texts/Iliad/iliad24.htm. Accessed on January 12, 2010.

"Homosexual Rights Around the World." 2006. http://www.asylumlaw.org/docs/sexualminorities/rights%20around%20the%20world-06.pdf. Accessed on January 12, 2010.

"Homosexuality in Greece and Rome: A Sourcebook of Basic Documents in Translation." 2010. http://www.laits.utexas.edu/ancienthomosexuality/bibliography.php. Accessed on January 12, 2010.

Human Rights Campaign. 2010. "Statewide Employment Laws and Policies." http://www.hrc.org/documents/Employment_Laws_and_Policies.pdf. Accessed on January 15, 2010.

Johansson, Warren, and William A. Percy. (2009). "Homosexuality in the Middle Ages." http://www.williamapercy.com/wiki/index.php/Homosexuality_in_the_Middle_Ages. Accessed on January 14, 2010.

Katz, Jonathan. 1976. *Gay American History: Lesbians and Gay Men in the U.S.A.* New York: Thomas Y. Crowell Company.

Kennedy, Dominic. 2007. "Gays Deserve Torture, Death Penalty, Iranian Minister Says." http://www.foxnews.com/story/0,2933,311025,00.html. Accessed on January 12, 2010.

"The Law in England, 1290–1885." 2010. http://www.fordham.edu/halsall/pwh/englaw.html. Accessed on January 14, 2010.

Lawrence v. Texas. 2003. http://caselaw.lp.findlaw.com/scripts/getcase.pl?court=US&vol=000&invol=02-102. Accessed on January 14, 2010.

Marjorie Jones et al., Appellants v. James Hallahan, Clerk of the Jefferson County Court, Appellee. 1973. http://marriagelawfoundation.org/cases%5CJones%20v.%20Hallahan.pdf. Accessed on January 5, 2010.

National Gay and Lesbian Task Force. 2009. "Employment Non-Discrimination Act." http://www.thetaskforce.org/issues/nondiscrimination/ENDA_main_page. Accessed on January 17, 2010.

Neill, James. 2009. *The Origins and Role of Same-Sex Relations in Human Societies.* Jefferson, NC: McFarland & Company.

No. 20371. 1996. http://hawaii.gov/jud/20371.pdf. Accessed on January 17, 2010.

Painter, George. 2004. "The Sensibilities of Our Forefathers: The History of Sodomy Laws in the United States." http://www.glapn.org/sodomylaws/sensibilities/virginia.htm. Accessed on January 14, 2010.

Partners Task Force for Gay and Lesbian Couples. 2002. http://www.buddybuddy.com/t-line-3.html. Accessed on January 17, 2010.

"Poll Results." 2007. http://atheism.about.com/gi/pages/poll.htm?linkback=http://atheism.about.com/b/a/250223.htm&poll_id=1770807142&poll=2&submit1=Submit+Vote. Accessed on January 12, 2009.

Rimmerman, Craig A. 2008. *The Lesbian and Gay Movements: Assimilation or Liberation?* Boulder, CO: Westview Press.

"Same Sex Marriage, Civil Unions and Domestic Partnerships." 2009. http://www.ncsl.org/IssuesResearch/HumanServices/SameSexMarriage/tabid/16430/Default.aspx. Accessed on January 6, 2010.

Shilts, Randy. 2007. *And the Band Played On,* rev. ed. New York: St. Martin's Griffin.

"Sodomy Laws: Virginia." 2004. http://www.glapn.org/sodomylaws/usa/virginia/virginia.htm. Accessed on January 14, 2010.

Teal, Donn. 1995. *The Gay Militants: How Gay Liberation Began in America, 1969–1971*. New York: St. Martin's Press.

"This Alien Legacy: The Origins of 'Sodomy' Laws in British Colonialism." 2008. New York: Human Rights Watch. Also available online at http://www.hrw.org/sites/default/files/reports/lgbt1208_web.pdf.

United Church of Christ. 1998. "Same-Sex Marriage Rights: A Timeline." http://www.ucc.org/assets/pdfs/emr9.pdf. Accessed on January 17, 2010.

"US Senate Candidate Wants Death Penalty for Homosexuals." 2006. http://www.wtol.com/Global/story.asp?S=4590031. Accessed on January 12, 2009.

Whitmore, William H. 1889. *The Colonial Laws of Massachusetts*. Boston: Rockwell and Churchill. Available online at http://books.google.com/books?id=Vzno-EGGVcoC&printsec=frontcover&dq=The+Colonial+Laws+of+Massachusetts&cd=1#v=onepage&q&f=false.

Williams, Walter L. 1986. *The Spirit and the Flesh*. Boston: Beacon Press.

2

Problems, Controversies, and Solutions

Introduction

On January 11, 2010, trial began in the U.S. District Court for the Northern District of California on a suit to overturn voter-approved Proposition 8, passed in November 2008. That proposition offered an amendment to the state constitution defining marriage as a contract between one man and one woman. In his opening statement for the defense, attorney Charles Cooper referred to "traditional marriage" 14 times. He said, among other comments, that

> [Traditional marriage is the union of a man and a woman, a] definition that has prevailed in virtually every society in recorded history, since long before the advent of modern religions.
> [T]he traditional age-old limitation of marriage to one man and one woman is worth preserving.
> [T]raditional marriage . . . has ancient and powerful religious connotations. (Beck 2010)

The debate over same-sex marriage involves arguments over a number of different issues. Proponents of the practice say that same-sex marriage is a civil right to which all American citizens are entitled, that same-sex marriage helps stabilize relationships between loving individuals of the same gender, and that same-sex marriage poses no threat to opposite-sex marriage that has been common for so many centuries. Opponents of same-sex marriage say that the practice legitimizes sinful behavior, that it sends the wrong message to children about an immoral type of sexuality, and that it gives special privileges to a certain class of American citizens.

No issue is more contentious, however, than the argument that marriage in Judeo-Christian culture has always been an institution between one man and one woman. Whether authorized by religious dogma or civil law, critics point out, marriage has always and without exception been permitted only between opposite-sex couples. Given the fundamental character of this argument, the place to begin in a review of the dispute over same-sex marriage is almost certainly a review of the nature of marriage in Judeo-Christian culture. Is it, in fact, true that opposite-sex marriage is the one and only legitimate type of relationship permitted in Jewish and Christian cultures, as far back as one can determine?

The issue as to how a society views same-sex marriage is a very different—and arguably much more fundamental—question than how it views same-sex relationships in general. One can imagine that a society tolerates, accepts, or even honors same-sex relationships (as discussed at length in Chapter 1) without its also acknowledging the right of same-sex couples to enter into a formal and legal relationship, such as marriage. The state of affairs in the United States today illustrates that point. Recent polls indicate that roughly 6 out of 10 Americans are willing to accept the proposition that same-sex relationships are morally acceptable. Even larger majorities (usually 80% and more) agree that gay men and lesbians should not be deprived of housing, employment, public accommodation, or other civil rights on the basis of their sexual orientation (see, for example, PollingReport .com 2010). However, a significant majority of Americans still believe that same-sex couples should not have the right to marry, with generally about 65 percent of respondents opposed to same-sex marriage and about 35 percent in favor of the practice (PollingReport.com 2010).

It may be that this disconnect in public opinion about same-sex relationships and marriage is an example of the view sometimes expressed that "I don't care what they [gay men and lesbians] do in the privacy of their own home, as long as they don't parade their sexual acts in public [that is, seek legal recognition of their 'lifestyle')." In view of this attitude, what is actually known about the legal status of same-sex marriage in the history of Western culture?

Same-Sex Marriage in Judeo-Christian History

Most opponents of same-sex marriage base their objections to a large extent on biblical injunctions on the topic. They usually cite one or more of the following passages to justify their stance on same-sex marriage:

- Thou shalt not lie with mankind, as with womankind: it is abomination. (Leviticus 18:22)
- If a man also lie with mankind, as he lieth with a woman, both of them have committed an abomination: they shall surely be put to death; their blood shall be upon them. (Leviticus 20: 13)
- Know ye not that the unrighteous shall not inherit the kingdom of God? Be not deceived: neither fornicators, nor idolaters, nor adulterers, nor effeminate, nor abusers of themselves with mankind. (I Corinthians 6: 9)
- For this cause God gave them up unto vile affections: for even their women did change the natural use into that which is against nature:
  And likewise also the men, leaving the natural use of the woman, burned in their lust one toward another; men with men working that which is unseemly, and receiving in themselves that recompence of their error which was meet. (Romans 1: 26–27)
- Knowing this, that the law is not made for a righteous man, but for the lawless and disobedient, for the ungodly and for sinners, for unholy and profane, for murderers of fathers and murderers of mothers, for manslayers,
  For whoremongers, for them that defile themselves with mankind, for menstealers, for liars, for perjured persons, and if there be any other thing that is contrary to sound doctrine. (1 Timothy 1: 9–10)

(It should be pointed out that the wording of these passages has been changed during a number of translations over hundreds of years, and a number of authorities differ as to the actual meanings of some terms, especially terms for which there is no precise comparable word in modern English.)

Some historians point out that these prohibitions arise relatively late in the history of Israelite culture, after the Israelites returned from Babylonian exile in the late sixth century BCE. Prior to this period, there appear to be no prohibitions on homosexual activity within the society. Indeed, one authority has written that "there is a distinct lack of preaching on sexual matters [of any type] among the Hebrews of the pre-exilic [pre-Babylonian exile] period" (Epstein 1948, 3–4).

The prohibitions found in modern versions of the Bible are generally construed as an effort by God (and/or his spokesperson on Earth) to warn the Israelites of any number of unapproved practices engaged in by their neighbors. They were a set of guidelines designed to make the Israelites a race of people that was different and special. Thus, in addition to prohibitions against same-sex relationships and same-sex marriage (which, by inference, were practiced by neighboring cultures), a very long list of other banned practices is to be found in the Bible, most of them in the book of Leviticus. Among these prohibitions are adultery (18: 20 and 20: 10), bestiality (18: 23 and 20: 15 and 16), theft (19: 11), lying (19: 11), profanity (19: 12 and 20: 9), hating another person (19: 17), taking vengeance on another person (19: 18), planting more than one type of seed in a field (19: 19), wearing a garment made of both linen and wool (19: 19), eating any food that contains blood (19: 26), cutting one's hair or beard (19: 27), having a tattoo (19: 28), and using false weights and balances (19: 36). A very large variety of foods are also prohibited in chapter 11 of Leviticus, including pigs, horses, camels, rats, cats, dogs, snakes, raccoons, squirrels, most insects, many birds (such as eagles, sparrows, owls, and crows), and many forms of seafood (such as catfish, sharks, scampi, octopus, squid, shellfish, and whales) (Divine Law 1999). Modern-day followers of a literal interpretation of the Bible presumably respect and observe all items on this list of prohibitions.

Many modern interpreters of scriptural proscriptions of same-sex relationships and same-sex marriage take a relatively simplistic view that biblical passages mean just what they say: same-sex relationships of all kind are prohibited. In fact, biblical scholars have historically held somewhat different views on the issue. In many instances, they have questioned whether

the story of Sodom and Gomorrah (Genesis 19), the laws of Leviticus, and the proscriptions against homosexual acts in I Corinthians, Romans, and I Timothy mean precisely what many church
leaders and the general public have come to believe that they
say, or whether these messages are more complex, requiring that
the modern world take a more careful look at the cultural context
in which those passages were written. As just one example, a
number of scholars have asked whether the proscription in Leviticus that "[t]hou shall not lie with mankind, as with womankind"
actually refers to same-sex acts as they are viewed in the modern
world. Instead, a long-held alternative is that, given the original
language used, the prohibition is actually against the practice of
using males as prostitutes in temple ceremonies, a practice
common among tribal neighbors of the Israelites (see, for example, Gay Christian Network 2010; Liberated Christians 1998; Religious Tolerance 2008; Walker 1999).

The appeal by some modern writers to the Bible as the source
of Western culture's one-man, one-woman model of "traditional
marriage" is also problematic on other grounds. Some scholars
have noted that the Bible mentions other types of marriages—
perhaps as many as eight in all—described and sanctioned by
the scriptures. For example, Jacob had two wives, Leah and
Rachel (Genesis 29: 1–30); Esau had three wives, Adah, Aholiba-
mah, and Bashemath (Genesis 36: 2–3); Abijah had 14 wives (II
Samuel 24: 9); and Solomon had 700 wives and 300 royal concu-
bines (I Kings 11: 1–3). Some scholars also recognize another type
of marriage, that which includes a man, his legal wife, and a
slave. Such a marriage is described in Genesis 16: 2–3, when
Sarah, who has been unable to bear a child with Abraham, offers
her slave, Hagar, as a "substitute wife," who may be able to have
offspring with him. Other types of nontraditional marriages
described in the Bible and apparently sanctioned by God include
contracts between a rapist and his victim, a male soldier and a
female prisoner of war, and two slaves (Religious Tolerance 2006).

In spite of any current controversy over the scriptural basis of
one-man, one-woman marriage, it is clear that over time, after the
death of Jesus, a Christian model of marriage similar to that promoted by most modern Christians evolved. That model is based
essentially on the union of one man and one woman for the purpose of producing children. The procreative element of Christian
marriage remains an essential component of the one-man, one-
woman standard for marriage. Both opponents of same-sex

marriage and jurists who have to rule on that issue tend to embrace this philosophy. For example, in the landmark case of *Baker v. Nelson* (191 N.W. 2d. 185), Justice C. Donald Peterson noted that "[t]he institution of marriage as a union man and woman, uniquely involving the procreation and rearing of children within a family, is as old as the book of Genesis" (*Baker v. Nelson* 1971, 185).

Given that Jesus himself said very little or nothing about marriage, and nothing at all about same-sex relationships, the Christian model of marriage is most commonly attributed to the philosophy and writings of Saint Paul. It was better, he said, to avoid all sexual contact in one's life whatsoever, as he himself had apparently been able to do. But, recognizing the powerful force of the sexual drive, Paul realized that most men (and probably women) could not follow his example. Therefore, he acknowledged that marriage was necessary to avoid having men and women involved in sexual activity outside the bonds of matrimony. Among his many admonitions on the subject, Paul wrote:

It is good for a man not to touch a woman.
Nevertheless, to avoid fornication, let every man have his own wife, and let every woman have her own husband.
For I would that all men were even as I myself. But every man hath his proper gift of God, one after this manner, and another after that.
I say therefore to the unmarried and widows, It is good for them if they abide even as I. (I Corinthians 7: 1–2, 8–9)

Even then, marriage was not officially affirmed a sacrament of the Roman Catholic Church until 1208, when the Council of Florence and Pope Innocent IV declared it so, intimating in the process that matrimony had always been a sacred rite of the church (Lehmkuhl 1910).

Rome and the Middle Ages

For the first three and a half centuries of its history, Christianity probably had relatively little impact on the world around it. In the world's most powerful nation at the time, Rome, same-sex relationships and same-sex marriage were not uncommon nor prohibited (see Chapter 1). With the ascension of the first

Christian emperor, Constantine, that situation changed. Christian doctrine on many issues, including same-sex relationships, became incorporated into Roman law. In 342 CE, for example, the emperor Constantius II issued a regulation making same-sex marriage illegal. The regulation survives in the Theodosian Code of 429, a compilation of laws adopted since the time of Constantine. It said in part anyone who " 'marries' in the manner of a woman ... when Venus is changed into another form" shall be subjected to "exquisite punishment" (Greenberg 1990, 229). The precise meaning of that law has been the subject of scholarly dispute, with some writers arguing that it was passed "facetiously," perhaps at least partly because an author of the law, the emperor Constans (Constantine's son), was himself accused of having a number of male lovers (Frakes 2006).

In any case, Roman law gradually became more clear over time about same-sex relationships in general, and same-sex marriage in particular. For example, in the year 390 CE, a law was passed specifying the death penalty (by public burning) for any man who "played the role of a woman" in a sexual encounter (Frakes 2006). For a period of time, Christianity battled with other religions and philosophies, such as Stoicism, Manicheism, and Neo-Platonism for dominance in setting moral and ethical standards in the Roman empire. But it eventually won out, with increasingly severe punishments for same-sex relationships and same-sex marriage. By 529, for example, Roman law no longer distinguished between active and passive participants in same-sex activities. The *Corupus Iurus Civilis* ("Body of Civil Law") promulgated by Emperor Justinian in that year called for the death penalty for all such individuals. According to one authority, that code, which summarized more than 200 years of Roman laws on a host of topics, "represent[s] the heritage which late Roman law was to leave to posterity [on the subject of same-sex relationships] (di Beradino 1997, 10). Christianity had triumphed. Same-sex relationships were damned, and same-sex marriage was beyond consideration.

And yet, such might not have been the case. While canon law (usually the dominant legal force in most countries of Western Europe) strictly prohibited same-sex relationships and same-sex marriages in civil society, the situation may have been quite different within the Roman Catholic Church (and, later, the Eastern Orthodox Church) itself. Such a dichotomy is hardly surprising. In the first place, members of the clergy were, in most cases, normal, healthy men themselves. They must often have had the same sexual appetites as ordinary men and indulged those appetites as did their lay brothers. (The issue with women was very different, of course, because women never held leadership positions in early Christianity.) Countless numbers of clergy, from local priests to popes, had spouses of the opposite sex and families, not so very different from those of the laity. For example, evidence suggests that at least 10 popes were married before receiving holy orders, and 5 were sexually active during their pontificate during the Middle Ages. The first in this list, Pope Sergius III, apparently had a son with his mistress, Marozia, a married woman. That son later became Pope John XI (Mann 1912). Somewhat later, one of Sergius's successor's sexual life was so blatant that his official entry in *The Catholic Encyclopedia* declares that he was "a coarse, immoral man, whose life was such that the Lateran was spoken of as a brothel, and the moral corruption in Rome became the subject of general odium" (Kirsch 1910).

In addition, members of the clergy who were attracted to other men were in, for them, an almost ideal—and perhaps seductive—situation, a community where one's only social contacts were with others of the same sex. In a very simplistic sense, one might ask what a man who was sexually attracted to other men would do with his life in the Middle Ages? If one remained in the secular world, he would almost certainly be expected to marry and raise a family. The clergy at least offered an escape from that option and, perhaps, an opportunity to develop one or more relationships with other individuals.

As might be expected, written records concerning same-sex relationships among the Roman Catholic clergy in the Middle Ages are sparse. But a few documents remain that suggest that the hypothesis in the preceding paragraph might have some validity. In his book *Christianity, Social Tolerance, and Homosexuality*, for example, Yale historian John Boswell reprints some letters between members of the clergy that have strong erotic overtones. For example, a leading theologian at the court of Charlemagne, Alcuin, wrote a number of erotic poems to other clergymen. In one, written to Arno, bishop of Salzburg, he says that

> I think of your love and friendship with such sweet memories, reverend bishop, that I long for that lovely time when I may be able to clutch the neck of your

sweetness with the fingers of my desires. Alas, if only it were granted to me, as it was to Habakkuk, to be transported to you, how would I sink into your embraces, . . . how would I cover, with tightly pressed lips, not only your eyes, ears, and mouth but also your every finger and your toes, not once but many a time. (Boswell 1980, 190; see remaining sections of this chapter for more examples of the same)

Given these two factors, it would hardly be surprising if same-sex relationships were not uncommon in the early church, as they have perhaps remained to the present day. (Based on a number of surveys, the best estimate appears to be that about one-third of all priests in the Roman Catholic Church today are attracted to members of the same sex; for a summary of those studies, see Religious Tolerance 2009.) A number of scholars have explored the world of same-sex relationships in the early Roman Catholic Church, with some discoveries having been made that are, perhaps, somewhat surprising. The evidence now suggests that not only were same-sex relationships relatively common among the clergy, but they were, in at least some instances, recognized, honored, and legitimized in formal ceremonies.

The person perhaps most closely associated with the study of same-sex unions in the Roman Catholic Church during the Middle Ages is probably John E. Boswell (1947–94), formerly A. Whitney Griswold Professor of History and chair of the Department of History at Yale University. In 1994, a few weeks before his death, Boswell's book *Same-Sex Unions in Premodern Europe* was published. The book summarized 12 years of Boswell's research at dozens of major libraries on original manuscripts in half a dozen languages. He came to the conclusion that "homosexual marriage ceremonies" were widely known in the Catholic world from the fifth century on. "Such ceremonies," he went on, "were performed in Catholic churches by priests and either established what the community regarded as marriages, or commemorated special friendships, in both cases in devoutly Christian terms."

In his book, Boswell lists 62 manuscripts that purportedly refer to same-sex unions. He also provides verbatim translations of 18 of those documents (Boswell 1994, 283–390). An example of the kind of ceremony that Boswell cites is the following, taken from a document entitled "Office for Same-Gender Union," currently held at the Mount Athos Panteleimon Monastery in Halkadiki, Greece:

> O Lord our God and Ruler, who madest humankind after thine image and likeness, and gavest them power of life everlasting, who approved it when thy holy apostles Philip and Bartholomew were united, bound together not be nature but in the communion of holy spirit, and who didst approve that thy holy martyrs Serge and Bacchus should be united, bless also these they servants, N. and N., joined not by nature but in the way of faith. Grant unto them, Lord, to love each other without hatred and to abide without scandal all the days of their lives, with the help of the Blessed Mother of God and all thy saints, because Thine is the power and the kingdom and the power and the glory, Father, Son and Holy Spirit. (Boswell 1994, 329)

Boswell is by no means the only scholar to have uncovered the institution of formal, at least quasi-legal unions among Roman Catholic clergy. For example, the Russian Orthodox theologian Pavel Florenskij (also Florensky, 1882–1937) wrote about the validation of similar same-sex unions in Orthodox churches. As described by William Eskridge in his review of the history of same-sex marriage, Florenskij described a series of steps in a process known as "brother-making," "enfraternization," or "spiritual brotherhood." Those steps included

- The couple stands in front of the altar, with the older brother on the right.
- The ceremony begins with prayers and litanies that celebrate similar ceremonies with other couples from the church.
- The couple is joined by a girdle that surrounds them both, signifying their union in Christ.
- The priest reads from the scripture a passage such as I Corinthians 12: 27 ("For as the body is one, and hath many members, and all the members of that one body, being many, are one body: so also is Christ.") and offers more prayers.
- The congregation joins in the Lord's Prayer, after which all assembled take part in communion.

- The priest leads the couple around the lectern while all sing a hymn.
- The couple exchange a kiss, and the service ends with all singing Psalm 133: 1 ("Behold, how good and how pleasant it is for brethren to dwell together in unity!"). (as cited in Eskridge 1993, 1450–51)

The publication of *Same-Sex Unions in Premodern Europe* in 1994 caused a sensation in the academic world. On the one hand Boswell's text provided a new and dramatically different view of the role of same-sex relationships and same-sex unions (including marriage) in the Middle Ages. One reviewer described the book as a "brilliant, learned, engaging, talkative, and insistent argument that the ancient and medieval church celebrated the same-sex equivalent of its heterosexual marriage ceremony" (Bennison 1995, 256). Other views were less complimentary. In one of the most hostile reviews, medieval historian Marian Therese Horvat called Boswell's book "advocacy scholarship" that had little redeeming value. She said the book revealed a "complete misunderstanding of the underlying spirit of the Age of Faith." The worst aspect of the book, she said, was that it was "bad history" that was "even more dangerous than the practice of bad medicine, because its poison seeps into the very soul of Christian Civilization" (Horvat 2002).

One of the most common criticisms of Boswell's book was that the ceremony he most commonly described, known as adelphopoiesis, really means just what the direct Greek translation suggest: "brother" (ἀδελφός; adelphos) "I make" (ποιέω; poieo). That is, critics suggested that the ceremonies Boswell described are really nothing more than affirmations of close friendship in Christ, rather than erotic love relationships.

Such may, of course, very well be true. This controversy illustrates once more the problems faced by modern scholars in translating ancient texts and trying to understand the subtle meanings contained in terms and phrases that may have no modern counterpart. Almost certainly, the questions raised by Boswell in his book can never be definitively answered, and scholars are likely to continue the debate over the true meaning of adelphopoiesis for years to come. The interesting point is that a scholarly and esoteric debate over religious ceremonies from the Middle Ages first published in 1994 has now become an important component of the modern-day debate over same-sex marriage, as proponents and opponents do battle over the concept of a Roman Catholic church that may (or may not) once have blessed same-sex unions with the same authenticity granted to opposite-sex marriages.

"Traditional Marriage"

The argument over same-sex unions in the Roman Catholic and Orthodox churches notwithstanding, there can be little doubt that an institution now labeled as "traditional marriage" did develop among the laity in Christian societies during the Middle Ages. That institution consisted of one man and one woman whose primary purpose it was to bear and raise children. But that "traditional marriage," which survived well into the twentieth century, was very different from what most people think of as a "conventional marriage" today.

In the first place, love was generally not considered to be a factor of any significance in the contracting of a "traditional marriage." Perhaps more than anything else, a "traditional marriage" was an economic transaction in which a man acquired a woman to be his companion and the mother of his children. Such transactions often involved the transfer of financial assets such as money and property in a contract arranged between a bridegroom and the prospective bride's father, a so-called *bride sale*. The symbol of the transaction was generally a ring, thought of as a "down payment" on the bride's dowry. The ring has, of course, remained a part of the modern marriage ceremony, although it no longer necessarily represents the purchase of a woman by a man. Without question, many husbands and wives grew to love each other over time, although love itself was almost never considered an issue in contracting a marriage ("Love, Marriage, Romance and Women . . . in Medieval and Celtic Culture" 1998).

Procreation was a critical issue for families in the Middle Ages and Renaissance for a number of reasons. The birth of a boy child, for example, ensured that the father's family line and name would be perpetuated. In addition, children were expected to begin work at an early age, certainly before puberty, helping in the fields and in cottage industries operated by the family. Children were, thus, an essential economic asset. Parents also depended on children for support and comfort during their own old age.

In many instance, marriages were arranged by some person, related or not related to a prospective bride and groom. These arranged marriages were designed to achieve some stable family unit, as interpreted by the arranger of the marriage. For example, in 1344 the ruler of an estate in Weitenau in the Black Force held the authority to arrange marriages for all girls over the age of 14 and all boys over the age of 18 living on his property (Youngs 2006, 137).

Among the nobility, marriage served other functions, such as extending the land over which a man had control, increasing his material wealth, and ensuring the maintenance of peace among neighboring states. Marriages were arranged by parents with political considerations such as these, often when the prospective bride and groom were very young ("Noble Life" 2010).

An important feature of "traditional marriages" was the unequal status of men and women in such arrangements. Generally speaking, when a woman married she lost all of her financial assets as well as much of her personal freedom. The English essayist, Daniel Defoe, regarded this type of marriage (a marriage without love) as "legalized prostitution" (Novak 2001, 68). The great English jurist, William Blackstone, provided the legal basis for this view of marriage in his monumental work on English law, *Commentaries on the Laws of England*. He wrote that "[b]y marriage, the very being or legal existence of a woman is suspended, or at least incorporated or consolidated into that of the husband, under whose wing, protection, or cover she performs everything" (Blackstone 1765, 430). In one famous example of this legal principle, a leader of the English suffragist movement, Millicent Garrett Fawcett, expressed her outrage when she reported to a local constabulary the theft of her purse. Her outrage was based on the court's charge that the theft had taken "£1, 18s. 6d., the property of Henry Fawcett," an action that, she later wrote, made her feel "as if I had been charged with theft myself" (Offen 2010).

One interesting manifestation of the role of women in "traditional marriage" involves the practice by which a bride gives up her maiden name to take her husband's surname at the wedding ceremony. Many people believe that this custom reflects the transfer of a piece of property (the bride) from one owner (her father, whose name she bears before marriage) to a new owner (her new husband, whose name she assumes). Thus the problem faced by many "liberated" women is whether to keep their maiden (paternal) surname or to assume the name of her new "owner," her husband (see, for example, "A New Perspective on Taking Your Husband's Name" 2010).

Over time, more and more women began to rebel against the position in which they found themselves in "traditional marriages," which limited their own freedom and independence. In colonial New England, for example, women who wished to remain financially and legally independent sometimes entered into a relationship with another woman that became known as a *Boston marriage* (Lewis 2010). A Boston marriage might consist of two unmarried women living together (almost certainly in a nonsexual relationships), which allowed them some of the benefits of a family unit without the constraints of the "master-slave" relationship they perceived in "traditional marriage."

The most severe aspects of "traditional marriage," such as the unreasonable constraints on wives in such relationships, gradually began to disappear in some places over a long period of time. An important factor in this evolution in the United States was the changes in sex roles that occurred during World War II. Largely because of the liberating opportunities made available during the war, women became less willing to give up the freedom they had found in war jobs, in the military, and in other positions of independence and responsibility. Many women began to seek a different kind of marriage in which they could become breadwinners, share housekeeping responsibilities and decision making, choose to have or not to have children, and even retain their own maiden names (see, for example, Bryant 2009; Baxandall and Gordon 2000; Rosen 2007).

By no means was this liberated view of marriage acceptable to all—or even most—women and men. The reaction among evangelical women, as an example, is reflected in the formation of the organization Concerned Women for America (CWA) in 1978. Founder Beverly La Haye has written that she was motivated to form the new group after watching a television appearance of Betty Friedan, one of the pioneers of the women's liberation movement in the United States. La Haye says that she jumped up and declared that "Betty Friedan doesn't speak for me and I bet she doesn't speak for the majority of women in this country." She decided that a new organization was needed to save traditional marriage in the United States against a movement that was "destroying the family and threatening the survival of the nation" (Faludi 1991, 247–48). CWA currently claims to have more than a half million members in all 50 states. The first among its six core issues is the family, on which its position is that "marriage consists of one man and one woman." The organization's goal is to "seek to protect and support the Biblical [sic] design of marriage and the gift of children," a position that is very consistent with that of the philosophy of "traditional marriage" outlined above (Concerned Women for America 2010a).

The example of CWA illustrates the fact that many individuals and groups that oppose same-sex marriage really do believe that the practice represents a threat to "traditional marriage" in the most classic sense. They often emphasize a number of other modern trends that threaten "traditional marriage," including divorce, cohabitation, adultery, premarital sex, and absentee fathers (Concerned Women for American 2010b). Such individuals and groups are, then, well within an important historical tradition of theological beliefs about the appropriate nature of marriage in Western culture (for a contemporary view of the role of women in "traditional marriages," see Rainey 1989).

Nontraditional Marriage in Western Culture

In spite of the dominant model of one-man, one-woman marriage in Western culture, a number of exceptions to this model have been attempted. For example, members of the so-called Shaker denomination believed that marriage was no longer a necessity since the second coming of the religion's founder, Mother Ann Lee, in 1747. Church dogma taught that celibacy was a more perfect state than marriage, and adherents to the religion were taught to remain abstinent if they possibly could. The church never specifically banned marriage among its members, but the strong emphasis on celibacy eventually led to the decline and near extinction of the religion. The only way to gain new members, children being virtually out of the question, was recruitment from nonmembers, a practice that resulted in declining numbers over time. Today, a relatively small number of Shaker communities remain in the United States and a few other nations ("Sabbathday Lake Shaker Village" 2010; Foster 1984, chapter 2).

A very different approach to marriage was an essential part of another religious community, a utopian commune founded in 1848 by John Humphrey Noyes in Oneida, New York. Noyes believed that Christ's second coming had already occurred, shortly after his death in 70 CE. He believed that the goal of modern Christians was to rid themselves of sin and become as perfect as possible in the present world, without waiting for death and an ascent to heaven. Noyes's philosophy is generally known as *perfectionism*.

From a practical standpoint, perfectionism implied for Noyes and his followers that Christians should share everything in common, their possessions, work responsibilities, and families. Noyes was convinced that the pattern of "traditional marriage" espoused by most Christians was responsible for most of the world's problems. That institution provided, in the first place, "only a scanty and monotonous allowance" for the natural sexual appetite, especially at an age (adolescence) when it is at its height (all quotations in this paragraph from Holloway 1966, 180–87). The bonding of one man to one woman also is responsible, he thought for "the natural vices of poverty, contraction of taste, and stinginess or jealousy." Noyes believed that the practice of "random procreation" guaranteed by "traditional marriage" would eventually be replaced by "scientific combination," such as that practiced so successfully with domestic animals. "The obvious remedy for these abuses," Noyes believed was "male continence combined with complete freedom of intercourse.'" By male continence, Noyes meant the practice of *coitus reservatus*, or self-control by a man that prevents fertilization of a woman. The concept of *complete freedom of intercourse* eventually became better known as *complex marriage*. In this system, every man had the right to have intercourse with every other woman in the community, and vice versa. Rules were established as to how such activities were to occur, but in principle, complete sexual freedom existed in the community.

The Oneida community survived as a thriving community for only a few decades. To a large extent, it died out when Noyes was unsuccessful in convincing his son, an atheist, to continue his mission. The practice of complex marriage was abandoned in 1879, and the community itself eventually confined its activities to the manufacture of cutlery, an industry in which it was famous until the first decade of the twenty first century (Hillebrand 2008; Klaw 1993).

Without much question, the best known and most successful system of nontraditional marriage is that previously endorsed by the Church of Jesus Christ of Latter-day Saints, more commonly known as the Mormon church. The denomination was founded in 1830 in Fayette Township, New York, by Joseph Smith. Smith had received his first vision of God 10 years earlier and been visited by the angel Moroni in 1823. The angel told Smith of a trove of golden plates containing a new scripture on which a new religion was to be based, the religion that was to become Mormonism (for an early history of Mormonism, see "Introduction to Church History" 2009).

One of the revelations received by Smith came in response to his question as to why prophets in the Old Testament were allowed more than one wife. The response to this question was that God permitted such forms of marriage under certain circumstances ("Origins of Polygamy among the Mormons" 2008). Provided with this information, Smith himself began to take multiple wives, a practice also adopted by other men of the denomination and one that the church did not formally acknowledge until 1852. Then, at a conference of the elders of the church held in Salt Lake City, president Brigham Young and elder Orson Pratt revealed that polygamy had been a common and approved practice in the church for many years ("Deseret News, —Extra, Containing a Revelation on Celestial Marriage" 1852, 1).

The 1852 announcement came only a few years after the Utah Territory was established by the Compromise of 1850. As the years went by, residents of the territory became more interested in being annexed to the United States as a full-fledged state. However, word of the religion's polygamous practices spread throughout the nation, and the federal government refused to consider statehood for the territory as long as the Mormon church recognized polygamy. After a number of battles between federal troops and state militia, a peaceful settlement was reached in 1890 when Wilford Woodruff, president of the church, issued a document now known simply as The Manifesto (and known within the church as Official Declaration—1). In this document, Woodruff said that the church was "not teaching polygamy or plural marriage, nor permitting any person to enter into its practice." He further stated that "[i]nasmuch as laws have been enacted by Congress forbidding plural marriages, which laws have been pronounced constitutional by the court of last resort, I hereby declare my intention to submit to those laws, and to use my influence with the members of the Church over which I preside to have them do likewise (Official Declaration—1 2006).

Although the Church of Jesus Christ of Latter-day Saints now officially disavows polygamy, the tradition lives on in an offshoot of the church known as Mormon fundamentalism (or fundamentalist Mormonism). This line of the denomination originated in the 1920s when a man by the name of Lorin C. Woolley declared that the mother church had been incorrect on a number of doctrinal issues, the most important of which was polygamy. He founded a new denomination in which the right of polygamy was restored to male members of the church (Hales 2008). That offshoot survives today with a nonscientific census placing its adherents at about 37,000 (Winslow 2007). A number of sects within the Mormon fundamentalist movement also exist. These include the Apostolic United Brethren, Church of Jesus Christ in Zion, Church of the Firstborn in the Fullness of Time, Fundamentalist Church of Jesus Christ of Latter Day Saints, Latter Day Church of Christ (Kingston clan), Righteous Branch of the Church of Jesus Christ of Latter-day Saints, School of the Prophets, True and Living Church of Jesus Christ of Saints of the Last Days, Centennial Park group, Nielsen/Naylor Group, and Independent Mormon fundamentalists ("The Latter-day Saint Movement" 2010). One of these branches, the Fundamentalist Church of Jesus Christ of Latter Day Saints, received some notoriety in 2007, when its leader, Warren Jeffs, was convicted of accessory to rape and sentenced to two consecutive terms of five years to life in prison ("Polygamist 'Prophet' to Serve at Least 10 Years in Prison" 2007).

An issue of special interest is the place of same-sex marriage in Native American cultures. Jack D. Forbes, professor emeritus of Native American Studies at the University of California at Davis, has noted that observers who talk about "traditional marriage" refer almost exclusively to that concept within Judeo-Christian culture, which traces back two to three thousand years. But, he points out, an important part of the American heritage is the Native American culture, which has been in existence at least 10 times that long (Forbes 2004). Unlike Judeo-Christian societies, Native American tribes have generally been much more open to a variety of marriage arrangements, include polygamy, cross-generational marriages, and same-sex marriages. "Native communities," Forbes has written, "usually were generally accepting of individual choices so long as they did not serve to damage others or the well-being of the whole" (Forbes 2004). The tradition of the berdache, described in Chapter 1, is one of the oldest and most honored sexual roles in Native American cultures, and same-sex unions between a berdache and another man were widely accepted and, in many cases, regarded as of special importance.

Interestingly enough, regardless of this tradition, modern-day Indian tribes are struggling with the issue of same-sex marriage in much the same way as are most American states. Some tribes have banned same-sex marriage by tribal degree, but one, the Coquille tribe of western Oregon, has approved same-sex marriage and granted full tribal spousal benefits to members of such relationships (Bushyhead 2009). In another instance, the legislative body of the Cherokee Nation has passed legislation banning same-sex marriage, but the nation's highest judicial court has overturned that legislation and ruled that an application for a marriage license by two women must be issued. (That case has been in dispute for a number of years, and the court agreed to rehear testimony again in 2010; see Rifkin 2008).

Same-Sex Marriage: Arguments Pro and Con

A number of arguments have been made, both for and against the legalization of same-sex marriage. Space prevents a complete discussion of all arguments pro and con on this topic. Instead, the following sections summarize some of the most common of those arguments *against* same-sex marriage, followed by rebuttals to those arguments and arguments *in favor of* same-sex marriage, again followed by rebuttals.

Arguments in Opposition to Same-Sex Marriage

Marriage Has Traditionally Been an Institution between One Man and One Woman in Western Culture and Most Other Human Societies

This argument has been presented in some detail in the preceding section. In summary, people who take this position are saying that one-man, one-woman marriage simply *is* the one and only correct legal relationship in human culture. For example, Jay Alan Sekulow, chief counsel for the American Center for Law and Justice, a group opposed to same-sex marriage, testified before the U.S. House of Representatives Judiciary Subcommittee on the Constitution in 2004 that the tradition of one-man, one-woman marriage goes back to the very origins of English and American law. He quoted Justice Blackstone, one of the great early commentators on English law, who said that "it is declared, that all persons may lawfully marry, but such as are prohibited by God's law; and that all marriages contracted by lawful persons in the face of the church, and consummate with bodily knowledge, and fruit of children, shall be indissoluble" ("Testimony of Jay Alan Sekulow" 2004, 14). To emphasize his point, Sekulow then quoted a possibly apocryphal story about Abraham Lincoln asking a friend how many legs a dog has, if you agree to the proposition that its tail counts as a leg. When his friend said, "Five legs, of course," Lincoln only laughed. "No matter what you called a tail," Lincoln said, "it was never going to be a leg" ("Testimony of Jay Alan Sekulow" 2004, 15–16). For Sekulow, the point is that no matter what you choose to call the union of two people *other than one man and one woman*, it will simply never be a marriage.

Rebuttal

The discussion of "traditional marriage" in the preceding section has shown that alternatives to one-man, one-woman marriages have existed in Western culture. Perhaps the best known and longest-lasting of these alternatives has been the practice of polygamy, a part of the Mormon tradition for about 70 years in the church as a whole, and for more than a century in at least some parts of the denomination.

Critics of this argument also point out that fact that many practices once regarded as inviolable and/or sacred because they had been around "forever" and were just simply the right way to do things have eventually been viewed in new a light. Slavery is perhaps the most obvious example. The practice of slavery dates to the earliest history of human society. Written records of the use of warriors and civilians captured in battle as slaves dates to at least the second millennium BCE in Egypt. Rules as to who may and may not be kept as a slave are also discussed at some length in the 25th chapter of the book of Leviticus. The practice of slavery in the United States and other Western nations is too well known to be repeated here. As late as the middle of the nineteenth century, before Lincoln's issuance of the Emancipation Proclamation, the practice of slavery was widespread and completely legal in the United States. Indeed, the practice was enshrined in the U.S. Constitution.

The fact that slavery had always been around and generally recognized as a legitimate right did not prevent a change in viewpoint. Eventually, slavery was outlawed in the United States and internationally, by act of the United Nations, in 1948 (which did not prevent a number of nations, such as Saudi Arabia, Yemen, Peru, and Mauritania, from retaining the practice for another 20 to 40 years) (Bales 2004).

Perhaps more to the point is the practice of miscegenation, marriage between two individuals of different races. That practice was illegal in the United States until 1967, when the U.S. Supreme Court ruled in *Loving v. Virginia* that the state of Virginia's 1924 miscegenation law was unconstitutional. The reasoning of the trial judge whose decision was overruled by the Supreme Court bears a familiar ring in the context of today's debate over same-sex marriage. Marriage between two people of different races is just simply wrong, Judge Leon Bazile wrote:

> Almighty God created the races white, black, yellow, malay and red, and he placed them on separate continents. And, but for the interference with his arrangement, there would be no cause for such marriage. The fact that he separated the races shows that he did not intend for the races to mix. (as cited in Cohen 2009)

Forty years after the Supreme Court's ruling, Jeter Loving spoke about same-sex marriage in the context of her own experience in defeating miscegenation laws in the United States. "Not a day goes by," she said, when she did not remember what it meant to have been given the right to marry the man with whom she was in love. As a result, she went on, "I believe all Americans, no matter their race, no matter their sex, no matter their sexual orientation, should have that same freedom to marry" (Nussbaum 2009).

For proponents of same-sex marriage, the history of miscegenation laws provide a lesson in thinking about laws that "have always been true" and are a "fundamental part of our society that can not be changed."

Same-Sex Marriage Poses a Threat to the Traditional Family

Some critics of same-sex marriage believe and argue that the goal of gay and lesbian activists is not simply to obtain the right to marry for same-sex couples; it is to destroy the very institution of marriage and the family itself. In many cases, the basis for this argument is that gay and lesbian activists have an "agenda" for the overthrow of American society as we know it. Although different writers vary in their approach to this subject, many base their views on a book written by two gay men, Marshall Kirk and Hunter Madsen, in 1989. In that book, *After the Ball: How America Will Conquer Its Fear and Hatred of Gays in the '90s,* Kirk and Madsen described a media campaign by which Americans could be convinced that same-sex relationships are normal and acceptable and that lesbians and gay men are fundamentally no different from people with other sexual orientations (Kirk and Madsen 1990). Some opponents of same-sex marriage view the proposals made by Kirk and Madsen (which generally do not speak of marriage issues directly) as the crystallization of a social agenda laid out by the leaders of the gay and lesbian civil rights movement.

For example, Peter Winn, associate editor of CitizenLink, online news magazine of the conservative evangelical group Focus on the Family, has written that "[t]hey don't just want marriage. They want to destroy marriage—and the family—as we know it" (Winn 2003). It is not clear from Winn's article to whom the "they" in this quotation refers. It could conceivably be all gay men and lesbians, all gay and lesbian activists, only some gay and lesbian activists, or only the specific individuals who are cited in Winn's article. His point seems clear, however, in that he feels that allowing same-sex marriage is likely to lead to the destruction of "traditional marriage" and the traditional family.

Critics who hold this view sometimes suggest that evidence already exists for the effects that same-sex marriage will have on "traditional marriage" and the family. For some reason, the example most commonly mentioned is that of France, which in 1999 adopted legislation granting to same-sex couples many of the rights and privileges enjoyed by opposite-sex couples. The result of that action, according to some observers, has been "the destruction of marriage" (Lutzer 2004, 27). As one speaker at the 2007 World Congress of Families IV noted, one consequence of the new legal rights granted same-sex couples in France has been a 40 percent increase in the number of children born outside marriage (Bull 2010). The speaker concluded from his observations that the issue of same-sex marriage is not really about gay men and lesbians at all; it is about the institutions of marriage and the family and their future chances of survival if same-sex marriage is permitted. Same-sex "marriage" and its variations, he argues, "will turn out in practice to mean the creation of an alternative form of legal coupling, which will over time result in the practical elimination of marriage and put a new, flimsier institution in its place" (Bull 2010).

Rebuttal

One of the problems that proponents of same-sex marriage have with this argument is its lack of specificity. The question they often ask is, "Please explain how granting the right of two men or two women to marry will affect the strength, viability, or sanctity or an opposite-sex marriage" (see, for example, "Mike in Maryland" at "Gay Marriage Is Fading as 'Values' Focal Point" 2009). A critic of Benjamin Bull's argument above might be whether he actually believes that a 40 percent increase in the number of children born out of legal marriage in France is the result of the adoption of civil solidarity pacts that are now available to French same-sex couples. If so, and it may well be true, the argument may then be subject to a variety of demographic tests.

In fact, such tests are already available and have been conducted on a limited basis. The reason such tests are limited, of course, is that same-sex relationships (marriages, civil unions, domestic partnerships, etc.) have been available for only a relatively short period of time. Data on long-term associations between same-sex unions and trends in the stability of marriage and families are still difficult to obtain. Still, some modest trends can be noted. In the first place, the one state in the United States where same-sex marriage has been legal for the longest period of time, Massachusetts, also has the lowest divorce rate of any state in the union. As of 2007, the divorce rate in Massachusetts was 2.3 per thousand. By contrast, the divorce rate in states that have taken some of the strongest stands against legal unions of any kind between same-sex couples are among the highest in the nation: 5.9 in Arkansas, 5.2 in Oklahoma, 4.7 in Kentucky, 4.9 in Idaho, 4.6 in Alabama, and 4.6 in Florida (Divorce Rates by State: 1990, 1995, and 1999–2007 2009).

Similar data are available from Europe. Yale law professor William N. Eskridge Jr. and Manhattan investment banker Darren R. Spedale have been studying data on marriage and divorce trends in Denmark, Norway, and Sweden, where various types of same-sex unions have been legal dating back nearly 20 years. In 2006, they published a book, *Gay Marriage: For Better or for Worse?: What We've Learned from the Evidence*, summarizing the results of their research. They found no evidence whatsoever that the availability of legal unions between same-sex couples had any effects at all on opposite-sex marriage and divorce rates. Indeed, if one were to hypothesize that any relationship at all exists between the two variables, Eskridge and Spedale concluded, it was that same-sex unions promote the stability of opposite-sex marriages (Eskridge and Spedale 2006). In a related paper, these authors summarized their conclusions by noting that "[l]ong-range trends in marriage rates, divorce rates, and nonmarital births either have been unaffected by the advent of same-sex part-nerships or have moved in a direction that suggests that the insti-tution of marriage is strengthening" (Eskridge, Spedale, and Ytterberg 2004, 2).

Very similar results have been obtained by other researchers. For example, Dr. Scot O'Grair has studied marriage, divorce, and birth rates in a number of countries and U.S. states and concluded that it seems that one would have to have "a significant streak of dishonesty" to come to the conclusion that "traditional marriage" is harmed by promoting same-sex marriage. "A more likely con-clusion, if one were force to make conclusions on such data," he concludes, "would be that same-sex marriage benefits the institution of marriage on whole" (O'Grair 2008).

Recognizing Same-Sex Marriage Will Lead to the Legalization of a Host of Other Disreputable Practices

This argument is a classic approach used in debates over many topics. It is based on the assumption that adopting one pol-icy logically requires one to adopt a second policy related to it, which in turn may lead to adopting yet a third, fourth, and other policies. The term used to describe this line of reasoning is the *slippery-slope* argument, suggesting that once one starts down a certain road, it is difficult to turn off that road until a number of related decisions have been made, some (or many) that one did not foresee or approve of at the beginning of the process.

With respect to same-sex marriage, the argument is that once marriage between two people of the same sex is legalized, what is to prevent legalization of a marriage between 2 men and a woman, or 2 woman and a man, or 1 man and 10 women (polyg-amy), or a brother and a sister (endogamy), or a man and his cat, or a woman and her dog? If one believes that marriage is a civil right, as do supporters of same-sex marriage, then how can that same right be denied to people who have other views of the nature of marriage? Supporters of this view generally do not emphasize the possibility of man-dog or woman-cat relation-ships, but do point out the logical necessity of extending marriage privileges to those who believe in polygamy (or polyandry). In a public statement on this issue with regard to the then-proposed (and since-passed) Defense of Marriage Act in 1996, Hadley Arkes, professor of jurisprudence and American institutions at Amherst College, pointed out that "[e]very argument for gay marriage is an argument that would support polygamy.... we can count on the fact that there will be someone, somewhere, ready to press this issue by raising a challenge in the court and testing the limits even further" (Fact Sheet on "Hate Crime" Legislation 2000, 7). Those who press this argument frequently point out that individuals and groups that support same-sex marriage often acknowledge and even endorse this possibility. The policy on polygamy of the American Civil Liberties Union, for example, specifically states that the organization "believes that criminal and civil laws prohibiting or penalizing the practice of plural marriage violate constitutional protections of freedom of expression and association, freedom of religion, and privacy for personal relationships among consenting adults" (National ACLU Policy on Plural Marriage 2008).

Rebuttal

The fact is that many people who support same-sex marriage hold the more general view that whom a person marries is her or his own business and that polygamy and polyandry are perfectly all right. But it is also possible to make an argument that the slippery-slope thesis does not apply in this case. Eugene Volokh, professor at the UCLA School of Law, suggests that what makes a difference is how people view marriage itself. If they think of marriage in terms of "it's none of my business whom people marry," they may have a very different view about the slippery-slope argument and polygamy than someone who believes that marriage between two people has social utility. In the latter case, Volokh argues, people can and probably will look at two different propositions—same-sex marriage and polygamy or polyandry— in very different lights. There is no reason, he says, why individuals cannot make intelligent and informed decisions about the two institutions that are different from each other (Volokh 2005).

The Primary Goal of Marriage Is Procreation, and Gay Men and Lesbians Cannot Procreate

This argument clearly has two parts. The first is very common among opponents of same-sex marriage. It states very simply that same-sex couples should not be allowed to marry because the primary purpose of marriage is to produce children. The second part of the argument is that same-sex couples are biologically not capable of having children. For opponents of same-sex marriage, these two parts go together almost inevitably. Typical of the kinds of comments in debates about same-sex marriage is the following: "A normative marriage of a man and a woman involves the consummation of the marriage and procreative act. A same sex couple will never be able to consummate a marriage and cannot procreate" ("Economic Reasons for Gay Marriage" 2010).

This argument about same-sex relationships has a very long history. In the late 1970s, popular singer Anita Bryant led a campaign in Dade County, Florida, against the adoption of an ordinance banning discrimination against lesbians and gay men in housing and public employment. Bryant mounted a campaign against the organization called Save Our Children, based on her thesis that "[a]s a mother, I know that homosexuals cannot biologically reproduce children; therefore, they must recruit our children" (Andreeva and Kit 2010). The argument continues to be persuasive today among antigay groups. In June 2009, the British far-right political party, National Front, used Bryant's statement as the lead-in to its weekly electronic newsletter outlining the upcoming campaign against "the enslavement of the White people of Britain" ("Now People Rise Up and Storm Break Loose!" 2009, 1).

The fundamental role of procreation in "traditional marriage" is by no means an argument limited to the fringes of the anti-same-sex-marriage movement. Indeed, it is a core argument for almost everyone who opposes any type of marriage other than that between one man and one woman. In a closely reasoned argument against same-sex marriage, Margaret A. Somerville, at the McGill Centre for Medicine, Ethics and Law in Montreal, claims that "traditional marriage" has evolved over millennia as the institution that "establishes the values that govern the transmission of human life to the next generation and the nurturing of that life in the basic societal unit, the family" (Somerville 2003, 3). Marriage never has been, is not, and cannot be, she says, a relationship designed simply to validate a relationship between two individuals, satisfying only their own needs. Confirming the primary goal of marriage as a procreative institution is especially important now, Somerville argues, because of the growth in reproductive technologies that allow procreation to occur outside of the traditional male-female sexual act.

Rebuttal

Rebuttals to this argument typically deal with each of its two separate aspects. In the first place, it is obviously incorrect to say that gay men and lesbians cannot reproduce. That statement suggests that infertility is somehow a biological correlate of homosexuality. Such a conclusion is clearly wrong. The 2000 U.S. census found that 29.6 percent of all lesbians had previously been married to a man, and 18.0 percent of gay men had previously been married to a woman. That these individuals were not infertile is indicated by the fact that 60 percent of all lesbians had had one child, 26 percent had had two children, and 15 percent had had three or more children. Among gay men, the comparable figures were 52 percent for one child, 28 percent for two children, and 20 percent for three or more children ("2000 Census and Same-Sex Households: A User's Guide 2002" 26–28).

Considerably more controversial is the claim by opponents of same-sex marriage that procreation is the primary purpose of marriage. It is certainly true that many individuals, organizations, legislative bodies, and courts hold to this position. For example, the Washington State Supreme Court ruled by a five-to-four vote in 2006 that the state's defense of marriage act (DOMA) was not unconstitutional. A fundamental part of the court's decision was that

> DOMA is constitutional because the legislature was entitled to believe that limiting marriage to opposite-sex couples furthers procreation, essential to survival of the human race, and furthers the well-being of children by encouraging families where children are reared in homes headed by the children's biological parents. Allowing same-sex couples to marry does not, in the legislature's view, further these purposes. ("In the Supreme Court of the State of Washington" 2006)

(Interestingly enough one response to this decision was the filing of a petition by same-sex-marriage advocates for a state law making procreation a legal requirement for all marriages in the state (Washington Secretary of State 2007).

Although a number of courts have agreed with the Washington supreme court majority, a number have also taken a different view. In its now-classic decision overturning the state's restriction of marriage to opposite-sex couples in 2008, the California Supreme

Court noted that procreation may, indeed, be an important function of marriage. It ought not to be, however, the defining criterion that determines whether or not two individuals should have the right to marry. In its four-to-three May 2008 decision on the issue, the court ruled that "[t]hus, although the state undeniably has a legitimate interest in promoting 'responsible procreation,' that interest cannot be viewed as a valid basis for defining or limiting the class of persons who may claim the protection of the fundamental constitutional right to marry" ("In the Supreme Court of California" 2008, 75).

The U.S. Supreme Court has not yet ruled on the issue of same-sex marriage and, therefore, on the associated issue of the role of procreation in marriage. The highest judicial body in Canada, the Superior Court of Justice, has, however, made its views known on the subject. In the case of *Halpern v. Canada*, the court ruled unanimously that restrictions on same-sex marriage violated that country's Charter of Rights and Freedoms. With regard to the issue of procreation, the court said that

> The objective of procreation cannot support the restriction against same-sex marriage. The evidence demonstrates that it was only recently, when same-sex couples began to advance claims for equal recognition of their conjugal relationships, that some courts began to infer that procreation was an essential component to marriage. It is well-established in annulment cases that a marriage is valid and not voidable despite the fact that one spouse refuses to have sexual intercourse, or is infertile, or insists on using contraceptives. Moreover, in cases where a husband is unable to consummate the marriage due to impotence resulting from advanced age, Canadian courts have consistently ruled that the marriage is understood to be for the purpose of companionship and is therefore valid and not voidable. . . . Procreation is not a pressing and substantial objective of the rule of marriage. (*Halpern v. Canada [Attorney General]*, 2002 CanLII 49633 [ON S.C.] 2002, 3)

A Family with One Man and One Woman Is the Best Environment in Which to Raise Children

This argument has two aspects. In many cases in which it is presented, the opponent of same-sex marriage simply makes the value judgment that, in her or his opinion, allowing same-sex couples to raise children is just plain wrong. This view has been expressed well by Erwin W. Lutzer, senior pastor of the Moody Church. In his book, *The Truth about Same-Sex Marriage*, Lutzer writes that many people who think about the possibility of allowing gay and lesbian couples to raise children "feel a profound sense of unease," even though, he goes on, "we cannot exactly say why" (Lutzer 2004, 57). (Critics of this position have an answer to that question, given below.) Lutzer's fellow opponents of same-sex marriage usually continue that children need an environment in which one man and one woman are present to provide the optimal environment for proper upbringing. A writer for the Catholic Education Resource Center says, for example, that "[e]xposure to both sexes is vitally important to the developmental needs of children because it helps them to form their sexual identity, but there are many more areas where children are affected by the parenting of a mother and father" (Brinkmann 2004). The author bases part of her argument on an official pronouncement of the Roman Catholic Church, which said that "as experience has shown, the absence of sexual complementarity in these unions creates obstacles in the normal development of children" (Congregation for the Doctrine of Faith 2003).

Proponents of this view often realize that these value judgments are not entirely adequate to make their case. The question as to how children fare in same-sex households is, after all, one that can be answered to a significant degree by means of careful research in the social sciences. One article purporting to review the evidence on same-sex parenting cited seven ways in which children are harmed by same-sex marriage: higher incidence of violence, higher incidence of mental health problems, reduced life expectancy, higher incidence of same-sex orientation, greater risk of sexual involvement with parents, greater risk of social or psychological problems, and higher incidence of child molestation ("Same-Sex Parenting Is Harmful to Children" 2004). The article concludes with the suggestion that the members of the Canadian Psychological Association, who hold a very different view on this subject, may be "just plain mad."

Rebuttal

In many instances, this dispute very quickly turns into a question of "he says, she says," with each side citing extensive scientific research to support its position, and providing rebuttals to the other side's claims of validity. What is a layperson to do in such a case? One possibility is to turn to professional organizations who might be expected to take an informed and impartial position on the topic. For example, the American Pediatric Association appointed a committee in 2005 to review the research on the effects on the legal, financial, and psychosocial health and well-being of children being raised in gay and lesbian households. The committee concluded that research conducted over a period of more than 25 years shows that "there is no relationship between parents' sexual orientation and any measure of a child's emotional, psychosocial, and behavioral adjustment." These studies found "no risk to children as a result of growing up in a family with 1 or more gay parents" (Pawelski et al. 2006).

Similar conclusions have been reached by a number of other professional organizations concerned with the welfare of children, including the American Academy of Child and Adolescent Psychiatry, American Academy of Family Physicians, American Family Therapy Academy, American Medical Association, American Psychiatric Association, American Psychological Association, American Academy of Child & Adolescent Psychiatry, American Psychoanalytic Association, Child Welfare League of America, National Adoption Center, National Association of Social Workers, and North American Council on Adoptable Children ("Resource Links—Parenting/Family Issues: Policy Statements of Professional Organizations" 2010).

Other Arguments

A number of other arguments offered in opposition to same-sex marriage are as follows. These arguments cover the range from carefully thought out, logical objections to the practice to more personal and emotional complaints.

1. Same-sex relationships are immoral. Therefore, relationships between gay men or lesbians should not be validated by making them legal.
2. Same-sex marriage is still just a social experiment. Society and children should not be asked to suffer the burdens of such an experiment.
3. Granting lesbians and gay men the right to marry provide them with a special privilege, since they are already allowed to get married, except not to someone of the same gender.

4. If same-sex marriage is legalized, churches, synagogues, mosques, and other places of worship may be required to conduct marriage ceremonies of which they do not approve.
5. The legalization of same-sex marriage will lead to the promotion of same-sex lifestyles in public schools.
6. Same-sex marriage is just another way of recruiting young children to the homosexual lifestyle.
7. Same-sex marriage violates my own personal religious beliefs.
8. Personally, I just do not like the idea of same-sex relationship and do not think they should receive legal sanction.

(For an extended discussion of any one or all of these arguments, see the section Arguments Opposed to Same-Sex Marriage and Adoption in Chapter 8.)

Arguments in Favor of Same-Sex Marriage

Many of the arguments in favor of same-sex marriage are either stated explicitly or appear implicitly in the rebuttal sections above. In addition, however, other arguments have been suggested in support of same-sex marriage. These include the following:

The Right to Marry Is Guaranteed to Same-Sex Couples by Provisions of the U.S. Constitution and State Constitutions That Contain "Equality under the Law" Provisions (As They All Do)

This argument is perhaps the keystone of the case in favor of same-sex marriage in the United States. The position could perhaps be phrased in the following terms:

Suppose that an opposite-sex couple that considers itself to be legally married is challenged (for some reason) to *prove* that they are married. What document or documents would that couple normally provide to supply such proof? The answer, of course, is a marriage license, a document issued by each of the 50 states certifying that the couple's marriage has satisfied state requirements for the marriage. Every state sets its own requirements for marriage, which vary from state to state. The age at which males and females, for example, differs from state to state and within some states, with a minimum age for a male differing from that of a female. People applying for a marriage license may be required to be a resident of the state or not, and special provisions are established for people who have been previously married. Until quite recently, states had no provisions for or against marriage between two individuals of the same sex.

A great many couples choose to have religious ceremonies in connection with their legal marriage. A religious ceremony in and of itself, however, does not constitute a legal marriage. That is, a man and woman might go through a formal wedding in a church, synagogue, or mosque, but without a legal document from the state, that couple is not legally married.

The question raised by advocates of same-sex marriage is whether a state can constitutionally refuse to issue a marriage license to two individuals of the same sex. The argument is that state constitutions generally have some type of provision requiring that individuals not be discriminated against on the basis of a number of characteristics, such as age, sex, national origin, or religion. Does that constitutional provision mean, then, that the state can refuse to grant a marriage license to two individuals, solely on the basis of their genders?

This question is a complex legal issue about which some of the finest legal minds in the nation have argued. Courts at all levels (except the U.S. Supreme Court) have now weighed in on one side or another of the issue. In September 2007, for example, the Maryland Supreme Court ruled that the state's 34-year-old law banning same-sex marriage did not violate the state constitution's equal protection provision because the state had a legitimate interest in promoting heterosexual marriage as a way of having children and raising families (Rein and Otto 2007). By contrast, the California Supreme Court took the opposite view. In their 2008 decision on same-sex marriage, the court ruled that "the California Constitution properly must be interpreted to guarantee this basic civil right to all Californians, whether gay or heterosexual, and to same-sex couples as well as to opposite-sex couples" (*In re Marriage Cases* 2008, 7). In contrast to the Maryland court, the California court decided that the state's "interest in retaining the traditional and well-established definition of marriage" was not a sufficient reason to deny marriage licenses to couples of the same gender (*In re Marriage Cases* 2008, 11). The difference between these two decisions, reflected in differing opinions among other state courts, is the standard used in considering the cases. The Maryland court used a more lenient standard, called the "rational basis" standard, while the California court used a more severe standard, called the "strict scrutiny" standard. Those states in which courts have used the "strict scrutiny" standard in considering same-sex marriage have tended to find that laws prohibiting the granting of marriage licenses to same-sex couples are unconstitutional, while those that apply the looser "rational basis" standard tend to support existing state marriage laws.

Rebuttal

As noted above, some legal experts say that limiting marriage to opposite-sex couples serves a very important function of the state: protecting traditional marriage and families consisting of one man and one woman, and their children. States have a right to limit a person's rights, they say, when public interest is of greater interest.

Same-Sex Couples Deserve the Same Economic Benefits as Those Granted to Opposite-Sex Couples

People who are legally married are entitled to a number of economic benefits not available to unmarried individuals. Some examples include the right to adopt children, the right to inherit property, the right to visit one's spouse in the hospital, the right to file joint income tax returns, the right to receive Social Security benefits on the death of a spouse, and the right to have joint life, health, and vehicle insurance policies. In 1997, the U.S. General Accounting Office (GAO) conducted a study of the federal benefits available to legally married couples in the United States not available to individuals or nonmarried cohabiting couples. The agency found 1,049 federal statutory provisions that fell into this category, a number that had increased to 1,138 when the study was updated in 2004 (United States General Accounting Office 2004, 1 and Appendix). Proponents of same-sex marriage say that same-sex couples should have the same civil and economic rights as those available to opposite-sex couples.

Rebuttal

As noted above, opponents of same-sex marriage argue that the state has a right to pass legislation that promotes, encourages, and supports institutions in which children are born and raised and "traditional" families are maintained. In that regard, restricting these rights to opposite-sex couples is both sensible and reasonable.

Allowing Same-Sex Couples to Marry Causes No Harm to Opposite-Sex Marriage or to "Traditional" Families

This argument is a simple one: Suppose that a legally married, same-sex couple moves into a neighborhood. How does the presence of that couple and any children they may have affect the stability of opposite-sex couples in the same neighborhood? Or, more broadly, how does it affect the stability of "traditional marriages" in the community as a whole, in the state, or in the nation?

Rebuttal

Opponents of same-sex marriage believe that allowing two men or two women to marry reduces the status and quality of "traditional marriage." Rather than pose no harm to the "traditional family," same-sex marriage will actually result in the destruction of "traditional marriage," according to this view. James Dobson, founder of Focus on the Family, has said on more than one occasion that "[i]f marriage is everything, it is absolutely nothing" (see, for example, Hodel 2003).

Other Arguments

As is the case against same-sex marriage, a number of additional arguments in favor of same-sex marriage have been advanced. These include the following:

1. Allowing same-sex couples to marry is likely to reduce the rate of promiscuity among gay males. Some heterosexual critics have long criticized gay males for their promiscuity, so marriage would almost certainly provide a way of dealing with this issue, allowing two men to remain together in a committed relationship similar to that enjoyed by nongay men. (This argument is less relevant to lesbians who, as a rule, tend to be less promiscuous than gay males.)
2. As a concomitant of the previous point, the availability of same-sex marriage would probably contribute to a decrease in the number of HIV/AIDS cases, since the disease is often spread by promiscuous, anonymous sex.
3. For some people, the main criterion for permitting two individuals to marry is whether or not they love each other, a standard that can be met by both same-sex and opposite-sex couples.

4. Allowing same-sex couples to marry would actually increase the strength of the modern institution of marriage, since a much larger number of men, women, and children would become part of the institution.
5. If same-sex marriage is permitted, a greater number of orphans and abandoned children will have an opportunity to have a real family.

In conclusion, supporters of same-sex marriage sometimes raise questions as to the sincerity of their opponents' arguments. As an example, a number of state and federal legislators and other government officials have had an opportunity to take a public stand on same-sex marriage. When they do so, these individuals often offer a common theme, outlined above, that marriage and family are the foundation of American society, and allowing same-sex marriage will bring about the destruction of both institutions. Yet, the record of some of these individuals raises questions as to how deeply they really hold these pro-marriage, pro-family beliefs. For example:

- President Bill Clinton, who signed the Defense of Marriage Act (DOMA) in 1996, was impeached by the U.S. House of Representatives in 1998 for lying about having sexual relations with a young woman in the White House.
- Henry Hyde (R-IL) voted for DOMA. In 1998, Hyde admitted to fathering a child out of wedlock with a married mother of three children when he was in his 40s, an affair he called "a youthful indiscretion" (D. Talbot 1998).
- Larry Craig (R-ID) voted for DOMA. In 2007, he was convicted of "lewd conduct" for soliciting a police officer in a bathroom at the Minneapolis airport (Orr 2009).
- Strom Thurmond (R-SC) voted for DOMA. After his death in 2003, Thurmond's family acknowledged that he had fathered a child out of wedlock with a 16-year-old maid in his home in 1925 ("Thurmond's Family 'Acknowledges' Black Woman's Claim as Daughter" 2003).
- Mark Sanford (R-SC) voted for DOMA. In 2009, he admitted to having had a long-term affair with a women in Argentina while he was governor of South Carolina and still married ("Mark Sanford" 2010).
- David Vitter (R-LA) was cosponsor of a bill to amend the U.S. Constitution to define marriage as between one man

and one woman. In 2005, Vitter admitted that he had been a client of an escort service known as D.C. Madam ("Hustler Says It Revealed Senator's Link to Escort Service" 2007).

- Miss California 2009, Carrie Prejean, was a spokesperson for the anti-same-sex marriage campaign in the state. She was removed from her position in late 2009 at least partly because of a sexually explicit video she made.
- Hiram Monserrate, Democratic senator in the state of New York, has been a leader in opposition to same-sex marriage in the state senate. In 2010, he was expelled from the senate by his colleagues because of a misdemeanor conviction for assaulting his girlfriend (Blain and Lovett 2010).
- Mark Foley (R-FL) voted for DOMA. He resigned from the U.S. House of Representatives in 2006 for having made sexual approaches to a number of House pages ("Three More Former Pages Accuse Foley of Online Sexual Approaches" 2006).
- Iris Robinson, wife of Ireland's First Minister Peter Robinson, has long campaigned against gay men and lesbians, claiming that homosexuality is "an abomination." In 2010, the BBC program *Spotlight* revealed that the 59-year-old Mrs. Robinson had had a long-term relationship with a then-19-year-old man, Kirk McCambley. Robinson reportedly gave McCambley $80,000 to set up a restaurant, but then asked for $8,000 back to donate to her church (Coll 2010).
- Mark Souder (R-IN) resigned his office on May 18, 2010, admitting an extramarital affair with a staff member. Souder had been a strong opponent of same-sex marriage, voted for DOMA, and signed an amicus curiae brief against the District of Columbia's proposal to approve same-sex marriage, all actions he defended as being necessary to protect traditional marriage in the United States (Sudbay 2010).
- Rev. George Allen Rekers is co-founder of the Family Research Council, which campaigns against same-sex marriage, and expert witness (for which he was paid well over $100,000) in opposition to same-sex adoption in Florida and Arkansas. In May 2010, he was found to have hired a male escort from a web site called rentboy.com to accompany him on a ten-day trip to Europe.

- The hierarchy of the Roman Catholic Church has been at the forefront of virtually every anti-same-sex marriage campaign in the United States and other parts of the world. For more than a decade, the church has also been involved in a seemingly ongoing series of sexual scandals involving priests and underage boys and girls. Those scandals, by early 2010, had become widespread in the United States, the Netherlands, Austria, and Germany, in at least one case involving questionable judgments made by Pope Benedict XVI himself about clergy under his control (Kulish and Donadio 2010).

(For further information on this issue, see the film *Outrage*, released in May 2009.)

The Status of Same-Sex Marriage in the United States

Same-sex marriage is now legal in five states and the District of Columbia. It is also recognized by the Coquille Indian tribe of Oregon. The five states in which same-sex marriage has been recognized are Connecticut, Iowa, Massachusetts, New Hampshire, and Vermont. In addition two states, New York and Rhode Island, recognize same-sex marriages performed in other states, although same-sex marriage is not legal in those states. In February 2010, the attorney general of Maryland issued an advisory opinion that the state could recognize same-sex marriages performed in other states, although Maryland itself has not yet changed its own marriage license law in this regard.

A state can legalize marriage between individuals of the same-sex in one of three ways. First, the citizens of the state can vote to approve such an arrangement. Every state has some type of provision, usually a referendum or initiative petition, by which an issue can be placed on the ballot on which all citizens of the state can vote. In theory, it would be possible for some individual(s) or group(s) to propose an initiative or referendum question asking for the voters' approval of a law legalizing same-sex marriage. Such an action has never occurred in the United States. On the other hand, initiative or referendum petitions can also be offered in opposition to same-sex marriage, usually defining by law that a marriage is legal only between one man and one woman or by adopting a constitutional amendment to that effect. As of mid-2010, 41 states had adopted laws defining marriage as an institution existing between one man and one woman; 30 states had passed constitutional amendments to the same effect (National Conference of State Legislatures 2010). (States often pass both a law and a constitutional amendment banning same-sex marriage. The reason is that opponents of same-sex marriage often feel that courts can more easily overturn a state law than a constitutional amendment. Currently, 28 states have both state laws and constitutional amendments banning same-sex marriage.)

A second route to the approval of same-sex marriage is through action by a state legislature. Two states have taken this route thus far, Vermont and New Hampshire. In 2007, a bill was introduced into the Vermont House of Representatives amending the state's marriage laws to permit same-sex marriage. That bill was eventually passed by both houses of the legislature and vetoed by Republican Governor Jim Douglas in 2009. Douglas's veto was then overridden by both houses of the legislature (Goodnough 2009a).

A similar sequence of events was taking place in Vermont's neighbor, New Hampshire, at about the same time. In a much closer contest, New Hampshire legislators passed a law permitting same-sex marriage in the state and then worked out a compromise that allowed Democratic Governor Jim Lynch to sign the bill. The law went into effect on January 1, 2010 (Goodnough 2009b).

A third state, Maine, nearly joined its two New England neighbors, Vermont and New Hampshire, also in 2009. On May 6 of that year, Democratic Governor John Baldacci signed into law a bill just passed by both houses of the state legislature permitting same-sex marriage in the state. Opponents of same-sex marriage then filed a referendum petition to have this action repealed, an effort that succeeded in the November 3, 2009, election. Largely through a massive effort by the Roman Catholic Church in the state, voters rejected the new law by a margin of 52 percent to 48 percent (Goodnough 2009c).

In addition to Vermont and New Hampshire, one other legal entity, the District of Columbia, has legalized same-sex marriage through legislative action. On December 18, 2009, Democratic mayor Adrian Fenty signed a bill passed by the Council of the District of Columbia legalizing same-sex marriage in the district. The district is a unique entity in the United States, one whose actions require approval (or at least avoid disapproval) by the U.S. Congress. The citizens of the district were required to wait for 30 days to see if the Congress overturned their council's action. When it did not, the law went into effect, and marriage licenses to same-sex couples were first issued on March 3, 2010 ("D.C. Mayor Signs Same-Sex Marriage Bill" 2009).

The third mechanism by which same-sex marriage may become legal in a state is through judicial action. A judge or a court may determine that a law prohibiting same-sex marriage is constitutional and that, therefore, the state is required to permit such marriages. Same-sex marriage has become legal in three states by this route: Connecticut, Iowa, and Massachusetts. The pattern for this method of approving same-sex marriage was established in the early 2000s when a group of lesbians and gay men sued the Massachusetts Department of Public Health, claiming that the department's refusal to issue them marriage licenses was a violation of the state constitution's right to equal treatment of all its citizens. The trial judge rejected this argument in May 2002, and the plaintiffs appealed that decision to the State Supreme Judicial Court. On November 18, 2003, that court overturned the trial court's decision and announced that the state legislature had 180 days to change state marriage laws to permit same-sex couples to receive marriage licenses. When the legislature failed to act within that period of time, Republican Governor Mitt Romney ordered county clerks in the Commonwealth to begin issuing licenses to same-sex couples as of May 17, 2004. Opponents of same-sex marriage vowed to promote a constitutional amendment that would invalidate the State Supreme Judicial Court's action, but steps for that action are complex and time-consuming. As of mid-2010, the court's decision was still in effect, and same-sex marriage was still legal in Massachusetts. Given the complexity of Massachusetts law involving constitutional changes, existing law authorizing same-sex marriage cannot be considered again until 2012 at the earliest (Pew Forum on Religion & Public Life 2008).

Since the Massachusetts Supreme Judicial Court decision of 2004, two other state supreme courts have reached similar decisions. On October 28, 2008, the Connecticut Supreme Court struck down a state law allowing civil unions as violating the state constitution's guarantee of equal protection under the law, and on April 3, 2009, the Iowa State Supreme Court reached a similar decision (McFadden 2008; Davey 2009).

Alternatives to Same-Sex Marriage

An important element in the debate over same-sex marriage is the possibility of legal arrangements that are similar to, but not identical with, marriage. Such arrangements are generally known as civil unions or domestic partnerships. They provide same-sex couples with many, but usually not all, of the same rights and responsibilities. As of mid-2010, one state, New Jersey, had a civil union law for same-sex couples, while similar laws in three other states (Connecticut, New Hampshire, and Vermont) had become moot because of the availability of marriage in those states. Seven other states have laws permitting domestic partnerships: California, Hawaii, Maine, Nevada, Oregon, Washington, and Wisconsin. The District of Columbia's domestic partnership law became moot when it made same-sex marriage legal in 2009. Domestic partnership laws vary widely in terms of the rights they provide, including typically such things as state tax benefits, hospital visitation rights, adoption and parenting rights, and inheritance rights. Thus far, the most comprehensive law passed is that in the state of Washington, the so-called "Everything but Marriage" act, in which same-sex couples in a domestic partnership are granted essentially all the same rights under state law available to married couples. An effort to overturn this law by state referendum in November 2009 failed by a popular vote of 951,822 to 838,842 (Ammons 2009).

As with same-sex marriage, many individuals oppose the institutions of civil union and domestic partnership. States that have passed laws or constitutional amendments banning same-sex marriage sometimes include all other legal entities that might be considered comparable to marriage, such as civil unions and domestic partnerships. Currently, 15 of the constitutional amendments passed by states to ban same-sex marriage have included explicit bans against civil unions, and four other amendments include bans on both civil unions and domestic partnerships. An example of the provisions included in such amendments is the Louisiana law:

> Marriage in the state of Louisiana shall consist only of the union of one man and one woman. No official or court of the state of Louisiana shall construe this constitution or any state law to require that marriage or the legal incidents thereof be conferred upon any member of a union other than the union of one man

and one woman. A legal status identical or substantially similar to that of marriage for unmarried individuals shall not be valid or recognized. No official or court of the state of Louisiana shall recognize any marriage contracted in any other jurisdiction which is not the union of one man and one woman. (Lambda Legal 2008)

The Future of Same-Sex Marriage in the United States

The future for marriage and similar unions for same-sex couples in the United States is difficult to predict. On the one hand, there was a rush to approve marriage, civil unions, and domestic partnerships in the last half of the first decade of the twenty-first century. On the other hand, opponents of such arrangements had achieved signal success in banning, both by law and by constitutional amendment, same-sex marriage and its substitutes in nearly all 50 states.

Public opinion polls also offer little guidance as to the future direction of same-sex marriage, civil unions, and domestic partnerships. Although public opinion polls differ to some extent on this question, long-term trends appear to point to a slow increase in the number of Americans who are willing to legalize marriage and similar institutions for same-sex couples. When the Gallup poll first asked questions about this topic in 1996, it found that 27 percent of respondents had no objection to same-sex marriage, while 68 percent opposed the practice. It its most recent poll, Gallup found those numbers to have narrowed to 40 percent in favor of same-sex marriage and 57 opposed (Gallup 2009). On the other hand, there was a significantly greater willingness to permit same-sex couples to enter into "marriage-like" arrangements, with 56 percent supporting such arrangements and 40 percent opposing them (Gallup 2009).

Most observers now agree that the key to the future of same-sex arrangements in the United States lies in a case working its way through the courts in the matter of the state of California's actions on same-sex marriage. Those actions had their beginnings in June 2004 when a superior court judge in San Francisco consolidated a group of separate lawsuits on the legality of same-sex marriage under the California constitution. The judge eventually ruled that the state's ban on same-sex marriage violates the state's constitutional guarantees of equal rights for all citizens of the state. In the fall of 2006, a state appeals court reversed the trial judge's decision, and said that restricting marriage to opposite-sex couples is not unconstitutional under the state constitution. The city of San Francisco then appealed that decision to the state supreme court, which, on May 15, 2008, reversed the appeals court decision, and declared that bans on same-sex marriage violated the equal protection provisions of the state constitution.

Acting under the supreme court's decision, county clerks in California began issuing marriage licenses to same-sex couples on June 16, 2008. At the same time, opponents of same-sex marriage had begun a campaign to place on the November 2008 ballot a proposition, Proposition 8, that would amend California's constitution to specifically prohibit same-sex marriage, thereby overriding the supreme court's decision of May 2008. The vote on Proposition 8 was held on November 4, 2008, and passed by a margin of 52 percent to 48 percent. Although that action appeared to end the battle over same-sex marriage in California, it did not. Instead, opponents of the proposition filed suit in federal district court in San Francisco, asking that the result of the election be overturned. The petitioners' argument was essentially that certain rights are guaranteed to citizens of the United States under the U.S. Constitution, and that those rights are not subject to voter approval; they are a fundamental prerogative of American citizens.

As of mid-2010, that case is being heard by Judge Vaughn Walker, chief judge of the district court. It is unclear when a decision will be reached in that case, but there is no question that whichever side loses will appeal the decision. Eventually, no matter how long it takes, the case will reach the U.S. Supreme Court, which will ultimately decide as to the legality of same-sex marriage in the United States (M. Talbot 2010).

References

Ammons, David. 2009. "Gregoire, Reed Certify R-71 and November Returns." http://blogs.sos.wa.gov/FromOurCorner/index.php/2009/12/gregoire-reed-certify-r-71-November-returns/. Accessed on March 23, 2010.

Andreeva, Nellie, and Borys Kit. 2010. "HBO Eyes Biopic about Anti-Gay Activist." http://www.hollywoodreporter.com/hr/content_display/news/e3i8decb5ca03594f57ac71c73740127394. Accessed on February 25, 2010.

Baker v. Nelson 1971. http://marriagelawfoundation.org/cases%5CBaker%20v.%20Nelson.pdf. Accessed on February 14, 2010.

Bales, Kevin. 2004. *Disposable People: New Slavery in the Global Economy*, 2nd ed. Berkeley: University of California Press.

Baxandall, Rosalyn, and Linda Gordon. 2000. *Dear Sisters: Dispatches from the Women's Liberation Movement*. New York: Basic Books.

Beck, Amanada. 2010. "For the Record: Defendants' Opening Statement." Prop 8 on Trial. http://prop8.berkeleylawblogs.org/2010/01/16/for-the-record-defendants-opening-statement/. Accessed on February 13, 2010.

Bennison, Charles. 1995. "Book Reviews." *Anglican Theological Review* 77 (April 1, 1995): 256.

Blackstone, William. 1765. *Commentaries on the Laws of England*. Book 1, Chapter 15. Yale Law School. Avalon Project. http://avalon.law.yale.edu/18th_century/blackstone_bk1ch15.asp. Accessed on February 17, 2010.

Blain, Glenn, and Kenneth Lovett. 2010. "State Senate Votes to Boot Sen. Hiram Monserrate, Citing His Misdemeanor Assault Conviction." *New York Daily News*. http://www.nydailynews.com/news/2010/02/09/2010-02-09_state_senate_to_vote_to_expel_sen_hiram_monserrate_over_misdemeanor_assault_conv.html. Accessed on March 15, 2010.

Boswell, John. 1980. *Christianity, Social Tolerance, and Homosexuality*. Chicago: University of Chicago Press.

———. 1994. *Same-Sex Unions in Premodern Europe*. New York: Villard Books.

Brinkmann, Susan. 2004. "Gay Marriage: Who's Minding the Children?" *Catholic Standard & Times*. http://www.catholiceducation.org/articles/homosexuality/ho0090.html. Accessed on February 25, 2010.

Bryant, Joyce. 2009. "How War Changed the Role of Women in the United States." http://www.yale.edu/ynhti/curriculum/units/2002/3/02.03.09.x.html. Accessed on February 17, 2010.

Bull, Benjamin W. 2010. "Attack on Traditional Marriage." http://www.worldcongress.org/wcf4.spkrs/wcf4.bull.htm. Accessed on February 23, 2010.

Bushyhead, Julie. 2009. "The Coquille Indian Tribe, Same-Sex Marriage, and Spousal Benefits: A Practical Guide." *Arizona Journal of International & Comparative Law* 26 (2): 509–46.

Cohen, Andrew. 2009. "Interracial Marriage and the Long Arc of Justice." *Vanity Fair*. http://www.vanityfair.com/online/daily/2009/10/interracial-marriage-and-the-long-arc-of-justice.html. Accessed on February 22, 2010.

Coll, Bryan. 2010. "Mrs. Robinson: Northern Ireland's Own Sex Scandal." *Time*. http://www.time.com/time/world/article/0,8599,1952511,00.html. Accessed on March 15, 2010.

Concerned Women for America. 2010a. "Our Core Issues." http://www.cwfa.org/coreissues-short.asp. Accessed on February 17, 2010.

———. 2010b. "Top 10 Reasons to Support the Marriage Affirmation and Protection Amendment." http://www.cwfa.org/articles/5351/CFI/family/index.htm. Accessed on February 17, 2010.

Congregation for the Doctrine of Faith. 2003. "Considerations Regarding Proposals to Give Legal Recognition to Unions between Homosexual Persons." http://www.vatican.va/roman_curia/congregations/cfaith/documents/rc_con_cfaith_doc_20030731_homosexual-unions_en.html. Accessed on February 25, 2010.

Davey, Monica. 2009. "Iowa Court Voids Gay Marriage Ban." http://www.nytimes.com/2009/04/04/us/04iowa.html. Accessed on March 23, 2010.

"D.C. Mayor Signs Same-Sex Marriage Bill." 2009. CNN Politics. http://www.cnn.com/2009/POLITICS/12/18/same.sex.marriage/index.html. Accessed on March 23, 2010.

"Deseret News, —Extra, Containing a Revelation on Celestial Marriage." 1852. http://relarchive.byu.edu/MPNC/descriptions/extra.html. Accessed on February 18, 2010.

di Beradino, Angelo. 1997. "Homosexuality in Classical Antiquity." *L'Osservatore Romano*, March 19, 1997, 10.

Divine Law. 1999. "Dietary Laws in Scripture." http://atschool.eduweb.co.uk/sbs777/laws/diet.html. Accessed on February 14, 2010.

Divorce Rates by State: 1990, 1995, and 1999–2007. 2009. National Center for Health Statistics. http://www.cdc.gov/nchs/data/nvss/Divorce%20Rates%2090%2095%20and%2099-07.pdf. Accessed on February 23, 2010.

"Economic Reasons for Gay Marriage." 2010. mndaily.com. http://www.mndaily.com/2010/02/21/economic-reasons-gay-marriage. Accessed on February 23, 2010.

Epstein, Louis M. 1948. *Sex Laws and Customs in Judaism*. New York: Bloch Publishing Company.

Eskridge, William N., Jr. 1993. "A History of Same-Sex Marriage." *Virginia Law Review* 79 (7): 1419–513.

Eskridge, William N., Jr., and Darren R. Spedale. 2006. *Gay Marriage: For Better or for Worse?: What We've Learned from the Evidence.* New York: Oxford University Press.

Eskridge, William N., Darren R. Spedale, and Hans Ytterberg. 2004. "Nordic Bliss? Scandinavian Registered Partnerships and the Same-Sex Marriage Debate." Issues in Legal Scholarship. http://asemus.asef.org/go/subsite/ccd/documents/nordicbliss-ytterberg.pdf. Accessed on February 23, 2010.

Fact Sheet on "Hate Crime" Legislation. 2000. http://www.us2000.org/cfmc/Homosexual%20Fact%20sheet.pdf. Accessed on February 23, 2010.

Faludi, Susan. 1991. *Backlash: The Undeclared War Against American Women.* New York: Crown Books.

Forbes, Jack D. 2004. "What Is Marriage? A Native American View." *New from Indian Country,* May 3, 2004. http://www.westgatehouse.com/art161.html. Accessed on February 20, 2010.

Foster, Lawrence. 1984. *Religion and Sexuality: The Shakers, the Mormons, and the Oneida Community.* Champaign-Urbana: University of Illinois Press.

Frakes, Robert. 2006. "Why the Romans Are Important in the Debate about Gay Marriage." http://hnn.us/articles/21319.html. Accessed on February 14, 2010.

Gallup. 2009. "Majority of Americans Continue to Oppose Gay Marriage." http://www.gallup.com/poll/118378/majority-americans-continue-oppose-gay-marriage.aspx. Accessed on March 23, 2010.

The Gay Christian Network. 2010. "What I Believe." http://gaychristian.net/justins_view.php. Accessed on February 14, 2010.

"Gay Marriage Is Fading as 'Values' Focal Point." 2009. http://www.fivethirtyeight.com/2009/09/gay-marriage-is-fading-as-values-focal.html. Accessed on February 23, 2010.

Goodnough, Abby. 2009a. "Gay Rights Groups Celebrate Victories in Marriage Push." *New York Times.* http://www.nytimes.com/2009/04/08/us/08vermont.html. Accessed on March 23, 2010.

———. 2009b. "New Hampshire Legalizes Same-Sex Marriage." *New York Times.* http://www.nytimes.com/2009/06/04/us/04marriage.html. Accessed on March 23, 2010.

———. 2009c. "A Setback in Maine for Gay Marriage, but Medical Marijuana Law Expands." *New York Times.* http://www.nytimes.com/2009/11/05/us/politics/05maine.html. Accessed on March 23, 2010.

Greenberg, David F. 1990. *The Construction of Homosexuality.* Chicago: University of Chicago Press.

Hales, Brian C. 2008. *Mormon Fundamentalism—Setting the Record Straight.* Orem, UT: Millennial Press.

Halpern v. Canada (Attorney General), 2002 CanLII 49633 (ON S.C.). 2002. http://www.canlii.org/en/on/onsc/doc/2002/2002canlii49633/2002canlii49633.html. Accessed on February 25, 2010.

Hillebrand, Randall. 2008. "The Shakers/Oneida Community. Part Two: The Oneida Community." http://www.nyhistory.com/central/oneida.htm. Accessed on February 18, 2010.

Hodel, Donald Paul. 2003. "Judicial Tyranny." http://www2.focusonthefamily.com/docstudy/newsletters/A000000770.cfm. Accessed on March 15, 2010.

Holloway, Mark. 1966. *Heaven on Earth*. New York: Dover Books.

Horvat, Marian Therese. 2002. *The Daily Catholic*. 13 (95; May 23). http://www.dailycatholic.org/issue/2002May/may23.htm. Accessed on February 15, 2010.

"Hustler Says It Revealed Senator's Link to Escort Service." 2007. http://www.cnn.com/2007/POLITICS/07/10/vitter.madam/index.html. Accessed on March 15, 2010.

In re Marriage Cases. 2008. http://www.courtinfo.ca.gov/opinions/archive/S147999.PDF. Accessed on March 12, 2010.

"In the Supreme Court of California." 2008. http://www.courtinfo.ca.gov/opinions/archive/S147999.PDF. Accessed on February 25, 2010.

"In the Supreme Court of the State of Washington." 2006. *Andersen v. King County.* 138 P.3d 963. Available online at http://www.courts.wa.gov/newsinfo/content/pdf/759341opn.pdf. Accessed on February 25, 2010.

"Introduction to Church History." 2009. http://www.lds.org/churchhistory/content/0,15757,4071-1-2132,00.html. Accessed on February 18, 2010.

Kirk, Marshall, and Hunter Madsen. 1990. *After the Ball: How America Will Conquer Its Fear and Hatred of Gays in the 90's*. New York: Plume Books.

Kirsch, Johann Peter. 1910. "Pope John XII." *The Catholic Encyclopedia*. Vol. 8. New York: Robert Appleton Company, http://www.newadvent.org/cathen/08426b.htm. Accessed on February 15, 2010.

Klaw, Spencer. 1993. *Without Sin: The Life and Death of the Oneida Community.* New York: Allen Lane.

Kulish, Nicholas, and Rachel Donadio. 2010. "Abuse Scandal in Germany Edges Closer to Pope." *New York Times*. http://www.nytimes.com/2010/03/13/world/europe/13pope.html. Accessed on March 15, 2010.

Lambda Legal. 2008. "Text of State Constitutional Amendments and Revisions Targeting Same-Sex Relationships." http://data.lambdalegal.org/pdf/legal/state-constitutional-amendments/text-state-by-state-constitutional-amendments-same-sex-relationships.pdf. Accessed on March 23, 2010.

"The Latter-day Saint Movement." 2010. http://www.ils.unc.edu/
~unsworth/inls181/exercise1/fundamentalist.html. Accessed on
February 18, 2010.

Lehmkuhl, Augustinus. 1910. "Sacrament of Marriage." *The Catholic
Encyclopedia*. Vol. 9. New York: Robert Appleton Company, http://
www.newadvent.org/cathen/09707a.htm. Accessed on February 14,
2010.

Lewis, Jone Johnson. 2010. "Boston Marriage: Women Living Together in
the 19th Century." http://womenshistory.about.com/od/bostonmarriage/
a/boston_marriage.htm. Accessed on February 17, 2010.

Liberated Christians. 1998. "Serious Study Of Leviticus: Has Nothing to
Do with Today's Homosexuality." http://www.libchrist.com/other/
homosexual/leviticus.html. Accessed on February 14, 2010.

"Love, Marriage, Romance & Women . . . in Medieval & Celtic Culture."
1998. http://www.dfwx.com/medieval_cult.html. Accessed on
February 17, 2010.

Lutzer, Erwin W. 2004. *The Truth about Same-Sex Marriage*. Chicago:
Moody Publishers.

Mann, Horace. 1912. "Pope Sergius III." *The Catholic Encyclopedia*. Vol. 13.
New York: Robert Appleton Company, http://www.newadvent.org/
cathen/13729a.htm. Accessed on February 15, 2010.

"Mark Sanford." 2010. "Times Topics." *The New York Times*. http://
topics.nytimes.com/top/reference/timestopics/people/s/mark
_sanford/index.html. Accessed on March 15, 2010.

McFadden, Robert D. 2008. "Gay Marriage Is Ruled Legal in
Connecticut." http://www.nytimes.com/2008/10/11/nyregion/
11marriage.html. Accessed on March 23, 2010.

National ACLU Policy on Plural Marriage. 2008. ACLU Policy #91.
http://www.acluutah.org/pluralmarriage.htm. Accessed on
February 23, 2010.

National Conference of State Legislatures. 2010. "Same Sex Marriage,
Civil Unions and Domestic Partnerships." http://www.ncsl.org/
IssuesResearch/HumanServices/SameSexMarriage/tabid/16430/
Default.aspx. Accessed on March 23, 2010.

"A New Perspective on Taking Your Husband's Name." 2010. http://
community.feministing.com/2009/03/a-new-perspective-on-taking-yo
.html. Accessed on February 17, 2010.

"Noble Life." 2010. http://www.mnsu.edu/emuseum/history/
middleages/nlife.html. Accessed on February 17, 2010.

Novak, Maximilian E. 2001. *Daniel Defoe: Master of Fictions: His Life and
Ideas*. Oxford: Oxford University Press.

"Now People Rise up and Storm Break Loose!" 2009. *Weekly ENews of the National Front*. 9 (June 27). http://74.125.95.132/search?q=cache:QFf6 AnfzbGYJ:www.nationalfrontnorth.com/multimedia/ezine/pdf/ nfnews9.pdf+%22I+know+that+homosexuals+cannot+biologically +reproduce+children%22&cd=1&hl=en&ct=clnk&gl=us. Accessed on February 25, 2010.

Nussbaum, Martha. 2009. "A Right to Marry? Same-sex Marriage and Constitutional Law." *Dissent*. http://www.dissentmagazine.org/article/ ?article=1935. Accessed on February 22, 2010.

Offen, Karen. 2010. "A Brief History of Marriage." http://www.imow.org/ economica/stories/viewStory?storyId=3650. Accessed on February 17, 2010.

"Official Declaration—1." 2006. http://scriptures.lds.org/en/od/1#. Accessed on February 18, 2010.

O'Grair, Scot. 2008. "Effects of Same-Sex Unions." http://isocrat.org/ science/demog/mar_stats.php#ymde. Accessed on February 23, 2010.

"Origins of Polygamy among the Mormons." 2008. http:// www.mormon-polygamy.org/origins_mormon_polygamy. Accessed on February 18, 2010.

Orr, Jimmy. 2009. "Ex-Senator Larry Craig Gives Up Appeal of Bathroom Sting." *Christian Science Monitor*. http://www.csmonitor.com/USA/ Politics/The-Vote/2009/0108/ex-senator-larry-craig-gives-up-appeal -of-bathroom-sting. Accessed on March 15, 2010.

Pawelski, James G., et al. 2006. "The Effects of Marriage, Civil Union, and Domestic Partnership Laws on the Health and Well-Being of Children." *Pediatrics* 118 (1, July): 349–364.

The Pew Forum on Religion & Public Life. 2008. "Gay Marriage Timeline." http://pewforum.org/Gay-Marriage-and-Homosexuality/ Gay-Marriage-Timeline.aspx. Accessed on March 23, 2010.

PollingReport.com. 2010. "Law and Civil Rights." http://www .pollingreport.com/civil.htm. Accessed on February 13, 2010.

"Polygamist 'Prophet' to Serve at Least 10 Years in Prison." 2007. http:// www.cnn.com/2007/US/law/11/20/jeffs.sentence/. Accessed on February 18, 2010.

Rainey, Barbara. 1989. "What Should Be the Wife's "Role" in Marriage?" Family Life. http://www.familylife.com/site/apps/nlnet/ content3.aspx?c=dnJHKLNnFoG&b=3781167&ct=4639651. Accessed on February 16, 2010.

Rein, Lisa, and Mary Otto. 2007. "Md. Ban On Gay Marriage Is Upheld: Law Does Not Deny Basic Rights, Is Not Biased, Court Rules." *The Washington Post*. http://www.washingtonpost.com/wp-dyn/content/

article/2007/09/18/AR2007091802177.html. Accessed on March 12, 2010.

Religious Tolerance. 2006. "Bible Passages Describing Eight Family/ Marriage Types." http://www.religioustolerance.org/mar_bibl0.htm. Accessed on February 14, 2010.

———. 2008. "Context and Analysis of Leviticus 18:22." http:// www.religioustolerance.org/hom_bibh4.htm. Accessed on February 14, 2010.

———. 2009. "Homosexual Orientation among Roman Catholic Priests." http://www.religioustolerance.org/hom_rcc.htm. Accessed on February 15, 2010.

"Resource Links—Parenting/Family Issues: Policy Statements of Professional Organizations." 2010. Rockway Institute, Alliant International University. http://www.alliant.edu/wps/wcm/connect/ website/Home/Research+and+Public+Services/Research+Institutes/ Rockway+Institute/For+the+Media/Resource+Links+on+Parenting -Family+Issues. Accessed on February 25, 2010.

Rifkin, Mark. 2008. "Native Nationality and the Contemporary Queer: Tradition, Sexuality, and History in Drowning in Fire." *The American Indian Quarterly* 32 (4; Fall 2008): 443–70.

Rosen, Ruth. 2007. *The World Split Open: How the Modern Women's Movement Changed America*, Rev. ed. New York: Penguin Books.

"Sabbathday Lake Shaker Village." 2010. http://www.shaker.lib.me.us/. Accessed on February 18, 2010.

"Same-Sex Parenting Is Harmful to Children." 2004. REALity. 23 (2; March/ April). http://www.realwomenca.com/archives/newsletter/2004_mar _apr/article_1.html. Accessed on February 25, 2010.

Somerville, Margaret A. 2003. "The Case against 'Same-Sex Marriage.' " A Brief Submitted to the Standing Committee on Justice and Human Rights [of the Canadian Parliament]. http://www.catholiceducation.org/ articles/homosexuality/ho0063.html. Accessed on April 15, 2010.

Sudbay, Joe. 2010. " 'Family Values' GOP Rep. Mark Souder to Resign over Affair with Staffer." http://www.americablog.com/2010/05/ family-values-gop-rep-mark-souder-to.html. Accessed on May 18, 2010.

Talbot, David. 1998. "This Hypocrite Broke Up My Family." http:// www.salon.com/news/1998/09/cov_16newsb.html. Accessed on March 15, 2010.

Talbot, Margaret. 2010. "A Risky Proposal." *The New Yorker*. January 18: 40–51.

"Testimony of Jay Alan Sekulow, Chief Counsel, the American Center for Law and Justice Before the Judiciary Subcommittee on the Constitution

May 13, 2004." 2004. http://www.aclj.org/media/pdf/040513_FMA HearingTestimony.pdf. Accessed on February 22, 2010.

"Three More Former Pages Accuse Foley of Online Sexual Approaches." 2006. http://blogs.abcnews.com/theblotter/2006/10/three_more_form .html. Accessed on March 15, 2010.

"Thurmond's Family 'Acknowledges' Black Woman's Claim as Daughter." 2003. http://www.foxnews.com/story/ 0,2933,105820,00.html. Accessed on March 15, 2010.

"2000 Census and Same-Sex Households: A User's Guide." 2002. http:// www.thetaskforce.org/downloads/reports/reports/2000Census.pdf. Accessed on February 25, 2010.

United States General Accounting Office. 2004. "Defense of Marriage Act: Update to Prior Report." http://www.gao.gov/new.items/d04353r.pdf. Accessed on March 15, 2010.

Volokh, Eugene. 2005. "Same-sex Marriage and Slippery Slopes." *Hofstra Law Review* 33 (October): 1155–1201.

Walker, Jonathan P. 1999. "Reconsidering Homosexuality and the Bible." http://www.gsafe.org/jonathan_walker.htm. Accessed on February 14, 2010.

Washington Secretary of State. 2007. "Proposed Initiatives to the People —2007." http://www.sos.wa.gov/elections/initiatives/people.aspx?y =2007. Accessed on February 25, 2010.

Winn, Pete. 2003. "Q&A: The Homosexual Agenda." http://www .citizenlink.org/CLFeatures/A000000562.cfm. Accessed on February 23, 2010.

Winslow, Ben. 2007. "37,000 'Fundamentalists' Counted in and Near Utah." *Deseret Morning News*. August 1, 2007. http://www.rickross.com/ reference/polygamy/polygamy684.html. Accessed on February 18, 2010.

Youngs, Deborah. 2006. *The Life-Cycle in Western Europe, c.1300–c.1500.* Manchester: Manchester University Press.

3

Worldwide Perspective

Introduction

One of the risks facing any scholar of social customs is the temptation to view other cultures through the prism of one's own history
and one's own social framework. If marriage has "always" been
an institution reserved for one male and one female in Judeo-
Christian societies, one might reason, then is it not logical to
assume that such has universally been the case in human history?
The only certain way to answer that question, of course, is to survey as many human societies as possible and discover what other
cultures have accepted as a "marriage." When one does so, one
finds that opposite-sex unions between one woman and one
man are certainly a very common model of marriage in human
history. On the other hand, alternative models of the institution
are also known.

In fact, the most common form of marriage known to anthropologists is probably some form of polygyny, the practice of an
individual having two or more spouses. In the case of a man
who takes two or more wives, the practice is known as polygyny,
and that of a woman who takes two or more husbands, the practice is called polyandry. In perhaps the most definitive study of
its kind, the Ethnographic Atlas Codebook provides demographic
data on 1167 societies, published in 29 successive installments in
the journal *Ethnology* between 1962 and 1980. The resource reports
on 98 societies in which marriage was the monogamous association between one man and one woman, 263 societies in which that
form of marriage was at times augmented by polygyny, 280

societies in which the standard form of association was polygynous, three that were polyandrous, and 595 that involved extended families consisting of a variety of male and female relationships simultaneously (Gray 1998).

Same-Sex Marriage in History

Of greater interest to readers of this book is to what extent, if at all, same sex marriages have existed in cultures outside Judeo-Christian cultures (discussed in Chapter 1), in general, and North America, in particular. It is worth noting at the outset of this discussion that information about same-sex marriages in cultures other than those of the Judeo-Christian tradition is often incomplete or inaccurate. Even trained anthropologists are not immune from the tendency mentioned in the first paragraph of this chapter to impose their own moral and ethical precepts on their research. This point has been made by scholars over and over again in the professional literature. For example, the authors of the highly respected work *Family in Transition*, Arlene S. and Jerome H. Skolnick, have written that

> The assumption of universality has usually defined what is normal and natural both for research and therapy and has subtly influenced our thinking to regard deviations from the nuclear family as sick or perverse or immoral. (Skolnick and Skolnick 1989, 7)

A modern writer on same-sex marriages in Africa reinforces this view. She writes that "the topic [of same-sex marriage] is pushed to the extreme margins [of anthropological research] by an historical fixation on western nuclear families as a universal ideal" (Njambi and O'Brien 2000, 4). The author also illustrates in her article how strongly the forces of Western culture are still operating to suppress and eliminate forms of marriage (and other cultural customs) in Africa. In 1991, for example, the Roman Catholic bishops association of Kenya issued a set of guidelines about same-sex marriage, suggesting that this practice be "given up completely," that women involved in such relationships be denied the sacraments, and that every effort be made to separate the members of a same-sex marriage, after which each woman would be provided with assistance individually and their children baptized (Kenya Catholic Bishops 1991; as cited in Njambi and O'Brien 2000, 18). Given the antipathy and bias with which even trained researchers approach the issue of same-sex marriage, then what is it that can be said about the this practice in various cultures throughout history?

First of all, there is evidence that same-sex marriages have existed at least in some cultures at some times in history for many centuries. One example frequently mentioned by writers on the subject is that of the southern Chinese province of Fujian during the Yuan and Ming dynasties (1264–1644). For some reason, the men of this province appear to have been inordinately interested in developing long-term relationships with other men, relationships that often were formalized through ceremonies virtually identical with those used for opposite-sex couples. The male-male marriages into which Fujian men entered were apparently remarkable similar to those of their heterosexual counterparts. (The best source for detailed information about these relationships is the 1990 book *Passions of the Cut Sleeve*, by Bret Hinsch.)

The record of same-sex marriage among Fujian men includes an important component present in virtually all accounts of such arrangements throughout history. Although it seems clear that such marriages were similar to and, generally, a replacement for opposite-sex marriage, participants always left those arrangements at some time for the purpose of entering into an opposite-sex marriage with the goal of producing children. In no same-sex marriage, of course, can the members of a couple reproduce by conventional biological means to produce children. So in any society in which children are important (and that probably includes every human culture that has ever existed), some arrangement is necessary for the continuation of the species, even if same-sex marriages are permitted or encouraged. Still, the record indicates that even after Fujian men had become involved in heterosexual couplings with a women, they retained very close relationships with their previous partners and continued to take part in a variety of same-sex traditions, such as all-male retirement parties, liaisons with other men, and even worship of a same-sex marriage god (Neil 2009, 261).

Perhaps the greatest volume of research on same-sex marriage outside Western culture is that dealing with that institution in various parts of Africa. In the vast majority of these cases, these marriages involve two women who join together in an arrangement that appears to be identical (except for biological roles) to opposite-sex marriage. Until the 1930s, these same-sex marriages were noted by a number of anthropological researchers, but not given serious attention. Then, two researchers, Eileen Jensen Krige and Melville J. Herskovits, began to take a more systematic and objective view of the same-sex marriage tradition in a variety of African tribes. In their individual research, Krige and Herskovits reported that these woman-woman relationships were apparently a form of legal marriage exactly like that of contemporaneous male-female marriages. Essentially the only role for men in such relationships was in the reproduction of children (see, for example, Herskovits 1937 and Krige 1937).

One of the interesting features of these relationships is that they have often been described by researchers as consisting of a woman and her "female husband" (see, for example, Haviland et al. 2007, 215). Some contemporary researchers note that this very phrase superimposes on native relationships a Western traditional view of what marriage should be like: an arrangement between a woman and a man (the "female husband"). Yet, participants in such marriages do not view their participation in these terms at all. In their important study of same-sex marriages among Gikuyu women, for example, Njambi and O'Brien point out that their interviewees never use the Gikuyu term for husband (*muthuri*), but always use the phrases *mutumia wakwa* or *muka wakwa* ("cowife") or *muiru wakwa* ("partner in marriage") (Njambi and O'Brien 2000, 16). Overall, Njambi and O'Brien provide a well-documented and clear-cut view of same-sex relationships between two women that appear to be a completely satisfactory (for the participants, at least) alternative to traditional opposite-sex or other forms of marriage (see also Roscoe and Murray 2001; Igwe 2009; O'Brien 1977).

Same-Sex Marriage: Recent Developments: Opposition

The status of same-sex marriage varies widely throughout the world. In some regions, there is no possibility of there begin a legal relationship between two individuals of the same gender for the foreseeable future. The Islamic religion, as an example, has very strong prohibitions against same-sex relationships (although such relationships are common among men, at least, in most Islamic nations; see, for example, FOXNews.com 2010). In nine nations with predominantly Muslim populations (Afghanistan, Iran, Mauritania, Nigeria, Pakistan, Saudi Arabia, Sudan, United Arab Emirates, and Yemen), same-sex relationships are penalized by death (Gay & Lesbian Archives of the Pacific Northwest 2007). Under such circumstances, any discussion of same-sex marriage is, obviously, impossible.

In other parts of the world, attitudes toward same-sex relationships have a mixed history. In many cultures, same-sex relationships were honored, largely ignored, treated as a normal variant of sexual behavior, or punished with relatively mild penalties. Historical and literary evidence suggests, for example, that same-sex relationships were common across the Indian subcontinent through most of history. Such penalties as were applied for such behaviors were generally mild and commonly less severe than penalties for certain opposite-sex behaviors (Vanita and Kidwai 2000, 25). The situation changed in India when that country was colonized by the British Empire, which brought with it the strong condemnations of homosexual behavior taught by Christianity. In 1860, the British colonial government in Delhi specifically prohibited homosexual activity in section 377 of the Indian Penal Code, a ban that remained in effect until it was overturned by the Indian Supreme Court in 2009 (Vanita 2002; Thottam 2009).

Similar patterns are apparent in Africa, where most modern nations retain attitudes and laws about homosexual behavior imported by colonizing nations from Western Europe that largely displaced traditional attitudes about same-sex behavior, in particular, and sexuality, in general (Epprecht 2008). The influence of religious beliefs from Islam and Christianity that so transformed native attitudes about same-sex behavior in Africa and other parts of the world in the nineteenth century have not yet disappeared. In April 2009, for example, Ugandan Member of Parliament David Bahati introduced legislation instituting new penalties for same-sex behavior. The legislation would have amended the current 14-year term in prison for homosexual activity to include the death penalty for anyone who was HIV/AIDS positive, who had been convicted of previous homosexual activity, or who had been found guilty of homosexual relations with a person under the age of 18. Bahati's actions came two days after a visit to Uganda by three American evangelical Christians who claimed to be experts on homosexuality. The message of the evangelicals was that the gay movement is an "evil institution" whose goal it is to "defeat the marriage-based society and replace it with a culture of sexual promiscuity" (Gettleman 2010, A9). The government's official response to complaints about its aggressive stand on same-sex behavior was reflected in a statement by the Ugandan Minister of Ethics and Integrity, James Nsaba Buturo, who said: "Homosexuals can forget about human rights" ("Hate Begets Hate" 2010, A12).

As in the United States, a number of nations have taken actions to restrict marriage to opposite-sex couples, usually by amending their national constitutions. It is not always clear whether constitutional amendments of this kind are written specifically to deter same-sex unions or whether the language of "one man and one woman" is simply simpler and, therefore, somewhat innocuous. As an example, a new constitution for the nation of Cuba was adopted at a national referendum with 97.7 percent of eligible voters approving the document. Article 36 of that constitution defines marriage as a "voluntarily established union between a man and a woman" ("The Text of the Constitution of the Republic of Cuba" 2003). A number of other nations have provisions in their national constitutions identical or similar to that of Cuba's, including Bulgaria (Bulgaria—Constitution 1991), Paraguay (Paraguay—Constitution 1992), and Cambodia (Cambodia Constitution 1993).

Since 2000, a number of countries have taken a somewhat different approach, adopting specific amendments to their constitutions to ban same-sex marriage and, often, same-sex adoption. These efforts are similar to those in the United States to promote an amendment to the U.S. Constitution defining marriage as an arrangement between one man and one woman. The first nation in the world to follow this avenue was Honduras. In 2005, the Honduran National Assembly voted unanimously to adopt a constitutional amendment banning marriage between and adoption by same-sex couples. The action was prompted by strong complaints from the Roman Catholic hierarchy in the country and from a number of Protestant evangelical groups concerned about the government's previous support for a variety of gay and lesbian organizations (GlobalGayz.com 2005; Constitution of Honduras—English Translation, Article 112). Since the action in Honduras, a number of other nations have taken similar actions, passing new constitutions or stand-alone amendments that specifically prohibit marriage between two individuals of the same gender. Such amendments are sometimes limited to same-sex marriage, while others include both marriage and any other kind of similar union, such as civil unions and domestic partnerships. These nations include Uganda (2005), Latvia (2005), Democratic Republic of Congo (2005), Serbia (2006), El Salvador (2007), Nigeria (2007), Ecuador (2008), Bolivia (2009), Dominican Republic (2009), Cayman Islands (2010), Jamaica (2010), and Zambia (2010).

Same-Sex Marriage: Recent Developments: Support

Thus far, the greatest support for same-sex marriage has occurred in Western Europe, with some important steps forward having occurred in other parts of the world.

Western Europe

The first nation in Europe—and the world—to take legal action to provide same-sex couples with marriage-like privileges was the Netherlands. In 1979, the Dutch parliament passed a law allowing same-sex couples to enter into common-law-type arrangements called unregistered cohabitation (*ongeregistreerd samenwonen*), in which they were accorded legal rights in a variety of areas, including rent law, social security, income tax, immigration rules, state pension, and death taxes (Waaldijk 2005, 104; Gay and Lesbian.net 2010). In 1997, the Dutch parliament revisited this issue and created a new category of association known as a registered partnership (*geregistreerd partnerschap*), which was available to both same- and opposite-sex couples. The new category was similar to unregistered cohabitation, except that it expanded the rights to which couples were admitted. Finally, in December 2000, the Dutch parliament became the first country in the world to open marriage to same-sex couples. The vote on this act was 49 to 26 in the upper house and 109 to 33 in the lower house of parliament ("Dutch Legislators Approve Full Marriage Rights for Gays" 2000). For trends in the number of same-sex couples taking advantage of the Dutch law, see Chapter 6.

Other European countries have followed similar pathways in recognizing the marital rights of same-sex couples. Denmark, for example, also recognized same-sex relationships as unregistered common-law arrangements in 1986, before creating the category of registered partnerships (*registreret partnerskab*) three years later. That law was extended to Greenland in 1996 and amended and expanded in 1999. Couples in a registered partnership have many of the same rights as those in an opposite-sex marriage, with a few exceptions:

- They may adopt children, but may not have joint custody of a child.
- They are not covered by Danish laws that refer specifically to opposite-sex couples.
- They are not provided with rights of international treaties unless all signatories to those treaties specifically agree (The Danish Registered Partnership Act 1996).

As of mid-2010, only minimal efforts have been made to take the next step in Denmark, extending full and equal rights of marriage to same-sex couples.

Two other Scandinavian countries, Sweden and Norway, have followed pathways toward approval of same-sex marriage similar to that of the Netherlands. Sweden extended the rights of a common-law marriage to same-sex couples in January 1988, and then expanded that right to a registered partnership (*registrerat partnerskap*) in June 1994. In April 2009, the Swedish parliament finally extended full marriage rights to same-sex couples by a vote of 261 to 22 (Nyberg 2009). Similarly, Norway approved common-law marriage status to same-sex couples in January 1989, registered partnership (*registrert partnerskap*) status in April 1993, and full and equal marriage rights in June 2008 ("Norway Passes Law Approving Gay Marriage" 2008).

Two other European nations have also approved same-sex marriage. Belgium approved common-law marriage rights for same-sex couples in November 1998, registered partnerships (*le partenariat enregistré*) in January 1999, and full marriage rights in February 2003 (Religious Tolerance 2003). For trends in same-sex marriages in Belgium, see Chapter 6.

The road to full marriage rights for same-sex couples in Spain was somewhat different from that of other European nations. Prior to 2004, a number of municipalities, including Aragon, Asturias, the Canary Islands, Catalonia, Madrid, Navarre, and Valencia, had established provisions for civil unions for same-sex couples. No federal action on the issue was taken, however, until the election of the Socialist government of President José Luis Rodríguez Zapatero in 2004. The following year, the president fulfilled a campaign promise by submitting to the national legislature a bill granting full marriage rights to same-sex couples. Although defeated by the Senate by a vote of 131 to 119, the bill was approved by the Congress of Deputies by a vote of 187 to 147. Since the latter body has veto power over the Senate, the bill was declared to have passed, and King Juan Carlos gave his royal assent to the bill on July 1, 2005. The bill's adoption prompted widespread demonstrations against the bill, organized by the Roman Catholic Church. Public opinion polls conducted at the time indicated, however, that 66 percent of the population supported their government's actions (Giles 2005). Data on the number of couples taking advantage of the Spanish same-sex marriage law are provided in Table 3.1.

As in the United States, a number of European nations have created alternative institutions designed to provide same-sex couples with some or many (but never all) of the rights enjoyed by opposite-sex couples in the institution of marriage. The most common term used to describe these arrangements is *registered partnerships*. Such arrangements have now been approved in Austria, Czech Republic, Finland, Hungary, Iceland, Liechtenstein, Slovenia, Switzerland, and the United Kingdom. Other designations that have been used for such arrangements (although they usually do not differ in substance) are life partnership (*Lebenspartnerschaft;* Germany), civil union (*união de facto;* Portugal), civil pact of solidarity (*pacte civil de solidarité;* France and Luxembourg), civil partnership (Ireland), and stable union of a couple (*unió estable de parella;* Andorra).

TABLE 3.1
Same-Sex Marriages in Spain, July 2005–8

Year	Marriages between Men	Marriages between Women	Same-Sex Marriages	Total Marriages	Percent Same-Sex Marriages
2005 (after July)	923	352	1,275	120,728	1.06
2006	3,190	1,384	4,574	211,818	2.16
2007	2,180	1,070	3,250	203,697	1.60
2008	2,299	1,250	3,549	196,613	1.81

Source: Instituto Nacional de Estadística (National Statistics Institute). Data for 2005, 2006, 2007, and 2008.

As of mid-2010, the status of same-sex marriage and similar institutions is very fluid in Europe. The situation in Portugal is a good example. Same-sex behavior was illegal in the country until 1982, and same-sex marriage is specifically prohibited by law. As recently as October 2008, the Portuguese parliament voted against extending marriage to same-sex couples by a vote of 196 to 28 ("Portugal Parliament Approves Gay Marriage" 2010). Still, same-sex couples were provided with the opportunity to participate in civil unions (*união de facto*) in 2001, and a number of nongovernmental organizations have long lobbied for equal marriage rights for lesbians and gay men. In September 2009, the newly elected government of Prime Minister Jose Socrates announced that it would make same-sex marriage a priority in its legislative agenda. Four months later, the government carried through on that promise and passed a same-sex marriage bill by a vote of 125 to 99. Rather than signing or vetoing the bill, Conservative president Anibal Cavaco Silva asked the nation's Constitutional Court to determine whether the new law would be constitutional. On April 8, 2010, the Constitutional Court ruled by a vote of 11-to-2 that the legislation was constitutional, and a month later, on May 18, 2010, Cavaco Silva finally signed the pending legislation, making Portugal the sixth country in Europe to legalize same-sex marriage ("Portugal's President to Ratify Same-sex Marriage Law 2010).

The United States and the United Kingdom have, of course, had a long and close social and political history. In the area of legal precedent, for example, U.S. attorneys and judges frequently cite the historic work of William Blackstone (1723–80), perhaps the most famous of all English jurists. Such has been the case in disputes over same-sex issues in the United States, much as it has been in debates over other major points of law in this country since the nation's founding (see, for example, REL: 02/15/2002 EX PARTE H.H. 2010, in which the chief justice of the Alabama Supreme Court refers to Blackstone eight times in a decision about a lesbian seeking custody of her biological child). The first law to deal specifically with same-sex marriage in the United Kingdom was apparently the Nullity of Marriage Act 1971, defining marriage as being between one man and one woman. Any marriage between two individuals of the same gender, according to this law, was to be declared null and void. The act had been passed as part of a legislative agenda based on recommendations of a special law commission established by the government to consider the status of family law in the United Kingdom. One commentator noted that it was "surely rather extraordinary" that no law had ever been passed in Great Britain stating when a marriage would or would not be void, a deficiency resolved by this act (Hall 1971).

The Nullity of Marriage Act 1971 was replaced two years later by the 1973 version of the Matrimonial Causes Act. The Matrimonial Causes Acts are a series of about two dozen laws dating to 1857 that codify marriage law in Great Britain. Section 11(c) of the Matrimonial Causes Act 1973 states that a marriage is void if "the parties are not respectively male and female" (Office of Public Sector Information 2010c, §11c). Similar laws prohibiting same-sex marriage are also in place in Scotland (Office of Public Sector Information 2010b, §5[4][3]) and Northern Island (Office of Public Sector Information. 2010a, §6[6]]3]). All of these laws remain in force in all parts of the United Kingdom, making same-sex marriage illegal throughout the nation.

Efforts to provide same-sex couples with some type of marriage-like legal arrangement in the United Kingdom have a relatively short history. Probably the first step in that direction occurred in 2001, when Ken Livingstone, mayor of London, announced that the city would initiate a London Partnerships Register, which would be available to both opposite- and same-sex couples. The register provided no legal rights to couples, but is generally regarded as the first time that any British governmental authority had granted legal recognition to same-sex couples ("Capital Move for Gay Couples" 2001).

The first comparable step on a national level occurred a year later when Lord Lester of Herne Hill introduced into the House of Lords a bill, the Civil Partnerships Bill, to provide same-sex couples with a number of rights comparable to those enjoyed by opposite-sex couples in a traditional marriage in England and Wales. The bill covered a number of topics, including sharing of communal property, property agreements, taxation, provision for health and welfare of partner without capacity to act for themselves, income-based benefits, working families' tax credit and disabled person's tax credit, and power of court for various purposes (Civil Partnerships Bill [HL] 2002). The bill passed a second reading in the House of Lords on January 25, 2002, but action was then suspended to allow the government to study the concept of civil partnerships and its implementation in the country. In June 2003, the Woman and Equality Unit of the Department of Trade and Industry published a paper, "Civil Partnership: A Framework for the Legal Recognition of Same-Sex Couples," that outlined the result of that study and gave the government's position on the issue ("Civil Partnership: A Framework for the Legal Recognition of Same-Sex Couples" 2003). The paper noted that

> Briefly, the Government proposes to create a new legal status of civil registered partner for same-sex partners who register under the new scheme. As well as their commitment to each other being respected, registered partners would also gain rights and responsibilities, reflecting the integral roles they play in each other's lives. (Civil Partnership: A Framework for the Legal Recognition of Same-Sex Couples 2003, 9)

When translated into a legislative bill, this report met general approval in both the House of Lords and the House of Commons. The primary objection it met came from members of the Conservative Party, who submitted a so-called "wrecking amendment" in the House of Lords that would have gutted the bill of its primary components. That amendment was approved by the House of Lords on a vote of 148 to 130. When the bill reached the House of Commons, it passed on a vote of 426 to 49 with instructions to the House of Lords to remove the wrecking amendment. The House of Lords did so by a vote of 251 to 126 on November 17, 2004, and the bill became law with the granting of Royal Assent on the following day (Gay and Lesbian.net 2009; text of the Civil Partnership Act 2004 is at http://www.opsi.gov .uk/acts/acts2004/ukpga_20040033_en_1).

In April 2009, the Office for National Statistics released the latest data on the number of civil partnerships formed in the kingdom from 2005 (based on the 11 days in England and Wales and 12 days in Scotland during which the option was available) through 2008. Those data are summarized in Table 3.2.

Generally speaking, the legal status of same-sex relationships has long been an issue of interest to governing bodies of the European Union. In January 2006, for example, the European Parliament adopted by a vote of 468 to 149 (with 41 abstentions) a document criticizing the continued existence of homophobia in member states of the Union and calling upon nations to

TABLE 3.2
Civil Partnerships Formed in the United Kingdom, 2005–2008

Year	United Kingdom	England and Wales	Scotland	Northern Ireland
2005	1,953	1,857	84	12
	(1,287; 666)[a]	(1,228; 629)	(53; 31)	(6; 6)
2006	16,106	14,943	1,047	116
	(9,648; 6,458)	(9,003; 5,940)	(580; 467)	(65; 51)
2007	8,728	7,929	688	111
	(4,770; 3,958)	(4,371; 3,558)	(339; 349)	(60; 51)
2008	7,169	6,558	525	86
	(3,824; 3,345)	(3,536; 3,022)	(245; 280)	(43; 43)

[a](male; female).
Source: Office for National Statistics. 2009. "Civil Partnership Formations: Numbers and Rates." http://www
.statistics.gov.uk/StatBase/Product.asp?vlnk=14675.

ensure that same-sex partners enjoy the same respect, dignity and protection as the rest of society; [and] enact legislation to end discrimination faced by same-sex partners in the areas of inheritance, property arrangements, tenancies, pensions, tax, social security etc. (European Parliament 2006; Belien 2006)

Other Regions of the World

Same-sex marriage is legal in two other nations of the world: South Africa and Canada. The first action by the South African government in this regard came in 1999 when the parliament adopted an act extending to same-sex couples the right of common-law marriage, similar to that enjoyed by opposite-sex couples in the nation. There then followed, however, a series of judicial pronouncements indicating that laws that distinguished between opposite-sex and same-sex couples were discriminatory under the nation's constitution. Finally, in 2005 the nation's highest judicial body, the Constitutional Court, ruled that the federal legislature was required to pass a law extending full marriage benefits to same-sex couples. The legislature did so on November 14, 2006, an act that was then signed by Acting President Phumzile Mlamblo-Ngcuka on December 30, making South Africa the fifth country in the world to approve of same-sex marriage (Alexander 2006).

Progress toward the approval of same-sex marriage in Canada has been similar to, although earlier than, that in the United States. That is, court actions requiring individual provinces to recognize same-sex marriages in Canada first appeared as early as 2003, although the federal government itself did not take action on the issue until 2005. Between June 10, 2003, when the Court of Appeals for Ontario ruled that Canadian law on marriage violated the Canadian Charter of Rights and Freedoms, and February 1, 2005, when the federal legislature first began debate on the subject, 8 of 10 provinces and one of three territories had changed their laws to permit same-sex marriage. More than 90 percent of the nation's populations live within these jurisdictions. Only the provinces of Alberta and Prince Edward Island and the territories Nunavut and Northwest Territories had not approved of same-sex marriage during this period ("The Supreme Court and Same-Sex Marriage" 2005).

The debate that took place in the federal legislature over same-sex marriage in 2005 was, therefore, somewhat anticlimatic. Although the parliament had overwhelmingly adopted a bill declaring that marriage was an institution between one man and one woman "to the exclusion of all others" as recently as 1999 ("Same-Sex Marriage in Canada" 2007), the 2005 bill moved quickly through both houses of parliament, passing the House on June 28 by a vote of 158 to 133 and the Senate on July 19 by a vote of 47 to 21. Deputy Governor General Beverly McLachlin then provided the Royal Assent needed to make the bill law. A year later, under a new Conservative government, the issue of same-sex marriage was once more raised with a government resolution asking for reconsideration of the subject in the House and Senate. That resolution was defeated on December 6, 2006, by a vote of 175 to 123 in the House, essentially putting the question of same-sex marriage in Canada to rest (Hurley 2005).

Canada counted the number of same-sex couples officially for the first time in its 2006 census. That census found that 45,300 same-sex couples were officially registered in the nation, of whom 7,500 (16.5%) were legally married and 37,900 (83.5%) were in common-law relationships (Statistics Canada 2007, 6; no explanation is given for the modest discrepancy in totals provided here). The number of same-sex couples grew at five times the rate of opposite-sex couples between 2001 and 2006, from 34,200 to 45,300 (an increase of 32.6%, compared to 5.9% for opposite-sex couples). Half of the same-sex couples who were legally married lived in just three cities, Montréal, Toronto, and Vancouver (also the three largest cities in Canada). Census officials reported that same-sex couples accounted for 0.6 percent of all legal marriages in Canada, a rate comparable to that for New Zealand and Australia districts where same-sex unions are permitted (0.7% and 0.6%, respectively) (Statistics Canada 2007, 12).

As of mid-2010, data on the number of same-sex marriages performed in South Africa, Norway, and Sweden are not available, largely because such marriages have become legal so recently.

Marriage-like legal entities have also been created in a small number of other countries around the world. For example, New Zealand passed legislation in 2000 creating a same-sex alternative to common-law legislation previously intended for opposite-sex couples. That law was modified in 2004, establishing the category of civil unions for same-sex couples. It provides nearly all of the same rights and responsibilities available to opposite-sex couples in a traditional marriage. In 2005, conservative members of the New Zealand introduced the Marriage (Gender Clarification) Amendment Bill designed to specifically define marriage as an institution between one man and one woman and to prohibit the recognition of civil unions in the country. That bill was defeated by a vote of 73 to 47, and the legislature has apparently been satisfied since that vote with the status quo for same-sex couples (Department of Internal Affairs [New Zealand] 2010; Berry 2005).

Two additional nations in which same-sex unions have been implemented are New Caledonia and Wallis and Futuna, both in the South Pacific Ocean. Both countries are dependencies of France, and, although they have their own governments, they are subject to laws passed in the mother country. In April 2009, the French National Assembly voted to extend the nation's *pacte civil de solidarité* to the two South Pacific nations, requiring them to bring their marriage laws into consonance with that of France (SSO 2009).

In some ways, the most surprising developments in the field of same-sex unions have taken place in South America. In spite of the strong Roman Catholic influence on government policies in virtually all Latin American nations, approval for some form of same-sex unions has slowly begun to spread through the continent. Arguably the most liberal nation in this respect is Uruguay, which granted the right to form civil unions to same-sex couples in 2007. The unions, known as cohabitation unions (*los sindicatos de la cohabitación*), grant same-sex couples essentially all of the same rights as those available to opposite-sex couples in a traditional marriage, including inheritance and pension rights and rights of child custody (Grew 2008). In early 2010, a senator from the coalition of ruling parties in the country announced that, should they win reelection in fall balloting, they would introduce legislation providing full marriage rights to all same-sex couples (Hoffman 2010).

A second South American nation in which same-sex unions have been approved is Ecuador. In September 2008, the nation voted on a new national constitution consisting of 444 articles, some of which were quite controversial. Among the controversial articles was one granting the right to have civil unions to same-sex couples. The constitution was eventually adopted by a vote of 63 percent to 39 percent (Romero 2008; 365Gay 2008). One other South American nation in which the status of same-sex civil union is somewhat problematic is Colombia. In June 2007, the Chamber of Representatives of the Colombian Congress voted 62 to 43 for a bill granting civil unions to same-sex couples. The bill was defeated in the Senate, however, when a group of senators from the ruling party, normally expected to vote for the bill, cast their ballots instead against it. The bill was defeated, then, by a vote of 34 to 29, with 39 members not voting on the measure ("Colombian Conservatives Derail Gay Union Bill" 2007). In the meantime, the nation's highest court has issued a series of rulings that extend many, if not all, of the rights enjoyed by married opposite-sex couples to same-sex couples. In these rulings, the court has said that same-sex couples must have the same rights as opposite-sex couples in areas such as social security, health insurance, employment, inheritance, and property rights (GayLawNet 2009). Finally, in 2009 the court ruled that same-sex couples in a civil union must be granted virtually of the same rights as those enjoyed by married heterosexuals, establishing a de facto equality between the two forms of relationships (Martinez 2009).

Actions by Subnational Entities

Some forms of government permit governmental units below that of the national level to make decisions on a variety of policy issues. The United States is, of course, a good example of this situation. Individual states are allowed to make virtually all basic decisions about marriage, including the age at which a man or a woman may marry, the cost of a marriage license, blood tests that may be required, and waiting periods that may be necessary. They are also allowed to determine whether or not same-sex couples may be granted licenses to marry.

Apparently the first subnational governmental entity in the world to grant some form of marriage-like arrangement to same-sex couples was the Australian Capital Territory (ACT). In 1994, the ACT legislature passed the Domestic Relationships Act, which provided limited marriage-like rights to same-sex couples, including certain death benefits typically granted to opposite-sex couples (Domestic Relationships Act 1994). Over the next decade, a number of efforts were made to expand the range of privileges offered to same-sex couples, most of which failed because of strong opposition from the national government. Finally, in 2009 the legislature passed a domestic partnership act that included many of the rights and privileges usually reserved for married couples (Green 2009).

Currently, same-sex couples in all states of Australia are covered by a federally recognized entity known as a de facto relationship. Similar to a common law marriage, a de facto relationship allows same-sex couples to receive certain benefits typically available only to opposite-sex couples in a common-law marriage. These benefits include joint Social Security and veteran benefits, worker's compensation, inheritance rights, hospital visitation privileges, the right to file a joint income tax return, and immigration rights (Gay and Lesbian Rights Lobby 2008). Two Australian state, Tasmania and Victoria, have entities that more closely approximate opposite-sex marriage. The Tasmanian Domestic Partnerships 2003 Act provides for two levels of relationships, known as significant relationships and caring relationships, depending on the precise nature of the relationship between individuals in the association. The law has been modified and amended to provide to same-sex couples essentially all of the rights available to opposite-sex couples in the state ("Relationships Act: The Tasmanian Approach" 2006). The state of Victoria has also passed a same-sex relationship act similar to that of Tasmania's. Provision for domestic partnerships was made in two laws passed in 2001, the Statute Law Amendment (Relationships) Act 2001 and the Statute Law Further Amendment (Relationships) Act 2001. These laws are based on the presumption that "[a]ll Victorian couples, regardless of gender or marital status, have equal rights under the law" ("A Fair Go for All Victorian Couples" 2010). They amended 60 different state acts that originally provided benefits for opposite-sex couples that were not available to same-sex couples. (It should be noted that same-sex marriage is specifically prohibited in Australian law by an amendment to the 1961 Marriage Act adopted by the national legislature in 2004; see Marriage Amendment Act 2004.)

The other nation, in addition to Australia, where laws regarding same-sex relationships have been the source of considerable activity is Spain. In the period between 1998 and 2003, 11 separate governmental entities enacted some form of recognition of marriage-like arrangements for same-sex couples. The first of these was the government of Catalonia, which in 1998 established a category known as a stable union (*unión estable*), which provided same-sex couples with certain benefits generally available to opposite-sex couples (Merin 2002, 151–55; Leston 1998). Other governmental entities have used the same or other titles for legal arrangements of this kind, including stable couples (*parejas estables*; Aragon, Navarre, Asturias, Balearic Islands), de facto couples (*las parejas de hecho*; Andalusia, Extremadura, Canary Islands, and Basque Country), and de facto unions (*las uniones de hecho*; Valencia and Madrid) (Pichardo Galán 2010). All such arrangements became moot, of course, with the federal government's adoption of same-sex legislation in 2005.

A number of subnational governmental entities that have approved some form of same-sex unions for their citizens are the following:

Argentina

The city legislature of Buenos Aires established civil unions for residents of the city on December 13, 2002. Four days later, the provincial legislature of the province of Rio Negro adopted very similar legislation. Many rights are granted to same-sex couples by both bodies, with the primary exception of formal marriage and adoption of children "(Argentina: Civil Union Proposals Passed in Rio Negro Province and Buenos Aires City" 2002). Civil union legislation has also been approved by two other Argentine cities, Villa Carlos Paz, in 2007, and Rio Cuarto, in 2009

("Córdoba: Aprueban La Unión Civil Entre Homosexuales en Villa Carlos Paz" 2007; "Río Cuarto: Aprueban La Unión Civil De Parejas Gays" 2009).

Mexico

Two governmental bodies in Mexico have recognized some form of same-sex union. The first of these bodies was the Legislative Assembly of the Federal District (D.F.), which approved an entity known as coexistence partnerships (*sociedades de convivencia*) on November 9, 2007, by a vote of 43 to 17. The bill establishing this entity had first been proposed in 2000 by Enoé Uranga, an open lesbian member of the assembly. Although the bill had been passed four times by the Assembly, it did not receive final approval until 2007.

Two years later, legislative assemblyman David Razú introduced a bill legalizing same-sex marriage in the D.F. The bill passed the Assembly on December 21, 2009, by a vote of 39 to 20 ("Mexico City Lawmakers OK Gay Marriage" 2009). The main import of the bill was simply to change the wording of the city's marriage laws to refer to "a free union between two people," rather than "a free union between a man and a woman (official test of the law is available in Spanish at Jurist: Legal News and Research 2009).

Somewhat unexpectedly, the second governmental entity to approve same-sex marriages in Mexico was the state of Coahuila, which borders Texas. On January 11, 2007, the state legislature created the category of civil pact of solidarity (*pacto civil de solidaridad*), similar to the French entity of the same name. After the legislature approved the measure by a vote of 20 to 13, one legislator said that "[t]his does not have to do with morality. It has to do with legality" (Walker 2007).

One off-shore territory of the United Kingdom, the island of Jersey, approved a civil partnership bill similar to that of the home country on October 20, 2009. The vote was 48 to 1. In a second such territory, the Isle of Man, the House of Keys passed a civil partnership bill like that of the United Kingdom in the spring of 2010, and final adoption of the legislation was pending as of the summer of 2010.

Finally, two territories in the Caribbean, Aruba and the Netherlands Antilles, are required to recognize marriages conducted in their parent nation, the Netherlands, although they do not allow such marriages on their own soil.

Court Decisions on Same-Sex Unions

Same-sex couples in a number of nations have appealed to the judicial system to obtain recognition of their rights to receive a marriage license or some similar arrangement, such as a civil union or registered partnership. Various courts have reached differing decisions on this issue. In Israel, for example, courts have consistently ruled that same-sex couples have the same rights of common-law marriage as do opposite-sex couples (1994); that same-sex couples are eligible for a variety of social, political, and economic benefits generally available to opposite-sex couples (1995, 1996, 2000, 2001, and 2005); and that the government must recognize same-sex unions and marriages conducted in other nations (2006) (GayTLVGuide 2010).

Other national courts have followed the lead of the Israeli judiciary in recognizing the right of same-sex couples to enjoy identical or similar matrimonial rights as those of opposite-sex couples. The supreme court of Nepal, for example, ruled in November 2008 that the nation's new interim constitution required the government to treat all individuals in exactly the same way, whether they were gay, nongay, "third sex," or some other sexual orientation. It indicated that one consequence of this position was that all marriage rights would have to be available to same-sex couples, just as they were to opposite-sex couples. As of mid-2010, a legislative committee was working on a bill designed to achieve the requirements set out by the court's ruling (Parashar 2010). Other nations in which court rulings have been instrumental in the development of same-sex unions of one form or another include Canada (1999), South Africa (2005), the United Kingdom (2006), Colombia (2007 and 2009), Slovenia (2009), Portugal (2009), and Poland (2010).

This campaign has been less successful in other nations, where courts have ruled that same-sex couples do not have the same or equivalent matrimonial rights as do opposite-sex couples. Among the nations in which courts have issued such rulings are Costa Rica (2006), Russia (2010), and Italy (2010).

Public Opinion about Same-Sex Marriage

Many public opinion polls have been conducted to gauge the feeling of citizens about the possibility of same-sex marriage or comparable institutions in their countries. As might be expected, the results of those polls range widely, from very high approval of such entities for same-sex couples to very strong opposition. One of the most comprehensive polls was conducted in 2006 by the European Commission as part of its periodic Eurobarometer program, which gauges public opinion in the European Union on a wide variety of issues. The 2006 study found that 44 percent of respondents agreed with the statement "Homosexual marriages should be allowed throughout Europe," in comparison with 49 percent who disagreed with the statement (Eurobarometer 66 2006, 37). Citizens of various member states differed widely in their response to this question, with the Dutch, Swedes, Danes, and Belgians expressing the strongest support for same-sex marriage (82%, 71%, 69%, and 62%, respectively), and the Poles, Greeks, Cypriots, and Latvians expressing the lowest level of support (17%, 15%, 14%, and 12%, respectively). As perhaps might be expected, support for same-sex marriage was highest in nations that already have laws allowing lesbians and gay men to marry or join in civil unions and lowest in nations without such institutions (Eurobarometer 66 2006, 41).

The results of public opinion polls on same-sex marriage and civil unions vary so widely that it is virtually impossible to make any generalizations worldwide. Some of the trends from recent polls in specific countries can, however, be summarized:

- In a poll conducted about two weeks after the Portuguese parliament approved same-sex marriage, the Eurosondagem polling firm found that 52 percent of respondents approved of same-sex marriage, while 42 percent opposed (Wockner 2010).
- Two recent polls in Argentina produced dramatically different results. One conducted in November 2009 by the polling firm Analogías found that 66.3 percent of interviewees in six Argentine cities supported same-sex marriage, while 23.1 percent opposed the practice. But a poll conducted by the firm Poliarquía Consultores of 1,000 Argentine adults found most opposed to same-sex marriage, 60 percent to 35 percent (these results and those following are from Angus Reid Global Monitor 2010).
- Citizens of Canada are significantly more supportive of same-sex marriage than are those of Great Britain or the United States. The support for same-sex marriage was

reported to be 61 percent in Canada, 41 percent in Great Britain, and 33 percent in the United States in a study conducted by Angus Reid Strategies.

- In a somewhat surprising result, a narrow majority of Israelis said that they thought that homosexual behavior was an "aberration" (46% to 42%), but a significant majority (61% to 31%) supported the rights of same-sex couples to marry legally.
- A poll by GfK Polonia conducted in July 2009 found that 75 percent of 1,000 Polish adults queried opposed same-sex marriage, while 14 percent approved.
- Although same-sex marriage is not legal in Australia, 59 percent of 1,100 adult Australians polled in May 2009 supported same-sex marriage in their country, while 36 percent opposed.
- Two-thirds (65.2%) of Chileans polled in March and April 2009 opposed granting marriage rights to same-sex couples, while one-third (33.2%) approved.

The results of these polls must be viewed with the same caution recommended for any public opinion polling, namely that they reflect not only the opinions of interviewees, but also the implicit and often unacknowledged biases of the interviewers and the precise wording of the questions being asked.

The Future of Same-Sex Marriage

As is the case with almost any social issue, it is next to impossible to suggest the future of same-sex marriage and civil unions around the world. It seems safe to say that such institutions will not be permitted in very large parts of the globe, such as those in which the Islamic religion is dominate. There seems to be next to no chance that same-sex marriage will be approved in most parts of Africa either. The future of same-sex marriage in areas where Christianity has traditionally been strong, such as Latin America, is more difficult to predict. One might suppose that the influence of the Roman Catholic Church would be sufficient to deter same-sex unions of any kind on the continent, but recent trends raise doubt as to whether such is the case or not. Same-sex unions are already available in at least three countries, Ecuador, Uruguay, and parts of Argentina, and are under serious consideration in other nations, such as Colombia and Venezuela. Only in Europe, especially Western Europe, does same-sex marriage appear to be a trend that will not be denied, especially given the strong support for the institution by the European Union (EU) itself. In retrospect, it is quite remarkable that six nations of the EU have adopted same-sex marriage over the last decade, and at least two other countries are expected to approve of the practice in the near future.

References

Alexander, Mary. 2006. "SA Legalises Gay Marriage." SouthAfrica.info. http://www.southafrica.info/services/rights/same-sex-marriage.htm. Accessed on March 26, 2010.

Angus Reid Global Monitor. 2010. "Issue Watch: Same-Sex Marriage." http://www.angus-reid.com/issue/C26/. Accessed on March 29, 2010.

"Argentina: Civil Union Proposals Passed in Rio Negro Province and Buenos Aires City." 2002. International Gay & Lesbian Human Rights Commission. http://www.iglhrc.org/cgi-bin/iowa/article/takeaction/globalactionalerts/597.html. Accessed on March 27, 2010.

Belien, Paul. 2006. "European Parliament Backs Gay Marriage." *The Brussels Journal*. January 22, 2006. http://www.brusselsjournal.com/node/696. Accessed on March 27, 2010.

Berry, Ruth. 2005. "Majority Happy with Civil Union, Prostitution Laws." nzherald.co.nz. http://www.nzherald.co.nz/nz/news/article.cfm?c_id=1&objectid=10333649. Accessed on March 26, 2010.

Bulgaria—Constitution. 1991. http://www.servat.unibe.ch/icl/bu00000_.html. Accessed on March 25, 2010.

Cambodia Constitution. 1993. http://www.servat.unibe.ch/icl/cb00000_.html#A045_. Accessed on March 25, 2010.

"Capital Move for Gay Couples." 2001. BBC News. http://news.bbc.co.uk/2/hi/uk_news/1411648.stm. Accessed on March 27, 2010.

"Civil Partnership: A Framework for Legal Recognition of Same-Sex Couples." 2003. http://www.equalities.gov.uk/pdf/civil%20partnership%20-%20a%20framework%20for%20the%20legal%20recognition%20of%20same-sex%20couples.pdf. Accessed on March 27, 2010.

Civil Partnerships Bill (HL). 2002. http://www.publications.parliament.uk/pa/ld200102/ldbills/041/2002041.pdf. Accessed on March 27, 2010.

"Colombian Conservatives Derail Gay Union Bill." 2007. MSNBC. http://www.msnbc.msn.com/id/19339227/. Accessed on March 27, 2010.

Constitution of Honduras—English Translation. 2005. http://www.honduras.com/honduras-constitution-english.html. Accessed on March 25, 2010.

"Córdoba: Aprueban La Unión Civil Entre Homosexuales en Villa Carlos Paz." 2007. Clarín.com. http://www.clarin.com/diario/2007/11/23/um/m-01547228.htm (in Spanish). Accessed on March 27, 2010.

The Danish Registered Partnership Act. 1996. http://users.cybercity.dk/~dko12530/s2.htm. Accessed on March 25, 2010.

Department of Internal Affairs [New Zealand]. 2010. Civil Unions. http://www.dia.govt.nz/diawebsite.nsf/wpg_URL/Services-Births-Deaths-and-Marriages-Civil-Unions?OpenDocument. Accessed on March 26, 2010.

Domestic Relationships Act. 1994. Australian Capital Territory Consolidated Acts. http://www.austlii.edu.au/au/legis/act/consol_act/dra1994253/. Accessed on March 26, 2010.

"Dutch Legislators Approve Full Marriage Rights for Gays." 2000. *New York Times*. http://www.nytimes.com/2000/09/13/world/dutch-legislators-approve-full-marriage-rights-for-gays.html?scp=2&sq=Norway+Gay+Marriages&st=nyt. Accessed on March 25, 2010.

Epprecht, Marc. 2008. *Heterosexual Africa?: The History of an Idea from the Age of Exploration to the Age of AIDS*. Athens: Ohio University Press.

Eurobarometer 66. 2006. http://ec.europa.eu/public_opinion/archives/eb/eb66/eb66_highlights_en.pdf. Accessed on April 29, 2010.

European Parliament. 2006. "Homophobia in Europe." http://www.europarl.europa.eu/sides/getDoc.do?pubRef=-//EP//TEXT+TA+P6-TA-2006-0018+0+DOC+XML+V0//EN. Accessed on March 27, 2010.

"A Fair Go for All Victorian Couples." 2010. http://www.equalopportunitycommission.vic.gov.au/publications/rights%20brochures/same%20sex%20relationships.asp. Accessed on March 26, 2010.

FOXNews.com. 2010. "Afghan Men Struggle with Sexual Identity, Study Finds." http://www.foxnews.com/politics/2010/01/28/afghan-men-struggle-sexual-identity-study-finds/. Accessed on March 25, 2010.

Gay & Lesbian Archives of the Pacific Northwest. 2007. "Sodomy Laws: Laws around the World." http://www.sodomylaws.org/. Accessed March 25, 2010.

Gay and Lesbian.net. 2009. "The Civil Partnership Act 2004." http://www.gay-and-lesbian.net/legal/8-civil-partnerships/18-the-civil-partnership-act-2004. Accessed on March 27, 2010.

———. 2010. "Gay and Lesbian Marriage: 1979–1999." http://www.gay
-and-lesbian.net/history/9-timeline-of-gay-marriage/5-1979-1999.
Accessed on March 25, 2010.

Gay and Lesbian Rights Lobby. 2008. "Your Rights Checklist." http://
glrl.org.au/index.php/Rights/Rights/Your-Rights-Checklist. Accessed
on March 26, 2010.

GayLawNet. 2009. Laws: Colombia. http://www.gaylawnet.com/laws/
co.htm#marriage. Accessed on March 27, 2010.

GayTLVGuide. 2010. "Gay Rights in Israel." http://www.gaytlvguide.com/
start-here/gay-rights-in-israel. Accessed on March 28, 2010.

Gettleman, Jeffrey. 2010. "After U.S. Evangelicals Visit, Uganda
Considers Death for Gays." *New York Times*. January 4, 2010, A1, A9.

Giles, Ciaran. 2005. "Spain: Gay Marriage Bill Clears Hurdle."
http://web.archive.org/web/20071227125726/http://www
.planetout.com/news/article.html?2005/04/21/5. Accessed on
March 26, 2010.

GlobalGayz.com. 2005. "Honduras Bans Gay Marriage & Adoption."
http://www.globalgayz.com/country/Honduras/view/HND/
gay-honduras-news-and-reports#article3. Accessed on March 25,
2010.

Gray, J. Patrick. 1998. "Ethnographic Atlas Codebook." *World
Cultures* 10 (1): 86–136. http://eclectic.ss.uci.edu/~drwhite/worldcul/
Codebook4EthnoAtlas.pdf. Accessed on March 24, 2010.

Green, Jessica. 2009. "Australian Territory Legalises Gay Civil
Partnership Ceremonies." pinknews. http://www.pinknews.co.uk/
2009/11/11/australian-territory-legalises-gay-civil-partnership
-ceremonies/. Accessed on March 26, 2010.

Grew, Tony. 2008. "Uruguay's First Gay Union, Four Months after They
Became Legal." pinknews. http://www.pinknews.co.uk/news/articles/
2005-7461.html. Accessed on March 27, 2010.

Hall, J. C. 1971. "The Nullity of Marriage Act 1971. *The Cambridge Law
Journal* 29:208–10.

"Hate Begets Hate." 2010. *New York Times* (editorial). January 4, 2010, A12.

Haviland, William A., et al. 2007. *Cultural Anthropology: The Human
Challenge*, 12th ed. Belmont, CA: Thomson Higher Learning.

Herskovits, Melville J. 1937. "A Note on 'Woman Marriage' in Dahomey."
Africa 10 (3): 335–41.

Hinsch, Bret. 1990. *Passions of the Cut Sleeve: The Male Homosexual Tradition
in China*. Berkeley: University of California Press.

Hoffman, Matthew Cullinan. 2010. "Uruguayan Socialists Prepare 'Homo sexual Marriage' Legislation." LifeSiteNews.com. http://www.lifesitenews.com/ldn/2009/may/09052509.html. Accessed on March 27, 2010.

Hurley, Mary C. 2005. Bill C-38: the Civil Marriage Act. http://www2.parl.gc.ca/Sites/LOP/LegislativeSummaries/Bills_ls.asp?Parl=38&Ses=1&ls=c38. Accessed on March 26, 2010.

Igwe, Leo. 2009. "Tradition of Same Gender Marriage in Igboland." *Nigerian Tribune*. http://revrowlandjidemacaulay.blogspot.com/2009/06/tradition-of-same-gender-marriage-in.html. Accessed on March 24, 2010.

Jurist: Legal News and Research. 2009. "Mexico City Legislature Approves Same-Sex Marriage Bill." http://jurist.law.pitt.edu/paperchase/2009/12/mexico-city-legislature-approves-same.php. Accessed on March 28, 2010.

Kenya Catholic Bishops. 1991. *Guidelines for the Celebration of the Sacrament of Baptism for Infants and Special Cases*. Nairobi: St. Paul Publications.

Krige, Eileen J. 1937. "Note on the Phalaborwa and Their Morula Complex." *Bantu Studies* 11: 357–66.

Leston, Cesar. 1998. "Catalonia Has Granted Domestic Partnership Rights." ILGA Euroletter 61, July 1998. http://www.france.qrd.org/assocs/ilga/euroletter/61.html#ES. Accessed on March 26, 2010.

Marriage Amendment Act. 2004. http://legislation.gov.au/comlaw/Legislation/Act1.nsf/0/91DFFD1199DF26D8CA2574170007CE06/$file/1262004.pdf. Accessed on March 26, 2010.

Martinez, Helda. 2009. "Colombia: Equal Rights for Same-Sex Partners." IPS. http://ipsnews.net/news.asp?idnews=45944. Accessed on March 27, 2010.

Merin, Yuval. 2002. *Equality for Same-Sex Couples: The Legal Recognition of Gay Partnerships in Europe and the United States*. Chicago: University of Chicago Press.

"Mexico City Lawmakers OK Gay Marriage." 2009. CBSNEWS. http://www.cbsnews.com/stories/2009/12/21/world/main6007081.shtml. Accessed on March 28, 2010.

Neill, James. 2009. *The Origins and Role of Same-Sex Relations in Human Societies*. Jefferson, NC: McFarland & Company.

Njambi, Wairimu Ngaruiya, and William E. O'Brien. 2000. "Revisiting 'Woman-Woman Marriage': Notes on Gikuyu Women. *NESA Journal* 12 (1): 1–23.

"Norway Passes Law Approving Gay Marriage." 2008. *Los Angeles Times*. http://www.latimes.com/news/local/la-on-norwaymarriage18-2008jun18,0,402614.story. Accessed on March 26, 2010.

Nyberg, Per. 2009. "Sweden Passes Same-Sex Marriage Law." CNN.com/europe. http://edition.cnn.com/2009/WORLD/europe/04/01/sweden.samesex/index.html. Accessed on March 26, 2010.

O'Brien, Denise. 1977. "Female Husbands in Southern Bantu Societies," in Alice Schlegel, ed. *Sexual Stratification: A Cross-Cultural View.* New York: Columbia University Press, 109–21.

Office of Public Sector Information. 2010a. The Marriage (Northern Ireland) Order 2003. http://www.opsi.gov.uk/si/si2003/20030413.htm#6. Accessed on March 27, 2010.

———. 2010b. Marriage (Scotland) Act 1977. http://www.uk-legislation.hmso.gov.uk/RevisedStatutes/Acts/ukpga/1977/cukpga_19770015_en_1#pt3-l1g5. Accessed on March 27, 2010.

———. 2010c. Matrimonial Causes Act 1973. http://www.opsi.gov.uk/RevisedStatutes/Acts/ukpga/1973/cukpga_19730018_en_2#pt1-pb2-l1g12. Accessed on March 27, 2010.

Paraguay—Constitution. 1992. http://www.servat.unibe.ch/law/icl/pa00000_.html#P001_. Accessed on March 25, 2010.

Parashar, Uptal. 2010. "Nepal Charter to Grant Gay Rights." *Hindustan Times.* http://www.hindustantimes.com/News-Feed/nepal/Nepal-charter-to-grant-gay-rights/Article1-499154.aspx. Accessed on March 28, 2010.

Pichardo Galán, José Ignacio. 2010. "Same-Sex Couples in Spain. Historical, Contextual and Symbolic Factors. http://www-same-sex.ined.fr/WWW/04Doc124Ignacio.pdf. Accessed on March 26, 2010.

"Portugal Parliament Approves Gay Marriage." 2010. MSNBC. http://www.msnbc.msn.com/id/34765160/. Accessed on March 26, 2010.

"Portugal's President to Ratify Same-sex Marriage Law. 2010. BBC News. http://news.bbc.co.uk/2/hi/europe/8688503.stm. Accessed on May 18, 2010.

REL: 02/15/2002 EX PARTE H.H. 2010. http://caselaw.lp.findlaw.com/scripts/getcase.pl?court=al&vol=1002045&invol=2. Accessed on March 27, 2010.

"Relationships Act: The Tasmanian Approach." 2006. http://www.buddybuddy.com/d-p-taz.html. Accessed on March 26, 2009.

Religious Tolerance. 2003. "Same-Sex (SSM) Marriage in Belgium." http://www.religioustolerance.org/hom_mar10.htm. Accessed on March 26, 2010.

"Río Cuarto: Aprueban La Unión Civil De Parejas Gays." 2009. La Voz.com.ar. http://archivo.lavoz.com.ar/09/05/07/Rio-Cuarto-aprueban-union-civil-parejas-gays.html. (In Spanish). Accessed on March 27, 2010.

Romero, Simon. 2008. "President Wins Support for Charter in Ecuador." *New York Times.* http://www.nytimes.com/2008/09/29/world/americas/29ecuador.html?_r=1. Accessed on March 27, 2010.

Roscoe, Will, and Stephen O. Murray. 2001. *Boy-Wives and Female Husbands: Studies of African Homosexualities.* London: Palgrave Macmillan.

"Same-Sex Marriage in Canada." 2007. http://www.mapleleafweb.com/features/same-sex-marriage-canada. Accessed on March 26, 2010.

Skolnick, Arlene S., and Jerome H. Skolnick. *Families in Transition,* 6th ed. Boston: Allyn & Bacon, 1989.

SSO. 2009. "New Caledonia Catches up with France." http://www.starobserver.com.au/soap-box/2009/06/09/new-caledonia-catches-up-to-france/13739. Accessed on March 27, 2010.

Statistics Canada. [2007]. "Family Portrait: Continuity and Change in Canadian Families and Households in 2006, 2006 Census." http://www.samesexmarriage.ca/docs/FamilyCensus2006.pdf. Accessed on March 29, 2010.

"The Supreme Court and Same-Sex Marriage." 2005. CBC News. http://www.cbc.ca/news/background/samesexrights/. Accessed on March 26, 2010.

"The Text of the Constitution of the Republic of Cuba." 2003. *Official Gazette of the Republic of Cuba.* Special Edition No.3 of January 31, 2003. http://www.walterlippmann.com/cubanconstitution.html. Accessed on March 25, 2010.

Thottam, Jyoti. 2009. "India's Historic Ruling on Gay Rights." *Time.* July 2, 2009. http://www.time.com/time/world/article/0,8599,1908406,00.html. Accessed on March 25, 2010.

365Gay. 2008. "New Ecuador Constitution Includes Gay Rights Guarantees." http://www.365gay.com/news/new-ecuador-constitution-includes-gay-rights-guarantees/. Accessed on March 27, 2010.

Vanita, Rith. 2002. "Homosexuality in India: Past and Present." *IIAS Newsletter.* No. 29. http://www.iias.nl/iiasn/29/IIASNL29_10_Vanita.pdf. Accessed on March 25, 2010.

Vanita, Ruth, and Saleem Kidwai. 2000. *Same-Sex Love in India: Readings from Literature and History.* New York: St. Martin's Press.

Waaldijk, Kees. 2005. "Others May Follow: The Introduction of Marriage, Quasi-marriage and Semimarriage for Same-Sex Couples in European Countries." *Judicial Studies Institute Journal.* 5: 104–27.

Walker, S. Lynne. 2007. "New Law Propels Gay Rights in Mexico." *San Diego Union Tribune*. http://legacy.signonsandiego.com/uniontrib/20070305/news_1n5gaylaw.html. Accessed on March 28, 2010.

Wockner, Rex. 2010. "Portuguese Support Same-Sex Marriage, by a Smidge." http://www.baywindows.com/index.php?ch=news&sc=glbt&sc2=news&sc3=&id=101526. Accessed on March 29, 2010.

4

Chronology

Although some form of legalized relationships between two individuals of the same gender has been known for hundreds of years, the details of specific events in that long history are not well documented. Most of the significant events in the history of same-sex marriages and their counterparts (civil unions, domestic partnerships, registered partnerships, and the like) and same-sex adoption issues date only to the 1990s. This chapter lists some of the most important events in that chronological history.

Where known and relevant, the specific month and day of an event is listed. In some cases, more than one date may be associated with an event. For example, legislative bodies typically pass laws on one date that are then signed by an executive on a different date. Those laws may then come into effect immediately or, more commonly, at some later date. The significance of the date chosen for listing is noted in each instance.

First century CE	Same-sex marriages among Roman upper classes are apparently relatively common and generally accepted. The emperor Nero legally married at least three young boys during his reign.
342	The Theodosian Code, issued by the Christian emperors Constantius II and Constans, declares same-sex marriages to be illegal and requires that any such couples be put to death.

Fourteenth to seventeenth century   Same-sex marriages were apparently common in the Chinese province of Fujian during the Ming Dynasty, 1368–1644.

1967   The U.S. Supreme Court, in the case of *Loving v. Virginia*, rules that the state of Virginia's law against marriage between two individuals of different races is unconstitutional. The vote is nine-to-zero. The court bases its decision on the proposition that "[m]arriage is one of the 'basic civil rights of man,' fundamental to our very existence and survival."

1970   Two Minnesota men, Jack Baker and James McConnell, apply for a marriage license in Hennepin County, Minnesota. They are refused and proceed to sue the county (*Baker v. Nelson*). Their case eventually is appealed to the U.S. Supreme Court, which declines to hear the case for lack of any "substantial federal question."

1971   Baker and McConnell (see 1970) are granted a marriage license in Blue Earth County, Minnesota, and are married by a Methodist minister, making them the first same-sex couple to be legally married in the United States.

1972   Two Kentucky women, Marjorie Jones and Tracy Knight, apply for a marriage license at the Jefferson County courthouse. They are denied a license, and their appeal to the U.S. Court of Appeals for Kentucky is also denied.

Camille Mitchell, a lesbian living in San Jose, California, is granted custody of her child in a divorce proceeding, although the judge rules that she may not spend time with her partner when the child is present.

1973   Maryland becomes the first state in the union to specifically ban marriage between two individuals of the same sex. Prior to this time, no specific prohibition of same-sex marriage existed in any state constitution or legal code.

1974   Under the equal rights amendment to the state's constitution, a same-sex couple in Washington State, John F. Singer and Paul Barwick, file suit against King County Auditor Lloyd Hara to force him to grant them a marriage license (*Singer v. Hara*). The King County superior court rules that the amendment does not apply to marriage, only to discriminatory treatment to individuals on the basis of their sex.

1975   Two gay men in Colorado, Richard Adams and Anthony Sullivan, sue Joseph D. Howerton, acting district director of the U.S. Immigration and Naturalization Service (INS), to force him to recognize their marriage, legally performed in the state (*Adams. v. Howerton*). The purpose of the recognition was to allow Sullivan, a citizen of Australia, to remain legally in the United States. The court ruled that immigration law prohibited the INS from admitting homosexuals to the country, so the Congress did not intend to recognize a marriage between homosexuals.

            Virginia becomes the fourth state to prohibit same-sex marriage.

1976   The citizens of Cuba, with a vote of 97.7 percent in favor, adopt a new constitution that specifically defines marriage as an institution between one man and one woman.

1977   In two separate cases, courts in Michigan and Colorado grant custody rights to lesbians (Jacqueline Stamper and Donna Levy) over the objections of their ex-husband, in one case, and their deceased partner's relatives in the other.

            The Florida legislature adopts a law stating that "[n]o person eligible to adopt under this statute may adopt if that person is a homosexual."

1979   The Dutch parliament grants same-sex couples the same rights of common-law marriage then available

1994
(*cont.*)
to opposite-sex couples. The action is the first of its kind in the world in which same-sex couples receive marriage-like rights comparable or identical to those for opposite-sex couples.

1984
The city of Berkeley, California, becomes the first legal entity in the United States to create a formal, legal recognition of same-sex relationships. It establishes an entity known as a domestic partnership that provides many of the same benefits for same-sex couples as are available in a traditional marriage. These benefits extend only to areas controlled by city law.

May 11
In the case of *De Santa v. Barnsley*, the Pennsylvania Superior Court rules that a divorce cannot be granted to two men (John DeSanto and William Barnsley) who have lived together in a common-law marriage for more than 10 years. The judge rules that a common-law marriage, recognized for opposite-sex couples by the state of Pennsylvania, cannot exist between two individuals of the same sex.

1985
The Alaska Supreme Court rules that the fact that a woman is a lesbian is irrelevant to her ability and right to adopt a child and awards a minor child to a lesbian mother and her partner rather than to the heterosexual father.

1986
The Danish parliament grants to same-sex couples the same rights of common-law marriage available to opposite-sex couples.

June 30
In the case of *Bowers v. Hardwick*, the U.S. Supreme Court rules that homosexual activity between adults in the privacy of their own home is not protected by the U.S. Constitution.

In one of the first cases of its kind in the United States, two lesbians, Annie Afflect and Rebecca Smith, are allowed to legally adopt a child.

1987   The National Center for Lesbian Rights (at the time, the Lesbian Rights Project) devises a strategy for allowing same-sex couples to adopt, a strategy known as second-parent adoption.

October 10   An estimated two thousand same-sex couples are "married" on the steps of the Internal Revenue Service building during the March on Washington as a statement against the unequal treatment of same-sex couples under the nation's tax laws.

1988   The Swedish legislature grants to same-sex couples
January   the same rights of common-law marriage available to opposite-sex couples.

October 20   The San Bernardino (California) superior court awards custody of Shawn Wallace to his father, Artie, a gay men with AIDS, after Wallace's ex-wife, a fundamentalist Christian, had earlier kidnapped the child to prevent his living with his father. Artie Wallace died a year later as a result of complications from AIDS.

1989   Norway approves common-law marriage rights for
January   same-sex couples identical to those for opposite-sex couples.

June   Denmark becomes the first country in the world to provide a form of marriage-like legal recognition for same-sex relationships called a registered partnership.

July   The New York Court of Appeals rules that a same-sex couple having lived together for at least 10 years can be considered a "family unit" for the purpose of rent control. The ruling is the first time that a state court has defined a same-sex couple as a "family."

1990   In the case *Matter of Cooper*, the New York Supreme Court rules that a gay man cannot sue to inherit from his deceased partner, who has left by will about

1990
(*cont.*)
80 percent of his estate to a former partner. The appellant claims that New York inheritance laws should apply even though the state refuses to grant marriage licenses to same-sex couples. The court rules that state laws do not apply, and that marriage in the state is limited to couples of the opposite sex.

1991 July
Bulgaria adopts a new constitution that includes a specific provision defining marriage as "a free union between a man and a woman."

1992
Levi Strauss & Company becomes the first Fortune 500 company to offer the same benefits to same-sex couples as it does to opposite-sex couples employed at the firm.

June
Paraguay adopts a new constitution that includes an article that limits marriage and all marriage-like institutions to one man and one woman.

1993 April
Norway approves registered partnership status for same-sex couples.

May 5
The Supreme Court of Hawaii rules that the state's ban on same-sex marriage is illegal unless the state can provide a compelling reason for the necessity of such a ban.

August 1
Norway becomes the second country in the world to establish registered partnerships for same-sex couples.

September
Cambodia's new constitution specifically restricts marriage to "one husband and one wife."

1994
The Australian Capital Territory adopts the Domestic Relationship Act 1994 granting to same-sex couples many of the same rights available to opposite-sex couples in the district. The act is the first of its kind in Australia and one of the first in the world by a governmental body.

The Israeli Supreme Court rules that same-sex couples are entitled to the same legal benefits as are opposite-sex couples in common-law relationships. Over the next three years, the court continues to expand the range of benefits available to same-sex couples.

June   Sweden establishes registered partnerships for same-sex couples.

1995   Utah becomes the first state to pass a so-called defense of marriage act (DOMA) specifically prohibiting any legal relationship between two individuals of the same sex.

April 21   In one of the most famous early cases of adoption by same-sex couples, *Bottoms v. Bottoms*, the Virginia Supreme Court rules that a lesbian, Sharon Bottoms, is not fit to have custody of her child, Tyler, and that the child is to be placed with his grandmother, Pamela Bottoms. Tyler's father has supported Sharon's request to retain custody of the child. Later appeals by the mother are all unsuccessful.

1996   The parliament of Greenland adopts registered part-
April 26   nership provisions of a Danish act passed in 1989.

May   Hungary approves common-law marriage rights for same-sex couples that are comparable to those available to opposite-sex couples.

June   Iceland approves registered partnerships for same-sex couples.

September   The U.S. Congress passes and President Bill Clinton signs the Defense of Marriage Act, which bans the U.S. government from recognizing same-sex marriages performed in any state or any other nation.

December   A trial judge in Hawaii rules that the state has pro-
3   vided no compelling reason for restricting marriage to opposite-sex couples. He delays implementation of his ruling a day later to allow the state supreme court to consider his decision.

1997 May A proposal to extend some marriage rights to same-sex couples in Slovakia is rejected by the cabinet of Prime Minister Vladimir Meciar.

July The Netherlands approves the creation of a marriage-like entity known as registered partnership for same-sex couples.

October 22 The Bergen County (New Jersey) superior court rules that the New Jersey Department of Youth and Family Services had violated three state adoption statutes in disallowing a homosexual couple from adopting a child, creating for the first time a right for same-sex adoption in the state.

1998 June The Czech parliament defeats a proposal to establish registered partnerships for same-sex couples by a margin of two votes.

June Catalonia becomes the first Spanish province to approve same-sex unions ("stable union of a couple"; *unión estable de una pareja*). Nearly all other provinces follow the Catalonian example over the next five years.

November The parliament of Belgium approves common-law marriage rights for same-sex couples.

November 3 Voters in the state of Hawaii approve by a vote of 69 percent to 31 percent an amendment to the state constitution limiting marriage to one man and one woman.

November 3 The voters of Alaska approve ballot measure 2, which amends the state constitution to restrict marriage to couples of the opposite sex.

February 27 Alaska superior court judge Peter A. Michalski rules that the state's marriage laws violate the state constitution and, therefore, the state must provide a compelling reason for withholding a marriage license from two men who wish to marry.

1999   The South African government grants to same-sex couples the same rights as those available to opposite-sex couples in a common-law marriage.

January   Only two months after extending common-law-marriage rights to same-sex couples, Belgium creates the new and more extensive category of registered partnership to cover such couples.

November The French parliament approves a registered-partnership-type entity for both gay and nongay couples called a *pacte civil de solidarité* (civil pact of solidarity) with many of the benefits typically available to married heterosexual couples.

May 4   The New Hampshire state legislature rescinds a ban on same-sex adoption and foster parenting that it had instituted in 1987. The action leaves Florida as the only state in the union with this type of legislation.

December The Vermont Supreme Court rules that same-sex marriage, or some equivalent institution, must be enacted by the state legislature within 100 days.

December The Czech parliament defeats a bill to establish registered partnerships for the second time, this time by a vote of 91 to 69.

2000   Same-sex couples in New Zealand are granted the same rights of common-law marriage as those available to opposite-sex couples.

April 1   A law in Vermont permitting civil unions between same-sex couples takes effect.

November Voters in Nebraska pass a constitutional amendment by a vote of 70 percent to 30 percent banning same-sex marriage, civil unions, and domestic partnerships.

November The German parliament, the Bundestag, approves a
10   bill creating registered life partnerships (*eingetragene*

November
10 (*cont.*)   *Lebenspartnerschaften*), providing benefits such as hospital visitation rights, the right to take the same surname, inheritance of pensions, right to act as next of kin, resident status for nonnational partners, rights to adopt children of one's partner, and all rights for insurance, tax purposes, and other financial matters identical to those of opposite-sex couples in a marriage.

December   The Dutch parliament approves by votes of 49 to 26 (upper house) and 109 to 33 (lower house) and Queen Beatrice grants royal assent to a bill granting full marriage rights to same-sex couples, an act that takes effect in April 2001.

2001
January 14   Kevin Bourassa is married to Joe Varnell and Elaine Vautour is married to Anne Vautour, both in Toronto, the first legal marriages of same-sex couples in Canada. As a result of legal challenges, the marriages are not fully approved until June 10, 2003.

March 15   Registered partnerships (*união de facto*) in Portugal, previously available only to opposite-sex couples, are made available to same-sex couples.

September   The Finnish parliament approves registered partnerships (*rekisteröidystä parisuhteesta*) for same-sex couples, an act that takes effect on March 1, 2002.

2002
June 5   A new Swedish law permitting same-sex couples to adopt children goes into effect.

October   The Italian parliament defeats a bill creating same-sex unions similar to those of the French civil pact of solidarity. As of mid-2010, the Italian government has yet to approve any form of same-sex marital entity.

October 26   The Czech parliament rejects a bill recommended by the cabinet to establish registered partnerships for same-sex couples. The parliament's action is its third rejection of registered partnerships for same-sex couples.

December 13 The city of Buenos Aires, Argentina, passes a law establishing a registry for same-sex civil unions in the city.

2003 January 30 A bill approving same-sex marriage passes the Belgian Chamber of Representatives by a vote of 91 to 22. The bill had previously (November 28, 2002) passed the Senate by a vote of 46 to 15. The act goes into effect on June 1, 2003, making Belgium the second nation in the world, after the Netherlands, to approve same-sex marriage.

March The provincial legislature of Rio Negros, Argentina, establishes civil unions for same-sex couples.

May 1 The supreme court of British Columbia rules that the federal government is required by the national constitution to recognize marriage between two individuals of the same sex.

June 10 The Ontario Appeals Court rules that bans on same-sex marriage violate the nation's Charter of Rights and Freedoms. The court's decision takes effect immediately, and the first same-sex marriages take place in Toronto the same day (see 2001).

June 26 In a decision reversing *Bowers v. Hardwick* (see 1986), the U.S. Supreme Court rules by a six-to-three vote that a Texas law criminalizing sodomy was unconstitutional and that, according to Justice Anthony M. Kennedy, "adults may choose to enter upon this relationship in the confines of their homes and their own private lives and still retain their dignity as free persons."

July 14 Croatia extends to same-sex couples the same rights afforded unmarried, cohabiting opposite-sex couples who have lived together for at least three years.

November 18 The Massachusetts Supreme Judicial Court issues its ruling in *Goodrich v. Department of Public Health* that

November 18 (*cont.*)	the prohibition on same-sex marriage in the Commonwealth violates the state constitution.
2004 February 20	Sandoval County (New Mexico) county clerk Victoria Dunlap issues marriage licenses to about 60 same-sex couples because she is unaware of any state law prohibiting same-sex marriages. Essentially all couples eventually marry, although the state quickly nullifies Dunlap's actions.
February 24	President George W. Bush announces his support for an amendment to the U.S. Constitution defining marriage as a civil right available only to couples of opposite sexes.
May	The government of Luxembourg recognizes civil unions (*pacte civil de solidarité;* civil pact of solidarity) between same-sex couples.
May 17	The first legal marriages between same-sex couples in the United States take place in Massachusetts.
August 14	The Australian parliament passes a law defining marriage as occurring between one man and one woman only.
November	Thirteen states pass constitutional amendments banning same-sex marriage, some of which also include civil unions and/or domestic partnerships.
November 18	Queen Elizabeth II grants a decree of Royal Assent to legislation passed by the House of Commons (by a vote of 426 to 29) and the House of Lords (by a vote of 251 to 136) granting the right of civil partnership to same-sex couples. The law takes effect on December 5, 2005.
November 18	A bill is introduced into the Norwegian parliament to make the nation's marriage laws gender neutral. It is later withdrawn with a request for the government to further study such an action.

November 29	The U.S. Supreme Court declines to hear a case from one citizen and 11 legislators from Massachusetts in an effort to overturn that state's law on same-sex marriage
December 8	The parliament of New Zealand enacts legislation permitting same-sex civil unions.
December 30	The Montana Supreme Court rules that the University of Montana system must provide the same health insurance benefits to same-sex couples as it does for opposite-sex couples.
2005 March	The coprinces of Andorra, the President of France, and the Bishop of Urgell, sign a new civil code that includes civil unions for same-sex couples.
April 7	New York City Mayor Michael Bloomberg orders city agencies to recognize legal same-sex marriages from other states and countries.
April	The state of Connecticut adopts legislation establishing civil unions for same-sex couples.
June 5	In a national referendum on a number of issues, Swiss voters approve by a vote of 58 to 42 registered partnerships for same-sex couples.
June 22	The Slovenian National Assembly adopts legislation creating registered partnerships (*registrirano partnerstvo*) by a vote of 44 to 3. Opposition parties boycott the vote claiming that the bill is too weak. This decision sets off a series of legislative actions that eventually lead to the passage of same-sex marriage legislation in early 2010.
June 28	The Canadian House of Commons passes bill C-38, legalizing same-sex marriage in Canada.
July 2	The Spanish Congress of Deputies votes 187 to 147 to override a decision by the Senate to reject a bill

July 2 (*cont.*)	establishing same-sex marriage in Spain. The first marriage between two women takes place in Barcelona 11 days later.
July 19	The Canadian Senate approves bill C-38, legalizing same-sex marriage in Canada.
July 20	Queen Elizabeth II grants Royal Assent for bill C-38, and same-sex marriage becomes fully legal in the country.
September	The parliament of Uganda passes the Constitutional Amendment Bill that revokes term limits for sitting president Yoweri Museveni. The bill also includes a section amending the constitution to prohibit the marriage of two individuals of the same sex.
December 5	The Civil Partnership Act takes effect in the United Kingdom (see 2004).
December 21	Vaira Vike-Freiberga, the president of Latvia, signs a constitutional amendment defining marriage as an institution between a man and a woman. Latvia becomes the first (and so far only) nation in Europe to include such an amendment in its constitution.
2006 January 26	A bill establishing registered partnerships (*registrovaného partnerství*) for Czech same-sex couples passes the Senate by a vote of 65 to 14. The bill had earlier passed the Chamber of Deputies by a vote of 86 to 54 on December 16, 2005. The bill was then vetoed by President Václav Klaus.
March 15	The Czech Chamber of Deputies overturns President Václav Klaus's veto of the registered partnership act by a vote of 101 to 76, exactly the number required for an override. The new law goes into effect on July 1, 2006.
March 30	The Massachusetts Supreme Judicial Court relies on a 1913 law to rule that out-of-state couples may not be

issued marriage licenses if they are not eligible to marry in their own states.

May 18   Legislation permitting adoption by same-sex couples is approved in Belgium. The law becomes effective on June 20.

July 6   The New York Court of Appeals, the state's highest court, rules that the state constitution does not guarantee same-sex couples the right to marry.

July 23   Same-sex civil unions become legal in Slovenia.

October 25 The New Jersey Supreme Court rules that same-sex couples are entitled to legal recognition equivalent to that of heterosexual marriage. In a four-to-three vote, the justices order the state legislature to establish some sort of equivalent legal entity, whether it be called marriage, civil union, or domestic partnership. The three dissenting justices do so because they would go even further and require that same-sex couples be allowed to marry in the state.

November   Voters in Arizona reject a constitutional amendment that would have banned same-sex marriages in the state. Voters in eight other states adopt such an amendment, and Arizona voters reconsider their decision in 2008.

            The Israeli Supreme Court rules that same-sex couples married in other nations are entitled to the same legal benefits as those available to opposite-sex couples married overseas.

November   For the first time anywhere in the country, Mexico
9   City approves a law establishing civil unions for same-sex couples living within the city.

November   The South African parliament approves by a vote of
14   230 to 41 legislation approving same-sex marriage in the nation. The action is the first of its kind on the

November 14 (*cont.*)	African continent and takes effect on December 1, 2006.
2007 **January**	The Mexico state of Coahuila establishes a category of civil pact of solidarity (*pacto civil de solidaridad*) for same-sex couples.
January 3	The Alaska Supreme Court rules that the state is required to provide the same benefits to same-sex couples in its employ as it does to opposite-sex couples. Governor Sarah Palin says she disagrees with the ruling, but will comply with it.
February	The Italian government of Prime Minister Romano Prodi approves a bill creating a form of union called "rights and duties of stable co-habitants" (*diritti e doveri delle persone stabilmente conviventi*). The government falls before the Senate, under the strong influence of the Roman Catholic Church and conservative politicians, is able to act on the bill. As of mid-2010, Italy has not yet adopted any form of matrimonial arrangement for same-sex couples.
February 7	Rhode Island state attorney general Patrick C. Lynch issues an advisory opinion to the effect that the state should recognize marriages performed in neighboring Massachusetts. Observers anticipate that the opinion may presage the state's passage of its own laws permitting same-sex marriage.
June 14	Massachusetts legislators vote to uphold its 2004 decision to approve same-sex marriage, making it impossible for further actions against that policy until 2012.
July	A proposal to legalize same-sex marriage in Luxembourg is defeated by a vote of 38 to 22 in the national legislature.
July 22	A law establishing domestic partnerships for same-sex couples takes effect in Washington State.

December 19	Uruguay becomes the first nation in Latin America to grant same-sex couples rights similar to those of opposite-sex marriage, an arrangement known as a cohabitation union (*convivencia unión*).
2008 January 1	A law establishing civil unions for same-sex couples goes into effect in New Hampshire. (Also see 2010.)
February 1	A law creating domestic partnerships for same-sex couples takes effect in Oregon. The law was passed by the state legislature in May 2007.
May 8	The Michigan Supreme Court rules that local governments and public colleges and universities are not allowed to offer same-sex couples the same benefits available to opposite-sex couples because of voters' earlier approval of a constitutional amendment banning marriage between two people of the same sex.
May 15	The California Supreme Court, in the case of *In re: Marriage Cases*, rules that the state's ban on same-sex marriage violates the state's constitutional guarantee of equality for all citizens. (Also see November 4, 2008.)
June	The Norwegian parliament approves same-sex marriage with a vote of 23 to 17 in the upper house and 84 to 41 in the lower house.
June 23	Largely through the efforts of the Roman Catholic Church, the senate of Colombia defeats a bill to legalize same-sex relationships.
July 1	A limited form of domestic partnership between same-sex couples becomes legal in Maryland.
August 19	The legislature of Argentina adopts legislation allowing one member of a same-sex couple to become eligible for a deceased partner's pension.

August 30   District Court justice Robert B. Hanson, in Polk County, Iowa, rules that the state's ban on same-sex marriage (Iowa Code §595.2[1]) is unconstitutional, and that same-sex couples are allowed to marry in the state. (Also see 2009.)

September   The people of Ecuador adopt a new constitution for the nation with a vote of 63.9 percent to 36.1 percent. The new constitution makes it legal for same-sex couples to form civil unions.

September 18   The Maryland Court of Appeals rules on a four-to-three vote that the state's ban on same-sex marriages does not violate the state's constitutional guarantees of equal treatment for all citizens.

October   The Portuguese Assembly of the Republic defeats a proposal to permit same-sex marriage by a vote of 196 to 28. (But see also April 2010.)

October 10   The Supreme Court of Connecticut rules that the state constitution guarantees same-sex couples equal right to marriage. The first same-sex marriages in the state are performed on November 12.

November   Voters in Arizona change their mind (see 2006) and approve a constitutional amendment banning same-sex marriage in the state.

November 4   Voters in California, Arizona, and Florida adopt constitutional amendments defining marriage as a contract between one man and one woman.

November 19   The Supreme Court of Nepal orders the national legislature to adopt legislation permitting marriage between two persons of the same sex.

2009 January 28   The Colombian Supreme Court rules that same-sex couples are entitled to virtually all of the same legal rights as opposite-sex couples (adoption being an exception).

March   The Nigerian House of Representatives adopts a bill by unanimous vote (360 to 0) banning marriage and all marriage-like institutions between individuals of the same sex. The bill has widespread provisions, calling for prison terms of up to five years not only for anyone who attempts to marry or join in a union with someone of the same sex, but also for anyone who performs, aids, abets, or witnesses such a ceremony or for anyone who has any type of association whatsoever with any type of same-sex organization or for anyone who is involved in "amorous displays" between same-sex individuals either in public or in private.

April   The Swedish parliament votes 261 to 22 to legalize same-sex marriage in the country. The bill goes into effect on May 1, 2009.

April 3   The Iowa Supreme Court affirms an earlier ruling by district judge Robert B. Hanson, declaring the state's ban on same-sex marriage to be unconstitutional. (Also see 2007.)

April 7   Same-sex marriage becomes legal in Vermont.

April 20   The parliament of Hungary passes a bill legalizing registered partnerships for same-sex couples.

May 6   The state legislature passes and Governor John Baldacci signs a law extending full marriage rights to same-sex couples in Maine. (See also November 4.)

May 18   The Washington State legislature passes and Governor Chris Gregoire signs an "everything-but-marriage" bill that grants same-sex couples all legal rights available to opposite-sex couples, with the one exception of the name given to the entity. (Also see November 4.)

May 26   The California Supreme Court upholds the results of the November 4, 2008, vote on Proposition 8, a constitutional amendment defining marriage as a contract between one man and one woman.

May 31   The legislature of Nevada overrides governor Jim Gibbons's veto of an act providing domestic partnerships for same-sex couples.

June 3   The New Hampshire legislature passes and governor John Lynch signs a bill legalizing same-sex marriage. The bill takes effect on January 1, 2010.

June 26   Ireland grants the right of registered partnership, with most of the same privileges associated with opposite-sex marriages, to same-sex couples.

July 1   Hungary's same-sex registered partnership law goes into effect.

August 3   Domestic partnerships for same-sex couples with limited legal benefits become available in Wisconsin.

October 22 The synod (ruling body) of the Swedish Lutheran Church, the nation's largest denomination, votes to participate in same-sex marriage ceremonies beginning on November 1, 2009.

November 4   Voters in Maine overturn the state legislature's act permitting same-sex marriage.

Voters in Washington State decline to overturn the state's "everything-but-marriage" law, making the state the sixth state in the union to provide same-sex couples with rights equal to those of opposite-sex couples (except for the name of the entity).

November 13   A local court in Buenos Aires, Argentina, rules that two men must be issued a marriage license. (Also see December 1.)

December   Both houses of the Austrian parliament vote to establish registered partnerships for same-sex couples by votes of 44 to 8 and 110 to 64.

December 1   The Buenos Aires city council rules that the marriage of Alex Freyre and José María Di Bello (see November 13) must be placed on hold until the nation's supreme court rules on the legality of the marriage license granted the couple.

December 15 The District of Columbia city council votes to approve legislation granting equal marriage rights to same-sex couples.

December 22 The Mexico City assembly passes legislation, by a vote of 39 to 20, granting same-sex couples the right to marry and to adopt children. The new law changes the definition of marriage as the union of a man and a woman to "the free uniting of two people."

December 28 Alex Freyre and José María Di Bello (see December 1) are married in a private civil ceremony in the registry office at Usuhaia, the capital of Tierra del Fuego province, Argentina.

2010 January A Russian court rules that two women married in Canada cannot be considered to be legally married in Russia since the Russian constitution does not recognize marriage between two individuals of the same gender.

January 7 By a vote of 20 to 14, the New Jersey state senate rejects a proposal to legalize same-sex marriage.

January 8 The parliament of Portugal votes 125 to 99 to legalize same-sex marriage, making the nation the sixth country in Europe to approve same-sex marriage.

February 10 The Australian Senate votes 45 to 5 against a proposal to legalize same-sex marriage. The action is taken despite current polls showing that Australians approve granting marriage rights to same-sex couples by a majority of 60 percent to 36 percent.

March 3 A law for a new family code, which recognizes the right of same-sex couples to marry and adopt children, passes its first reading in the Slovenia parliament

March 8   Judge Felix Gustavo de Igarzabal of Buenos Aires
           declares the marriage between Alex Freyre and José
           María Di Bello (see December 28, 2009) null and void.
           The couple is ordered to turn in their marriage license
           or face a fine.

May   Reporters learn that Revered George Alan Rekers, a
           founder of the anti-same-sex marriage Family
           Research Council, has hired a male escort from
           rentboy.com to accompany him on a ten-day trip to
           Europe. Rekers explains that he needed someone to
           carry his luggage.

May 18   Representative Mark Souder (R-IN), a vocal oppo-
           nent of same-sex marriage, resigns his post in the
           U.S. Congress because of the revelation of his extra-
           marital affair with a staffer.

May 18   Portuguese President Anibal Cavaco Silva announces
           that he will sign pending legislation to legalize same-
           sex marriage, making Portugal the sixth nation in
           Europe to permit such arrangements.

5

Biographical Sketches

This chapter contains brief biographical sketches of some individuals who have been important figures in the history of same-sex marriage and adoption. The majority of these individuals are not world-famous politicians, scientists, lawyers, or other renowned figures. Instead, they tend to be rather ordinary men and women who, at some time in their lives, decided that they wanted to work for equal civil rights available to their heterosexual friends and neighbors. Because they are often not otherwise famous, their biographical information may be someone limited. But they are included in the chapter because the actions they took moved forward the struggle for equal treatment for lesbians and gay men at some point in the history of that effort. Biographies of some individuals who have worked against equal civil rights in marriage and adoption are also included.

Barry T. Albin (1952–)

Albin wrote the majority opinion in the case of *Lewis v. Harris* (908 A.2d 196) in 2006, an opinion that held that withholding a marriage license from a same-sex couple violated the New Jersey state constitution. The court ruled that the state had to either issue such marriage licenses or find some alternative legal entity that provided same-sex couples with exactly the same rights as those enjoyed by married opposite-sex couples. The ruling was unanimous, although three justices wrote a dissenting opinion that argued that the court erred in simply not requiring the state to recognize same-sex marriages in the state.

Barry T. Albin was born in Brooklyn, New York, on July 7, 1952. He attended Rutgers College, from which he received his bachelor's degree in 1973, and Cornell Law School, which awarded him his JD in 1976. After graduation, he accepted an appointment as deputy attorney general in the Appellate Section of the New Jersey Division of Criminal Justice, where he served until 1978. He then became assistant prosecutor in Passaic and Middlesex Counties, a post he held until 1982. He then joined the law firm of Wilentz, Goldman & Spitzer, in Woodridge, New Jersey, where he was named a partner four years later. During his tenure at Wilentz, Albin was elected president of the New Jersey Association of Criminal Defense Lawyers and chosen by his peers to be listed in the "Best Lawyers in America" publication for 2000–2001.

In July 2002, governor James E. McGreevey nominated Albin for a seven-year term on the New Jersey Supreme Court. He was confirmed by the state senate on September 12, 2002. On May 15, 2009, governor Jon Corzine renominated Albin for a permanent position on the court, a nomination that was confirmed by the state senate on June 26, 2009. As a result of that action, Albin is eligible to remain on the court until he reaches mandatory retirement age of 70 in 2022.

Jack Baker (1942–)

Jack Baker and his life partner, Michael McConnell, were among the first same-sex couples in the United States to apply for a marriage license. They made that application on May 18, 1970, at the offices of the Hennepin County (Minnesota) Clerk of Court's office. They were denied that application and eventually sued the county on the grounds that they were being discriminated against on the basis of their gender. They lost that case in district court and again before the Minnesota Supreme Court. Finally, the U.S. Supreme Court declined to hear an appeal of the case on the grounds that it did not involve any substantial federal question. The decision issued by the Minnesota Supreme Court in *Baker v. Nelson* is generally regarded as one of the most influential court opinions on same-sex marriage, one that is still cited by courts today.

Jack Baker was born Richard John Baker in 1942. He attended the University of Minnesota, where he became politically active early in his career as a student. He was one of the founding members and a president of the group Fight Repression of Erotic

Expression (FREE), often called the first student gay group in the United States. The group was established a month before the Stonewall riots in New York City in 1969. In 1971, Baker ran for student body president in a campaign in which he appeared in high-heeled shoes with the slogan, "Put Yourself in Jack Baker's Shoes." To the surprise of almost everyone, he was elected and then, a year later, reelected, an accomplishment that no other student body president had achieved at Minnesota. Baker eventually earned his law degree from Minnesota in 1972. He then formed his own law firm in south Minneapolis, where he continued to work for more than 30 years.

In addition to his legal practice, Baker continued his work as a gay activist. Unable to obtain the marriage license they sought, Baker and McConnell decided to pursue another avenue, adult adoption. In August 1972, McConnell legally adopted Baker in Hennepin County. The action is generally thought to have been the first action of its kind by two adults of the same sex. The action brought Baker and McConnell a few of the legal rights usually reserved to opposite-sex couples, such as inheritance rights and reduced university fees at Minnesota, where they were both still students at the time. Also in 1971, Baker and McConnell applied for a marriage license a second time, this time in Mankato (Blue Earth County). With the license, they were married in Minneapolis by the Rev. Roger Lynn, a minister in the Methodist Church. Baker and McConnell relied on this marriage to file joint federal tax returns until 2004, when the Internal Revenue Service rejected their filing because of the newly passed Defense of Marriage Act.

As of 2010, Baker and McConnell continue to live in South Minneapolis.

Bob Barr (1948–)

Barr introduced the Defense of Marriage Act (DOMA) in the U.S. House of Representatives on May 7, 1996. The act defines marriage as a contract between one man and one woman, and gives all states, territories, possessions, and Indian tribes the right to ignore legal recognition of same-sex marriages, civil unions, domestic partnerships, and other arrangements enacted in other states, essentially excusing those governmental entities from the legal provisions of the Fifteenth Amendment to the U.S. Constitution. In 2004, Barr changed his position on same-sex marriage and testified before Congress in support of the Respect for Marriage Act, a bill to revoke DOMA.

Robert Laurence Barr Jr. was born in Iowa City, Iowa, on November 5, 1948. As a member of a military family, Barr moved frequently during his childhood, attending schools in Iraq, Malaysia, Pakistan, Panama, and Peru, before finally graduating from the Community High School in Teheran, Iran, in 1956. He then matriculated at the University of Southern California (USC), from which he received his bachelor's degree in 1970. Originally a liberal Democrat, Barr changed his political views at USC, eventually adopting a strongly conservative position that informed most of the rest of his political career.

Barr continued his educational career at George Washington University, from which he received his MA in international affairs in 1972 and at Georgetown University, which awarded him his JD in 1977. Barr then worked briefly as an analyst at the Central Intelligence Agency (CIA) before moving to Georgia and becoming politically active. After a failed run to the U.S. House of Representatives, he was appointed U.S. Attorney for the Northern District of Georgia by President Ronald Reagan in 1986, a post he held until 1990. Barr ran for the House of Representatives again in 1994, this time defeating six-term Democrat Buddy Darden for the seat in Georgia's seventh congressional district (north-central Georgia). Largely as the result of redistricting, Barr lost his seat in the election of 2002.

Since leaving Congress, Barr has been increasingly critical of the Republican Party and its policies. In 2006 he officially left the party and became a member of the Libertarian Party and in 2008 was the party's nominee for president of the United States. Barr remains an active spokesperson for many libertarian and conservative causes. He now practices law at the firm of Edwin Marger and operates a consulting firm, Liberty Strategies, Inc., both in Atlanta, Georgia.

David Boies (1941–)

Boies was paired with attorney Ted Olson representing the plaintiffs in the 2009 court case, *Perry v. Schwarzenegger*, that challenged the outcome of the November 2008 vote on Proposition 8, a constitutional amendment defining marriage as a legal institution between one man and one woman. The decision of Boies and Olson to work together on this case was the subject of considerable comment because the two men represent opposite poles of the legal spectrum and, in fact, argued the opposing sides in the 2000 U.S. Supreme Court case of *Bush v. Gore*, which determined the outcome of the 2000 U.S. presidential election.

David Boies was born in Sycamore, Illinois, on March 11, 1941. His family moved to California while Boies was still in high school, and he eventually graduated from Fullerton High School, in Fullerton, California. Boies then attended the University of Redlands, in Redlands, California, and Northwestern University, in Evanston, Illinois, from which he received his bachelor's degree in 1964. He the continued his education at Yale Law School, where he earned his LLB in 1966 and at the New York University School of Law, which awarded his LLM in 1967.

After graduating from Yale, Boies joined the law firm of Cravath, Swaine & Moore, in New York City, where he remained until 1997. He was made a partner in the firm in 1973. In 1997, Boies left Cravath, Swaine & Moore to found his own firm, Boies, Schiller & Flexner LLP, where he continues to work. Boies has also served briefly in the federal government, first as chief counsel and staff director of the United States Senate Antitrust Subcommittee in 1978, and then as chief counsel and staff director of the United States Senate Judiciary Committee in 1979. Boies was named Lawyer of the Year by *Time* magazine in 2000 and was awarded an honorary doctor of laws degree by New York University in 2007. Boies has been married three times and is the father of six children.

Mary Bonauto (1961–)

Bonauto was lead attorney in the case of *Goodrich v. Department of Public Health* in 2004 in which the Massachusetts Supreme Judicial Court ruled that the state could not withhold marriage licenses from same-sex couples. She was also very active in the 2009 campaign to uphold the Maine state legislature's passage of an act legalizing same-sex marriage in that state, a campaign that ultimately failed in the November election on the issue.

Mary Bonauto was born in Newburgh, New York, in 1961. She attended Hamilton College in Clinton, New York, from which she received her bachelor's degree in comparative literature and history in 1983. It was at Hamilton that she realized she was attracted to women and came out on campus as a lesbian. She continued her studies at the Northeastern University School of Law in Boston, where she earned her JD in 1987. Northeastern has a cooperative studies program in which students alternate their time between academic courses on campus and professional training in the field of their choice. During this period, Bonauto worked at the Public Protection Bureau of the Office of the Massachusetts Attorney General; the Divorce Unit of Greater Boston Legal Services; the law firm of Julian & Olsen, in Madison, Wisconsin; and the law firm of Sugarman & Sugarman, in Boston.

Bonauto's first job after graduation from Northeastern was with Mittle & Herrernan, a small law firm in Portland, Maine. In 1989, she was hired for a new position with Gay & Lesbian Advocates & Defenders (GLAD) in which she would be responsible for enforcing a new Massachusetts law prohibiting discrimination in jobs, housing, and public accommodation on the basis of sexual orientation. She has remained with GLAD ever since, currently serving as Civil Rights Project Director of the organization. She lives in Portland, Maine, with her partner of 19 years, Jennifer Wriggins, and their five-year-old twin daughters.

John E. Boswell (1947–94)

Boswell was one of the world's preeminent students of the history of same-sex relationships. In his book *Same-Sex Unions in Premodern Europe* (Villard Books, 1994), he argued that same-sex unions were relatively common during the period explored in the book (the eighth to sixteenth century) and were routinely blessed by the Roman Catholic Church. Although this thesis was strongly criticized by a number of scholars, Boswell's evidence for his contention is very strong indeed. It has, in any case, caused scholars to take a new and very different view of same-sex relationships, especially among members of the clergy in the Catholic church, during the Middle Ages.

John Eastburn Boswell was born in Boston on March 20, 1947, to Catharine and Colonel Henry Boswell Jr. He attended the College of William and Mary, from which he received his bachelor's degree in 1969, and Harvard University, which granted Boswell his PhD in 1975. He then joined the faculty of history at Yale University, where he was appointed full professor with tenure in 1982. He was named A. Whitney Griswold Professor of History in 1990. Boswell was an extraordinary philologist, with a mastery of 17 languages, including ancient Latin and Greek; Arabic; Catalan; Church Slavonic; Old Icelandic; and classical Armenian, Syriac, and Persian. In addition to *Same-Sex Unions in Premodern Europe*, Boswell authored a number of other ground-breaking books, including *The Royal Treasure: Muslim Communities Under the Crown of Aragon in the Fourteenth Century* (1977); *Christianity, Social Tolerance, and Homosexuality* (1980); *Rediscovering Gay History: Archetypes of Gay Love in Christian History* (1982); *The Kindness of Strangers: The Abandonment of Children in Western Europe from Late Antiquity to the Renaissance* (1989); *Homosexuality in the Priesthood and the Religious Life* (1991; coauthor); and *Forms of Desire: Sexual Orientation and the Social Constructionist Controversy* (1992).

Boswell converted from Episcopalian to Roman Catholic at the age of 16 and devoted much of his scholarship to demonstrating that the Roman Catholic Church was not historically opposed to same-sex relationships. In addition to his significant research contributions, he was highly regarded as a teacher, with his course in medieval history consistently receiving ratings among the 10 most popular at Yale. In 1987, Boswell was one of the founders of the Lesbian and Gay Studies Center at Yale, now the Research Fund for Lesbian and Gay Studies. He died in New Haven, Connecticut, on December 24, 1994, as the result of complications of AIDS.

Chris Bryant (1962–)

Bryant is a member of parliament for the Labour Party from the Rhondda district of Wales. He and his partner, Jared Cranney, made history in March 2010, when they were joined in a civil partnership in the Houses of Parliament, the first such event in British history.

Christopher John Bryant was born on January 11, 1962, in Cardiff, Wales, to a Scottish mother and a Welsh father, who was a computer engineer. He grew up in Wales, Spain, and England as his father moved from job to job. He attended Cheltenham College, in Cheltenham, England, and matriculated at Mansfield College, Oxford, from which he earned a BA in English in 1983. He later earned his master's degree at Oxford also. He then enrolled at Ripon College, in Cuddesdon, Oxfordshire, where he studied for the priesthood, earning his degree in theology. He was ordained a priest of the Anglican Church in December 1986 and spent two years as curate at All Saints parish, High Wycombe. He then was youth chaplain for the diocese of Peterborough, where he remained until leaving the priesthood in 1991. He is said to have been concerned about the problems of being openly gay and a member of the priesthood.

After leaving the church, Bryant decided to pursue a career in politics, working at first as an election agent for the Labour Party in the Holborn and St. Pancras constituency. He also pursued a career in writing, publishing biographies of Sir Stafford Cripps and Glenda Jackson. In his first run for a seat in parliament, he was narrowly defeated for the seat from Wycombe in the 1997 election. Three years later, however, he was selected to run for the safe Labour seat in Rhondda, a post he has held ever since. Over the past decade, Bryant has held a number of leadership positions in Labour governments, including parliamentary private secretary to the Secretary of State for Constitutional Affairs; deputy leader of the House of Commons; Parliamentary Under-Secretary of State for Foreign Affairs; and, most recently, Minister of State for Europe. Bryant and Cranney have been together since 2008.

Charles J. Cooper (1952–)

Cooper was lead attorney for the defense in the 2009–10 trial, *Perry v. Schwarzenegger*, that challenged the outcome of the November 2008 vote on Proposition 8. That proposition offered a constitutional amendment limiting marriage in California to opposite-sex couples. Cooper was at the time, and remains, a founding member and senior partner at the firm Cooper & Kirk, PLLC.

Charles J. Cooper was born in Dayton, Ohio, on March 8, 1952. He attended the University of Alabama at Birmingham, from which he received his BS in business administration in 1974. He then continued his studies at the University of Alabama School of Law, where he earned his JD in 1977. He was first in his class academically and editor of the school law review. After graduation, Cooper took a job as law clerk to judge Paul Roney, judge of the U.S. Circuit Court of Appeals for the Fifth Circuit (1977–78) and then as law clerk for Justice William H. Rehnquist, of the U.S. Supreme Court (1978–79). Cooper then joined the Civil Rights Division of the U.S. Department of Justice, where he remained until 1985. He was then appointed assistant attorney general in the Office of Legal Counsel at the Department of Justice, a post he held until 1988. He then returned to private practice with the Washington, DC, firm of McGuire Woods. After two years at McGuire Woods, he joined the firm of Shaw, Pittman, Potts & Trowbridge, where he was a partner and head of the firm's Constitutional and Government Litigation Group. In 1996, he became one of the founding members of Cooper & Kirk, PLLC. Cooper has been named by the *National Law Journal* as one of the 10 best civil litigators in the nation.

Irwin Cotler (1940–)

Cotler is member of parliament in the Canadian parliament for the district of Mount Royal, in Quebec, Canada. In February 2005, Cotler introduced bill C-38 to the House of Commons, a bill legalizing marriage between couples of the same sex in Canada. That bill passed in the House on June 28, 2005, in the Senate on July 19, 2005, after which it received Royal Assent from Queen Elizabeth II on the following day.

Irwin Cotler was born in Montreal, Quebec, Canada, on May 8, 1940. He attended McGill University in Montreal, from which he received his BA in 1961 and his law degree in 1964. He then continued his studies at Yale University before accepting an appointment as professor of law at McGill, where he also served as director of the university's Human Rights Program. He subsequently was visiting professor of law at Harvard University and Woodrow Wilson Fellow at Yale. In 1999, he was elected to the House of Commons with probably the largest margin of victory in Canadian history, winning 92 percent of the total vote. In 2003, he was appointed Minister of Justice and Attorney General of Canada, a post he held until the fall of the Liberal Party in the election of 2006. He continues to serve as a member of parliament while on leave of absence from McGill.

Cotler may be best known for his work in international human rights cases, where he has served as council for a number of individuals best known for their struggle in that area, individuals such as Nelson Mandela, Andrei Sakharov, Nathan Sharansky, Indonesian trade union leader Muchtar Pakpahan, Nigerian playwright and Nobel Laureate Wole Soyinka, Bangladeshi journalist Shoaib Choudhury, and Chinese-Canadian political prisoner, KunLun Zhang.

Dennis Damon (1948–)

Damon is a state senator who introduced legislation in January 2009 to legalize same-sex marriage in the state of Maine. The legislation later went on to be approved by the state house and senate and was signed by Governor John Baldacci on May 6, 2009. On November 4, 2009, the voters of Maine passed an initiative petition that revoked the act, leaving same-sex marriage illegal in the state.

Dennis Damon was born in Bar Harbor, Maine, on December 21, 1948. He earned his BS degree in education at the University of Maine at Orono in 1971 and then taught school for 14 years, first in Orono and then at Mount Desert High School. In 1985 he left teaching to become vice president of the Norumbeja Moving and Storage Company. Two years later, he opened his own company, Mount Desert Spring Water Company, which he ran for 10 years. In addition to his current senate seat, Damon has also been special project consultant to the Bureau of Rehabilitation Services of the Maine Department of Labor since 2001.

Damon served for one year as Hancock County Commissioner (1992) before being elected as a Democrat to the state senate in 2002. He was reelected in 2004, 2006, and 2008, which he says is his last term in the senate. In the senate he has served as chair of the Joint Standing Committee on Marine Resources, the Joint Standing Committee on Transportation, and a number of joint select committees, most recently the Joint Select Committee on Property Tax Reform. In introducing bill LD 1020, "An Act to End Discrimination in Civil Marriage and Affirm Religious Freedom," Damon noted that "[r]arely do we as legislators have the opportunity and the privilege to introduce legislation that so wholly corrects discrimination and provides the means for us to move forward as a civil society bound by laws."

Damon currently resides in Trenton, Maine, with his wife and three children.

James Dobson (1936–)

Dobson is an American evangelical Christian who founded the organization Focus on the Family in 1977. The purpose of Focus on the Family is to nurture and defend the traditional heterosexual family consisting of a husband, wife, and children. He served as chair of the organization until his resignation in 2003. He also founded the Family Research Council, an organization that promotes traditional marriage and the traditional heterosexual family, in 1981. Dobson has long taken a strong stand against same-sex relationships and the promotion of civil rights for gay men and lesbians. On one occasion, he stated that "[h]omosexuals are not monogamous. They want to destroy the institution of marriage. It will destroy marriage. It will destroy the Earth" (*The Daily Oklahoman*, October 23, 2004).

James Clayton Dobson Jr. was born in Shreveport, Louisiana, on April 21, 1936. His father, grandfather, and great-grandfather were all ministers in the Church of the Nazarene, so religion was an essential part of his life from his childhood. He said that he responded to a call from his father at the altar at the age of three, when he promised to devote his life to the Christian church. He attended the Church of the Nazarene's Pasadena College (now the Point Loma Nazarene College), where he earned his bachelor's degree in psychology. He then continued his studies at the University of Southern California (USC), which granted him his PhD in child psychology in 1967. After his graduation, Dobson was offered a position as associate professor of pediatrics at the USC school of medicine. Concurrently he served on the staff of the division of child development at Children's Hospital in Los Angeles.

In 1970, Dobson published his first book, *Dare to Discipline*, which has since sold more than two million copies. The book encouraged parents to use corporal punishment on their children in order to enforce an appropriate moral standard. The book was the first of a number of books that became very popular among evangelical and conservative Christians, including *Hide or Seek* (1974), *What Wives Wish Their Husbands Knew About Women* (1975), *Preparing for Adolescence* (1978), and *The Strong-Willed Child* (1978). Since then, Dobson has written dozens more books, pamphlets, brochures, and other materials. In 1977, he founded Focus on the Family, an organization that he headed for the next 26 years. In the same year, he began his radio program of the same name that began as a 15-minute broadcast and eventually expanded to a half-hour program.

Dobson resigned as president and CEO of Focus on the Family in 2003, although he continues to host his radio program and to write for the organization's newsletter.

William N. Eskridge, Jr. (1951–)

Eskridge is currently John A. Garver Professor of Jurisprudence at Yale Law School, in New Haven, Connecticut. He has written extensively about the history and legal aspects of same-sex marriage and has testified on a number of occasions in legal proceedings dealing with same-sex marriage. He is author and coauthor of two important books on the subject of gay marriage, *The Case for Same-Sex Marriage: From Sexual Liberty to Civilized Commitment* (The Free Press, 1996) and *Gay Marriage: For Better or for Worse?: What We've Learned from the Evidence* (with Darren R. Spedale; Oxford University Press, 2006).

William N. Eskridge Jr. was born on October 27, 1951, in Princeton, West Virginia. He attended Davidson College, from which he received his bachelor's degree in history summa cum laude in 1973. He then attended Harvard University, from which he earned his MA in history in 1974 and Yale University, which granted him his JD in 1978. He then served for one year as law clerk for Judge Edward Weinfeld and attorney with the firm of Shea & Gardner before accepting an appointment as assistant professor of law at the University of Virginia in 1982. He moved to Georgetown University, where he served as associate professor (1987–90) and professor (1990–98) of law before returning to Yale as John A. Garver Professor of Jurisprudence. Eskridge has also served as visiting professor of law at New York University (1993), Harvard University (1994), Stanford University (1995), and Yale University (1995). He has written a dozen books in addition to *The Case for Same-Sex Marriage* and *Gay Marriage*, and nearly 100 refereed papers on a variety of issues, including same-sex marriage. One of those papers, "A History of Same-Sex Marriage" (*Virginia Law Review*, volume 79, 1993), is one of the most comprehensive reviews of the subject currently available. Eskridge has also testified before a number of legislative bodies in the United States and Canada on a variety of issues, including same-sex marriage, asbestos compensation, ethics in government, military sales to Pakistan, and adjustable rate mortgages.

Maggie Gallagher (1960–)

Gallagher is a writer and political organizer who has advocated against the right of same-sex couples to marry. She is the president of two groups organized to work against the legalization of same-sex marriage, the National Organization for Marriage (NOM) and the Institute for Marriage and Public Policy (IMPP). In the 2009 New York Senate debate over the legalization of same-sex marriage in the state, NOM spent over $600,000 on behalf of the antimarriage position.

Margaret Gallagher was born on September 16, 1960, in Lake Oswego, Oregon. She attended Lakeridge High School in Lake Oswego before matriculating at Yale University. At Yale, she was a member of the conservative Party of the Right of the Yale Political Union. She received her bachelor's degree in religious studies from Yale in 1982.

Gallagher first became well known as the result of an anonymous editorial she wrote for the *New York Times* in September 1992. Entitled "An Unwed Mother for Quayle," Gallagher explained in her piece why she supported the position about women who have children out of wedlock Quayle had taken in criticizing the *Murphy Brown* television program. Gallagher later married Raman Srivastav, with whom she is raising her two children.

In an August 2003 article in the journal *Weekly Standard*, Gallagher explained her objection to same-sex marriage. The problem with same-sex marriage, she said, "is not that it would allow a handful of people to choose alternative family forms, but that it would require society at large to gut marriage of its central presumptions about family in order to accommodate a few adults' desires." Gallagher has authored and coauthored a number of books in support of her position on same-sex marriage and other social issues, including *The Abolition of Marriage; The Case for Marriage: Why Married People Are Happier, Healthier, and Better Off Financially* (with Linda Waite); *Enemies of Eros: How the Sexual Revolution Is Killing Family, Marriage, and Sex and What We Can Do About It; Can Government Strengthen Marriage?: Evidence from the Social Sciences;* and *The Age of Unwed Mothers: Is Teen Pregnancy the Problem?: A Report to the Nation.*

Julie Goodridge (1957–)

Goodridge and her partner, Hillary Goodridge, were lead plaintiffs in the case *Goodridge v. Department of Public Health*, which resulted in the Commonwealth of Massachusetts becoming the first state in the United States to legalize marriage between two individuals of the same sex. In their complaint, the Goodridges and the 12 other plaintiffs argued that the sole reason the state would not issue them a marriage license was because of their sex, and that position violated the equal rights provisions of the Massachusetts constitution, a position that was eventually upheld by the Massachusetts Supreme Judicial Court in November 2003.

Julie Goodridge was born in Greenwich, Connecticut, on July 14, 1957. She attended Boston University, from which she received her BA in philosophy in 1979, and Harvard University, which granted her an EdM in human development in 1983. After graduating from Harvard, she worked as a stock broker with E. F. Hutton and with Merrill Lynch. She later served as vice president at Dean Witter Reynolds. In 1984, she founded her own investment firm, Northstar Asset Management, Inc., with offices in Boston. The firm is dedicated to assisting its clients in placing their investments in socially responsible corporations. The firm's name was chosen to reflect the practice that African-American slaves escaping from their masters used in following the North Star to reach their freedom. In carrying out its mission, Northstar also participates in and contributes to a number of organizations that work for social justice and change, including Responsible Wealth, a project of United for a Fair Economy; the Social Investment Forum; Gay & Lesbian Advocates & Defenders (GLAD); the Gay, Lesbian, & Straight Education Network (GLSEN); the Boston Alliance of Gay, Lesbian, Bisexual and Transgendered Youth (BAGLY); Boston Women's Fund; Spontaneous Celebrations, an organization devoted to forging relationships between culturally diverse people; and Mass Equality, an organization working to achieve full equality for the lesbians, gay men, bisexuals, and transgendered individuals and to protect marriage equality in Massachusetts and other New England states.

At the time *Goodridge v. Department of Public Health* was being heard, Goodridge and her partner had been together for 19 years and were parents of a five-year-old girl. In 2006, two years after being married, the couple decided to separate and began to begin "amicably living apart."

Phyllis Lyon (1924–)

Lyon's name is inextricably linked with that of Del Martin, her domestic partner of 56 years. Lyon and Martin founded the Daughters of Bilitis in 1955, the first political and social organization in the

United States designed specifically for lesbians. Throughout their lives, Lyon and Martin were involved in a number of gay, lesbian, and feminist organizations, including the Council on Religion and the Homosexual, whose goal it was to encourage religious leaders to include gay men and lesbians in church activities, and the Alice B. Toklas Memorial Democratic Club, the first gay and lesbian political organization in San Francisco, and still one of the most influential such groups in the city.

Phyllis Lyon was born in Tulsa, Oklahoma, on November 10, 1924. She grew up in Seattle, Southern California, and San Francisco, graduating from Sacramento High School in 1943. She then attended the University of California at Berkeley, from which she received her BA in journalism in 1946. Like many women of her day, Lyon felt that her life would eventually have to center on a man. As she told historian John D'Emilio, "If you were a woman, you had to have a man. There was no other way." By the 1950s, however, she learned otherwise. After a stint as a general reporter for the *Chico Enterprise-Record*, Lyon moved to Seattle to work on a trade magazine. There she met Del Martin and fell in love. In 2004, they were the first same-sex couple to be married in San Francisco after Mayor Gavin Newsom had issued an order permitting same-sex marriage licenses in the city. Four years later, after the California Supreme Court ruled that same-sex marriages were legal in the state, the couple was married a second time.

In 1972, Lyon and Martin coauthored *Lesbian/Woman*, a book that discussed lesbian lives in a strongly positive tone, an approach that was virtually unknown at the time. *Publisher's Weekly* called the book one of the 20 most important women's book of its generation. In the last three decades, Lyon has been especially interested in the topic of human sexuality in general and, in 1970, cofounded the Institute for Advanced Study of Human Sexuality in San Francisco, from which she received her EdD in 1976. She also served on the San Francisco Human Rights Commission for more than a decade, acting as chairperson for two of those years.

Richard Malone (1946–)

Malone is bishop of the Roman Catholic Diocese of Portland, Maine. He was one of the leading voices in opposition to legislation legalizing same-sex marriage adopted by the Maine state legislature in Maine. His position on the issue, expressed in advertisements paid for by the diocese during the repeal campaign, was that same-sex marriage is a "dangerous sociological experiment that I believe will have negative consequences for society as a whole. Children will be taught in schools ... [that the logical concept that] marriage and reproduction are intrinsically linked is no longer valid." Malone said that these are "profound changes that will reverberate throughout society with tragic consequences."

Richard Joseph Malone was born in Salem, Massachusetts, on March 19, 1946. He attended St. John's Prep, in nearby Danvers, Massachusetts, and then continued his studies at Cardinal O'Connell Seminary in Jamaica Plain, Massachusetts. He received his BA in philosophy, his bachelor's degree in divinity, and a master's degree in theology, all from St. John Seminary, in Boston. In 1981, he was awarded his doctorate in theology (ThD) degree by Boston University. He then continued his studies at the Weston Jesuit School of Theology in Cambridge, Massachusetts, where he was awarded his licentiate in sacred theology in 1990.

Malone was ordained a priest of the Roman Catholic Church in May 1972. His first pastoral assignment was at the St. Patrick parish in Stoneham, Massachusetts. In 1974, he became a member of the faculty at St. Clement High School, in Somerville, Massachusetts. Two years later, he was appointed a member of the faculty and chaplain at the Xaverian High School in Westwood, Massachusetts. In 1979, he joined the faculty at St. John Seminary, where he taught religion and theology. During his years at St. John, Malone also served as chaplain at Wellesley College, in Wellesley, Massachusetts, and at Regis College, in Weston, Massachusetts. He later served also as chaplain at the Harvard-Radcliffe Catholic Student Center, as director of the office of religious education for the archdiocese of Boston, as secretary of education for the archdiocese, and as auxiliary bishop of Boston for the south region. In 2004, he was appointed the 11th bishop of Portland.

Del Martin (1921–2008)

With her longtime domestic partner, Phyllis Lyon, Martin had been deeply involved in the gay and lesbian political rights movement for more than half a century. In 1955, Martin and Lyon founded the Daughters of Bilitis, the first organization created to push for political rights of lesbians in the United States. A year later, they also founded and edited the nation's first lesbian periodical, *The Ladder*. The two women were also involved in creating the Council on Religion and the Homosexual in 1964 and San Francisco's Alice B. Toklas Memorial Democratic Club in 1972.

Martin was born Dorothy L. Taliaferro in San Francisco on May 5, 1921. Early in life, she became better known as Del. She attended George Washington High School in San Francisco before matriculating at the University of California at Berkeley. She later transferred to San Francisco State College (now San Francisco State University), where she met her future husband, James Martin. She then left San Francisco State, gave birth to a daughter, Kendra, and moved with her family to the suburbs. Before long, she realized that her long-standing attraction to women made her marriage impossible, and she was divorced from Martin (although she did keep her husband's surname).

In 1950, Martin moved to Seattle to take a job with a publisher of construction trade information. There she met Lyon, who was working with the same company. They made a commitment to each other in 1952 and, in 1955, moved to San Francisco. There they bought a house where they continued to live for more than 50 years.

In addition to her political activities, Martin wrote two important books, *Lesbian/Woman* (with Lyon) and *Battered Wives*, a book that became critical in the development of a national movement against domestic violence. Martin and Lyon were married twice, the first time in 2004, and again in 2008. She died in San Francisco on August 27, 2008, as the result of complications arising from a broken arm that exacerbated her already poor health.

Michael McConnell (dates not known)

Michael McConnell and his partner, Jack Baker, are generally recognized as being one of the first same-sex couples in the United States to apply for a marriage license. That application, to the Clerk of Courts in Hennepin County, Minnesota, was denied on May 18, 1970. McConnell and Baker then filed suit to force the county to issue them a marriage license, a case that eventually worked its way to the U.S. Supreme Court, which declined to hear the case for lack of a "substantial federal question." Baker and McConnell were later granted a marriage license by a clerk in a different Minnesota county (Blue Earth), which they used for a marriage conducted in Minneapolis in late 1970.

McConnell was born James Michael McConnell in Oklahoma, but has always been known simply as Michael McConnell. He attended the University of Oklahoma, from which he earned his bachelor of arts degree in library science (with a minor in pharmacy) in 1967. He then continued his studies at the University of Minnesota, which granted his master's degree in library science in 1968. After graduation, McConnell took a position as technical services librarian at the Park College Library, in Kansas City, Missouri, where he was also assistant professor. In 1971, the regents of the University of Minnesota offered McConnell a post as instructor and librarian, but then withdrew that offer when they heard about Baker and McConnell's efforts to obtain a marriage license.

After serving for a year as executive director of Youth Services Coalition, in Minneapolis, McConnell was offered a job with the Hennepin County Library system, where he served in the technical services division, as senior librarian in the Southdale-Hennepin Area Library, as principal librarian at the Rockford Road Community Library, as principal librarian for the Near North Cluster, and as coordinating librarian for the Hennepin County Library system. McConnell continues to live with his partner, Baker, in South Minneapolis.

Thomas S. Monson (1927–)

Monson is president of the Church of Jesus Christ of Latter-day Saints (LSD; Mormons), the 16th man to hold that title in the denomination. As leader of the church, Monson is, in principle, responsible for all policies promoted by and practices carried out by the church. In practice, he is generally assisted by other members of the First Presidency, the ruling cadre of the church, consisting of the first president himself and his counselors. During the campaign to pass Proposition 8 (an anti-same-sex marriage initiative) in California in November 2008, Monson distributed a letter to members of the church urging them to "do all you can to support the proposed constitutional amendment by donating of your means and time to assure that marriage in California is legally defined as being between a man and a woman." Ultimately, members of the Mormon church are thought to have made 48 percent ($15,305,050.17) of the donations to the "Yes" on Proposition 8 campaign, although they make up only about 2 percent of the state's population.

Thomas Spencer Monson was born on August 21, 1927, in Salt Lake City. He graduated from West High School in Salt Lake City in 1944 with plans to enroll at the University of Utah. Those plans were delayed, however, as he was called to service in the U.S. Navy for the last few months of World War II. After completing that tour of duty, he finally enrolled at the University of Utah, from which he received his bachelor's degree in business management in 1948. After leaving college, he received his first official appointment in the church, as a ward bishop and a counselor to the church bishopric. He also took a job in the advertising department of the Salt Lake City *Deseret News*, where he remained until his appointment as an apostle of the church in 1963. An apostle is the highest priesthood office in the LSD church with the task of acting as "special witness of the name of Jesus Christ who is sent to teach the principles of salvation to others." Since 1963, Monson has worked his way up through the hierarchy of the church, serving as chair of the Scripture Publication Committee, second counselor to first president Ezra Taft Benson, and first counselor to first president Gordon B. Hinckley. Upon Hinckley's death in February 2008, Monson was elected first president of the denomination, a post he continues to hold.

Marilyn Musgrave (1949–)

Musgrave was formerly a member of the U.S. House of Representatives from the fourth district of Colorado. In 2003, she introduced a bill to add an amendment to the U.S. Constitution defining marriage as a contract between one man and one woman. A similar bill had been introduced a year earlier by Representative Ronnie Shows (D-MS). Musgrave was chief sponsor of the so-called Marriage Amendment again in 2004 and 2005–6.

Musgrave was born Marilyn Neoma Schuler on January 27, 1949, in Greeley, Colorado. She attended Eaton High School, while working as a waitress and house cleaner to earn money during her free time. She matriculated at Colorado State University, from which she earned her bachelor's degree in social studies in 1972. She and her husband then opened a bale-stacking business in Fort Morgan, Colorado, while she also taught school full-time. When the couple began to have children, Musgrave quit working to spend her time as a full-time wife and mother.

Musgrave's first foray into politics came in 1990 when she won a seat on the Fort Morgan board of education. One of her major interests in this position was having the board adopt an abstinence-only program as its sole sex education program. During her tenure on the board, she also served as president of the Fort Morgan Right to Life chapter. In 1992, she successfully ran for a seat in the Colorado House of Representatives, where she served three terms before being elected to the Colorado Senate in 1998. In 2002, Musgrave ran successfully for the U.S. House of Representatives from the 4th district of Colorado. She was re-elected in 2004 and 2006, but was defeated for re-election in 2008. During her three terms in the U.S. House, Musgrave was especially interested in social issues related to same-sex couples, including adoption, marriage, and civil unions.

In March 2009, Musgrave was chosen by the Susan B. Anthony List to head an initiative aimed at defeating sitting members of the U.S. House of Representatives whose voting record on abortion was inconsistent with the expressed views of their constituents. She was quoting as defining her task in the office as "We're going to say very clearly that these votes [on abortion] do have consequences, and we will use every form of medium to defeat these people."

Jerry Nadler (1947–)

Nadler represents the eighth district of New York in the U.S. House of Representatives. He has long been a strong supporter of many liberal causes, one of which is same-sex marriage. In 2009, he was author and primary sponsor of the Uniting American Families Act, designed to alter immigration laws to be more accessible for same-sex couples, and the Respect for Marriage Act, an effort to revoke the Defense of Marriage Act passed in 1996 by the U.S. Congress and signed by President Bill Clinton.

Jerrold Lewis Nadler was born in Brooklyn, New York, on June 13, 1947. He graduated from Stuyvesant High School in 1965 and received his BA from Columbia University in 1969.

In 1978, he received his JD from Fordham Law School. His political career began when he was elected to the New York State Assembly in 1976, after which he was reelected seven more times. In 1992, he was selected to run for the U.S. House of Representatives when the sitting member, Theodore Weiss, died one day before the primary election, which he was expected to win handily. Nadler won the general election (in a district where no member of the Republic Party has been elected for more than a century) and has been reelected ever since. In the 111th Congress (2009–11), Nadler served as chair of the Judiciary Subcommittee on the Constitution, Civil Rights, and Civil Liberties of the U.S. House Committee on the Judiciary. He is a member of the American Jewish Congress, the American Civil Liberties Union, the National Abortion Rights Action League, America's Pro-Israel Lobby, and the National Organization for Women.

Theodore Olson (1940–)

Olson and attorney David Boies represented the plaintiffs in a court case initiated in 2009 to overturn the November 2008 passage of Proposition 8, amending the California state constitution to limit marriage to opposite-sex couples. Olson's role in this case was the subject of considerable speculation and discussion, since he has been a life-long Republican with a strong conservative bent who served as Solicitor General in the administration of President George W. Bush. He and his partner in this case, David Boies, were adversaries in the 2000 U.S. Supreme Court case, *Bush v. Gore*, that decided the presidential election of that year.

Theodore Bevry Olson was born in Chicago on September 11, 1940. His family moved to California, where Olson eventually graduated from Los Altos High School in 1958. He then attended the University of the Pacific, from which he received his bachelor's degree in 1962, and the University of California at Berkeley law school (Boalt Hall), from which he received his law degree in 1965. He then accepted a position as attorney at Gibson, Dunn & Crutcher, a firm with which he is still affiliated. He also served as assistant attorney general in charge of the Office of Legal Counsel in the U.S. Department of Justice from 1981 to 1984. In June 2001, Olson took a leave of absence from Gibson, Dunn & Crutcher to serve as President Bush's Solicitor General.

In July 2004, Olson resigned from that office to return to private practice in the Washington office of Gibson, Dunn & Crutcher.

The decision by Olson and Boies to work together on the same-sex marriage case in California raised a number of eyebrows, since the two men have long been about as far apart on most legal issues as two individuals can be. Olson has been quoted as saying, however, that "on matters of human decency, human rights, individual rights, fairness, due process and equal rights," there are no "liberal" and no "conservative" positions, just a willingness to do what is right.

Olson has been married four times. His third wife, the former Barbara Kay Bracher, a television commentator for Fox News, was killed in the crash of American Airlines Flight 77 on September 11, 2001.

David Paterson (1954–)

Paterson became governor of New York State on March 17, 2008, replacing former governor Eliot Spitzer, who had resigned because of personal ethical issues. Paterson became the first African-American governor of the state, and the second legally blind governor in the United States (after Bob C. Riley, of Arkansas, who served for 11 days in January 1975). Almost from his investiture, Paterson worked aggressively to promote the rights of lesbians and gay men. In April 2008, he introduced legislation in the state legislature that would legalize same-sex marriage in New York. The bill was eventually defeated in December 2008, largely through the efforts of Roman Catholic organizations in the state. In May 2008, Paterson also issued an executive order directing all state agencies to begin recognizing same-sex marriages performed outside the state of New York, effective no later than June 30.

David Alexander Paterson was born in Brooklyn, New York, on May 20, 1954, to Basil and Portia Paterson. At the age of three months, Paterson contracted an ear infection that spread to his optic nerve, leaving him blind in one eye, and with limited sight in the other. He has been legally blind ever since. He attended school in South Hempstead, Long Island, where his family moved to allow him to attend traditional classes, rather than special education classes, to which he would have been assigned in Brooklyn. He was the first special needs student to be mainstreamed in

South Hempstead, where he graduated from Hempstead High School in 1971. Paterson then enrolled at Columbia University, from which he received his BA in history in 1977. He then continued his education at Hofstra University, which awarded him his JD in 1982.

Paterson's first job was with the Queens district attorney's office, where he remained for three years. When state senator Leon Bogues died in August 1985, Paterson ran for and won the empty seat, a seat that his father had once held. At the time, at the age of 31, he was the youngest member of the state senate. He was reelected in 1986 and then eight more times. In 2002, Paterson was chosen minority leader of the senate, the first non-white to hold that position in New York State. Four years later, gubernatorial candidate Eliot Spitzer chose Paterson as his running mate for lieutenant governor, a position he assumed after a successful campaign on January 1, 2007. In late 2009, Paterson announced his intention to run for another term as governor of the state.

Jason West (1977–)

In February 2004, West announced that, as mayor of New Paltz, New York, he would begin conducting marriage ceremonies between same-sex couples. He performed 25 such ceremonies before New York state judge Vincent Bradley issued a temporary restraining order barring the mayor from conducting further marriage ceremonies for a month. That restraining order was later made permanent by Ulster County Supreme Court Judge Michael Kavanagh on June 7, 2004. West was defeated for reelection on May 1, 2007, by a vote of 514 to 379.

Jason West was born on January 1, 1977, in Latham, New York, where he attended Shaker High School. He attended the State University of New York at New Paltz, from which he received a BA in history and a BS in visual arts in 2000. After graduation, West formed his own company, Jason West Housepainting, which remains in existence today. He also became interested in politics and joined the New York State Green Party. He unsuccessfully ran for the state legislature under the banner of that party in 2000 and 2002. In 2003, he ran for mayor of New Paltz, and, to the surprise of many observers, was elected. West became the first member of the Green Party to win elective office in the state.

In general, his tenure of mayor seemed very successful. He was named Best Mayor of 2003 by *Hudson Valley Magazine*, and was honored by a number of political and community organizations, including the New York State Senate Democratic Conference and the California State Legislature. After losing his campaign for reelection, however, he returned to his previous career as a house painter. He has also remained interested and active in a number of environmental and political organizations, however. Since losing his position at New Paltz, he has served on the boards of directors of Certified Naturally Grown, a certification program for organically grown foods; Arm of the Sea Theater, which presents touring productions of socially significant programs; and Young Elected Officials' Network, an association of elected public officials under the age of 35 working to develop socially aware communities. In March 2010, West was guest speaker at a rally in New Paltz commemorating the sixth anniversary of the revoked marriages he conducted as mayor of the town.

6

Documents and Data

The evolution of the debate over same-sex marriage can be traced in a number of important documents related to that issue, documents such as laws, executive orders, reports, and court decisions. This chapter includes excerpts from a number of those documents. Included among these documents are three pieces of legislation and two court cases dealing with same-sex adoption. One of the major concerns among individuals who oppose same-sex marriage (as well as among proponents of same-sex marriage) is the possibility that same-sex couples may earn the right to adopt children, which they regard as inappropriate in and of itself, as well as being an argument against same-sex marriage. These documents provide an insight into the reasoning for and against allowing same-sex couples to adopt children.

The chapter concludes with a collection of statistics and data related to same-sex marriage in the United States and other nations around the world.

Legislation

Federal Defense of Marriage Act (1996)

In September 1996, the U.S. Congress passed and President Bill Clinton signed the federal Defense of Marriage Act, declaring that marriage was defined as a legal relationship between a man and a woman. The act was codified in two parts of the Federal Code, Chapter 1, Section 7, and Chapter 28, Section 1738C. Those sections are reprinted here.

TITLE 1. CHAPTER 1. §7. Definition of "marriage" and "spouse"
In determining the meaning of any Act of Congress, or of any ruling, regulation, or interpretation of the various administrative bureaus and agencies of the United States, the word "marriage" means only a legal union between one man and one woman as husband and wife, and the word "spouse" refers only to a person of the opposite sex who is a husband or a wife.

TITLE 28. PART V. CHAPTER 115. §1738C. Certain acts, records, and proceedings and the effect thereof
No State, territory, or possession of the United States, or Indian tribe, shall be required to give effect to any public act, record, or judicial proceeding of any other State, territory, possession, or tribe respecting a relationship between persons of the same sex that is treated as a marriage under the laws of such other State, territory, possession, or tribe, or a right or claim arising from such relationship.

Source: U.S. Code, Chapters 1 and 28

Alabama Marriage Protection Act (1998/2006)

As of early 2010, 41 states had passed legislation specifically prohibiting same-sex marriage. Thirty states had adopted constitutional provisions for the same purposes. Some states had laws, but not constitutional provisions; other states had constitutional provisions, but not laws; and some states had both laws and constitutional provisions. An example of a state with both kinds of provisions is Alabama, whose legislature passed the Alabama Marriage Protection Act in 1998. That act later became a model for a constitutional amendment, Amendment 774, which was adopted in 2006. The first five sections of both law and amendment are the same, while the constitutional amendment adds two additional sections, as shown in the excerpt below.

Code of Alabama
Section 30-1-19

Marriage, recognition thereof, between persons of the same sex prohibited.

(a) This section shall be known and may be cited as the "Alabama Marriage Protection Act."

(b) Marriage is inherently a unique relationship between a man and a woman. As a matter of public policy, this state has a special interest in encouraging, supporting, and protecting the unique relationship in order to promote, among other goals, the stability and welfare of society and its children. A marriage contracted between individuals of the same sex is invalid in this state.

(c) Marriage is a sacred covenant, solemnized between a man and a woman, which, when the legal capacity and consent of both parties is present, establishes their relationship as husband and wife, and which is recognized by the state as a civil contract.

(d) No marriage license shall be issued in the State of Alabama to parties of the same sex.

(e) The State of Alabama shall not recognize as valid any marriage of parties of the same sex that occurred or was alleged to have occurred as a result of the law of any jurisdiction regardless of whether a marriage license was issued.

[Constitutional additions:]

(f) The State of Alabama shall not recognize as valid any common law marriage of parties of the same sex.

(g) A union replicating marriage of or between persons of the same sex in the State of Alabama or in any other jurisdiction shall be considered and treated in all respects as having no legal force or effect in this state and shall not be recognized by this state as a marriage or other union replicating marriage.

Sources: Code of Alabama, Section 30-1-19, http://www.legislature .state.al.us/CodeofAlabama/1975/coatoc.htm; Constitution of Alabama—1901, Amendment 774, http://www.legislature.state.al.us/CodeofAlabama/Constitution/1901/Constitution1901_toc.htm

Federal Marriage Amendment (2003)

In 2003, Representative Marilyn Musgrave (R-CO) introduced into the U.S. House of Representative a proposed amendment to the U.S. Constitution dealing with the issue of same-sex marriage. The amendment, with a slight modification, has been reintroduced every year since then, except for 2007. (The modification consists of a deletion of the italicized phrase in the document below.) The most favorable action on the amendment thus far occurred in 2006, when the House voted 236 to 187 in favor of the amendment, although a cloture motion to force a vote on the amendment in the Senate failed 49 to 48. (A two-thirds vote is required in both houses for adoption of the amendment.)

Marriage in the United States shall consist only of the union of a man and a woman. Neither this Constitution or the constitution of any State, *nor state or federal law,* shall be construed to require that marital status or the legal incidents thereof be conferred upon unmarried couples or groups.

Source: 108th Congress, 1st Session, H. J. Res. 56, "Proposing an Amendment to the Constitution of the United States Relating to Marriage," http://thomas.loc.gov/cgi-bin/query/z?c108:H.J.RES.56

Oregon Family Fairness Act (2007)

Almost all states in the United States currently have prohibitions against same-sex marriage in their state constitutions or in laws dealing with the issue. However, a number of states have adopted or are considering legislation that provides all the benefits and responsibilities of marriage without calling the relationship by that name. The most common alternative to same-sex marriage thus far has been a domestic partnership. The most recent state to adopt domestic partnership legislation, an extract of which is provided here, is Oregon. In the final versions of the bill, the term "civil union" was replaced by the term "domestic partnership."

House Bill 2007

Summary

[The bill begins with a summary of its main features.]

Establishes requirements and procedures for entering into *[civil union]* domestic partnership contract between individuals of same sex.

Provides that any privilege, immunity, right or benefit granted by law to individual who is or was married is granted to individual who is or was in *[civil union]* domestic partnership. Provides that any responsibility imposed by law on individual who is or was married is imposed on individual who is or was in *[civil union]* domestic partnership.

Provides that any privilege, immunity, right, benefit or responsibility granted or imposed by law to or on spouse with respect to child of either spouse is granted to or imposed on partner with respect to child of either partner.

A Bill for an Act

Relating to same-sex relationships; creating new provisions; and amending ORS 107.615, 192.842, 205.320, 409.300, 432.005, 432.235, 432.405 and 432.408.

Be It Enacted by the People of the State of Oregon:

SECTION 1. Sections 1 to 9 of this 2007 Act may be cited as the Oregon Family Fairness Act.

[Section 2 lists the findings of the state legislature that have led to this bill. Only the first of those findings is listed here.]

SECTION 2. The Legislative Assembly finds that:

(1) Section 20, Article I of the Oregon Constitution, has always enshrined the principle that all citizens of this state are to be provided with equal privileges and immunities under the laws of the State. In addition, as provided in ORS 659A.006, it has long been the public policy of this state that discrimination against any of the citizens of this state is a matter of state concern that threatens not only the rights and privileges of the state's inhabitants but menaces the institutions and foundation of a free democratic state. These fundamental principles are integral to Oregon's constitutional form of government, to its guarantees of political and civil rights and to the continued vitality of political and civil society in this state.

[Section 3 provides definitions for important terms used in the bill.]

[Section 4 lists certain types of domestic partnerships that are prohibited.]

[Section 5 mandates the forms to be used in registering domestic partnerships.]

[Sections 6–8 state the requirements to be followed by individuals registering for a domestic partnership.]

[Section 9 provides a general overview of the rights and responsibilities associated with domestic partnerships, as extracted here.]

SECTION 9. (1) Any privilege, immunity, right or benefit granted by statute, administrative or court rule, policy, common law or any other law to an individual because the individual is or was married, or because the individual is or was an in-law in a specified way to another individual, is granted on equivalent terms, substantive and procedural, to an individual because the individual is or was in a domestic partnership or because the individual is or was, based on a domestic partnership, related in a specified way to another individual. because the individual is or was in a domestic partnership or because the individual is or was, based on a domestic partnership, related in a specified way to another individual.

(2) Any responsibility imposed by statute, administrative or court rule, policy, common law or any other law on an individual because the individual is or was married, or because the individual is or was an in-law in a specified way to another individual, is imposed on equivalent terms, substantive and procedural, on an individual because the individual is or was in a domestic partnership or because the individual is or was, based on a domestic partnership, related in a specified way to another individual.

(3) Any privilege, immunity, right, benefit or responsibility granted or imposed by statute, administrative or court rule, policy, common law or

any other law to or on a spouse with respect to a child of either of the spouses is granted or imposed on equivalent terms, substantive and procedural, to or on a partner with respect to a child of either of the partners.

(4) Any privilege, immunity, right, benefit or responsibility granted or imposed by statute, administrative or court rule, policy, common law or any other law to or on a former or surviving spouse with respect to a child of either of the spouses is granted or imposed on equivalent terms, substantive and procedural, to or on a former or surviving partner with respect to a child of either of the partners.

(5) Many of the laws of this state are intertwined with federal law, and the Legislative Assembly recognizes that it does not have the jurisdiction to control federal laws or the privileges, immunities, rights, benefits and responsibilities related to federal laws.

(6) Sections 1 to 9 of this 2007 Act do not require or permit the extension of any benefit under ORS chapter 238 or 238A, or under any other retirement, deferred compensation or other employee benefit plan, if the plan administrator reasonably concludes that the extension of benefits would conflict with a condition for tax qualification of the plan, or a condition for other favorable tax treatment of the plan, under the Internal Revenue Code or regulations adopted under the Internal Revenue Code.

(7) Sections 1 to 9 of this 2007 Act do not require the extension of any benefit under any employee benefit plan that is subject to federal regulation under the Employee Retirement Income Security Act of 1974.

(8) For purposes of administering Oregon tax laws, partners in a domestic partnership, surviving partners in a domestic partnership and the children of partners in a domestic partnership have the same privileges, immunities, rights, benefits and responsibilities as are granted to or imposed on spouses in a marriage, surviving spouses and their children.

[Remaining sections of the bill deal with "housekeeping" issues and with bringing this act into agreement with other relevant state laws.]

Source: 74th Oregon Legislative Assembly—2007 Regular Session, A-Engrossed, House Bill 2007, Available online at http://www.leg.state .or.us/07reg/measpdf/hb2000.dir/hb2007.a.pdf)

Arkansas Same-Sex Adoption Law (2008)

Five states in the United States have laws that specifically prohibit the adoption of a child by a same-sex couple. The most recent of these laws was adopted in the general election of November 4, 2008, by the voters of Arkansas. The vote was on an initiative brought before the electorate by the Arkansas Family Council. The proposed initiative passed by a vote of 57 percent to 43 percent. The somewhat lengthy title and full text of that initiative are reprinted here.

Popular Name
AN ACT PROVIDING THAT AN INDIVIDUAL WHO IS
COHABITING OUTSIDE OF A VALID MARRIAGE MAY NOT ADOPT
OR BE A FOSTER PARENT OF A CHILD LESS THAN EIGHTEEN
YEARS OLD

Ballot Title
A PROPOSED ACT PROVIDING THAT A MINOR MAY NOT BE
ADOPTED OR PLACED IN A FOSTER HOME IF THE INDIVIDUAL
SEEKING TO ADOPT OR TO SERVE AS A FOSTER PARENT IS
COHABITING WITH A SEXUAL PARTNER OUTSIDE OF A
MARRIAGE WHICH IS VALID UNDER THE CONSTITUTION AND
LAWS OF THIS STATE; STATING THAT THE FOREGOING
PROHIBITION APPLIES EQUALLY TO COHABITING OPPOSITE-SEX
AND SAME-SEX INDIVIDUALS; STATING THAT THE ACT WILL
NOT AFFECT THE GUARDIANSHIP OF MINORS; DEFINING
"MINOR" TO MEAN AN INDIVIDUAL UNDER THE AGE OF
EIGHTEEN (18) YEARS; STATING THAT THE PUBLIC POLICY OF
THE STATE IS TO FAVOR MARRIAGE, AS DEFINED BY THE
CONSTITUTION AND LAWS OF THIS STATE, OVER UNMARRIED
COHABITATION WITH REGARD TO ADOPTION AND FOSTER
CARE; FINDING AND DECLARING ON BEHALF OF THE PEOPLE
OF THE STATE THAT IT IS IN THE BEST INTEREST OF CHILDREN
IN NEED OF ADOPTION OR FOSTER CARE TO BE REARED IN
HOMES IN WHICH ADOPTIVE OR FOSTER PARENTS ARE NOT
COHABITING OUTSIDE OF MARRIAGE; PROVIDING THAT THE
DIRECTOR OF THE DEPARTMENT OF HUMAN SERVICES SHALL
PROMULGATE REGULATIONS CONSISTENT WITH THE ACT; AND
PROVIDING THAT THE ACT APPLIES PROSPECTIVELY
BEGINNING ON JANUARY 1, 2009.

BE IT ENACTED BY THE PEOPLE OF THE STATE OF ARKANSAS:

Section 1: Adoption and foster care of minors.

(a)   A minor may not be adopted or placed in a foster home if the individual seeking to adopt or to serve as a foster parent is cohabiting with a sexual partner outside of a marriage which is valid under the constitution and laws of this state.

(b)   The prohibition of this section applies equally to cohabiting opposite-sex and same-sex individuals.

Section 2: Guardianship of minors.
This act will not affect the guardianship of minors.

Section 3: Definition.
As used in this act, "minor" means an individual under the age of eighteen (18) years.

Section 4: Public policy.
The public policy of the state is to favor marriage, as defined by the constitution and laws of this state, over unmarried cohabitation with regard to adoption and foster care.

Section 5: Finding and declaration.
The people of Arkansas find and declare that it is in the best interest of children in need of adoption or foster care to be reared in homes in which adoptive or foster parents are not cohabiting outside of marriage.

Section 6: Regulations:
The Director of the Department of Human Services, or the successor agency or agencies responsible for adoption and foster care, shall promulgate regulations consistent with this act.

Section 7: Prospective application and effective date.
This act applies prospectively beginning on January 1, 2009.

Source: NOTICE TO THE PUBLIC. http://www.sos.arkansas.gov/elections/elections_pdfs/proposed_amendments/2007-293_Adopt_or_Foster_parent.pdf

Uniting American Families Act (2009)

Under U.S. immigration law, a man or woman may sponsor his or her wife or husband from a country other than the United States to live and work permanently in this country. Same-sex spouses do not have the same privilege. Even couples that have been legally married in the United States or some other country are not eligible to take advantage of the privileges offered by immigration law to heterosexual couples. In 2000, Representative Jerry Nadler (D-NY) introduced legislation to revise immigration law so that it would apply to same-sex couples as well as to opposite-sex couples. Rep. Nadler's bill was never reported out of committee, and he reintroduced the bill in 2001, 2003, 2005, 2007, and 2009. Beginning in 2003, Senator Patrick Leahy (D-VT) has introduced a comparable bill into the U.S. Senate. None of the bills has ever been reported out of committee, let alone been debated on the floor of the House or Senate. The wording of the bill has remained essentially the same upon each reintroduction, as given below. The extract provided here shows

how changes in definition and terminology in the original immigration laws would accomplish the objective of providing equal treatment for same-sex couples.
[Section 2 of the bill provides the fundamental changes required to make the necessary adjustments in existing immigration law:]

SEC. 2. DEFINITIONS OF PERMANENT PARTNER AND PERMANENT PARTNERSHIP.

Section 101(a) (8 U.S.C. 1101(a)) is amended—

(1) in paragraph (15)(K)(ii), by inserting "or permanent partnership" after "marriage"; and
(2) by adding at the end the following:
    "(52) The term 'permanent partner' means an individual 18 years of age or older who—

> "(A) is in a committed, intimate relationship with another individual years of age or older in which both individuals intend a lifelong commitment;
> "(B) is financially interdependent with that other individual;
> "(C) is not married to, or in a permanent partnership with, any individual other than that other individual;
> "(D) is unable to contract with that other individual a marriage cognizable under this Act; and
> "(E) is not a first, second, or third degree blood relation of that other individual.
>
> > "(53) The term 'permanent partnership' means the relationship that exists between 2 permanent partners."

SEC. 3. WORLDWIDE LEVEL OF IMMIGRATION.

Section 201(b)(2)(A)(i) (8 U.S.C. 1151(b)(2)(A)(i)) is amended—

(1) by "spouse" each place it appears and inserting "spouse or permanent partner";
(2) by striking "spouses" and inserting "spouse, permanent partner,";
(3) by inserting "(or, in the case of a permanent partnership, whose permanent partnership was not terminated)" after "was not legally separated from the citizen"; and
(4) by striking "remarries." and inserting "remarries or enters a permanent partnership with an other person."

SEC. 4. NUMERICAL LIMITATIONS ON INDIVIDUAL FOREIGN STATES

(a) PER COUNTRY LEVELS.—Section 202(a)(4) (8 U.S.C. 1152(a)(4)) is amended—

    (1) in the paragraph heading, by inserting ", PERMANENT PARTNERS," after "SPOUSES";

    (2) in the heading of subparagraph (A), by inserting ", PERMANENT PARTNERS," after "SPOUSES"; and

    (3) in the heading of subparagraph (C), by striking "AND DAUGHTERS" inserting "WITHOUT PERMANENT PARTNERS AND UNMARRIED DAUGHTERS WITHOUT PERMANENT PARTNERS"

(b) RULES FOR CHARGEABILITY.—Section 202(b)(2) (8 U.S.C. 1152(b)(2)) is amended—

    (1) by striking "his spouse" and inserting "his or her spouse or permanent partner";

    (2) by striking "such spouse" each place it appears and inserting "such spouse or permanent partner"; and

    (3) by inserting "or permanent partners" after "husband and wife"

[The following sections make changes in the allocation of immigrant visas, procedures for granting immigrant status, admission of immigrants for emergency purposes, inadmissible aliens, conditional permanent resident status, and related issues.]

Source: H. R. 1024, Uniting American Families Act of 2009, http://thomas.loc.gov/cgi-bin/query/F?c111:1:./temp/~c111imxoE0:e5119

An Act to End Discrimination in Civil Marriage and Affirm Religious Freedom (2009)

As of early 2010, same-sex marriage was legal in five states: Connecticut, Iowa, Massachusetts, New Hampshire, and Vermont. In each of these states, approval of same-sex marriage was achieved by an act of the legislature or by court decree. In no state was same-sex marriage approved by a vote of the general electorate. The closest that event came to occurring was in Maine, where the state legislature passed a bill on May 6, 2009, legalizing same-sex marriage in the state. That action was overturned, however, by a vote of the general electorate on November 3, 2009. The act's name indicates efforts by the legislature to placate

*religious leaders who were concerned that they would be required to per-
form or otherwise support same-sex marriages. An extract of the original
act follows.*

Be it enacted by the People of the State of Maine as follows:

Sec. 1. 19-A MRSA §650, as enacted by PL 1997, c. 65, §2, is repealed.

Sec. 2. 19-A MRSA §650-A is enacted to read:

§ 650-A. Codification of marriage

Marriage is the legally recognized union of 2 people. Gender-specific
terms relating to the marital relationship or familial relationships,
including, but not limited to, "spouse," "family," "marriage,"
"immediate family," "dependent," "next of kin," "bride," "groom,"
"husband," "wife," "widow" and "widower," must be construed to be
gender-neutral for all purposes throughout the law, whether in the
context of statute, administrative or court rule, policy, common law or
any other source of civil law.

Sec. 3. 19-A MRSA §650-B is enacted to read:

§ 650-B. Recognition of marriage licensed and certified in another
jurisdiction

A marriage of a same-sex couple that is validly licensed and certified in
another jurisdiction is recognized for all purposes under the laws of this
State.

[Section 4 outlines the process by which applications for marriage must be filed.]

Sec. 5. 19-A MRSA §655, sub-§3 is enacted to read:

3. Affirmation of religious freedom. This Part does not authorize any
court or other state or local governmental body, entity, agency or
commission to compel, prevent or interfere in any way with any
religious institution's religious doctrine, policy, teaching or
solemnization of marriage within that particular religious faith's
tradition as guaranteed by the Maine Constitution, Article 1, Section 3
or the First Amendment of the United States Constitution. A person
authorized to join persons in marriage and who fails or refuses to join
persons in marriage is not subject to any fine or other penalty for such
failure or refusal.

*[Section 6 modifies the section of the state's original marriage law dealing with
"prohibitions" to marriage in the state, one of which involves individuals of the
same gender.]*

Source: SP0384, LD 1020, item 1, 124th Maine State Legislature, An
Act to End Discrimination in Civil Marriage and Affirm Religious
Freedom, http://www.mainelegislature.org/legis/bills/bills_124th/
billpdfs/SP038401.pdf

Reports

United States General Accounting Office (2003)

*In January 1997, the U.S. General Accounting Office (GAO) responded
to an inquiry from Representative Henry Hyde (R-IL) about federal benefits available to married couples under U.S. law. The GAO found
"1,049 federal statutory provisions classified to the United States Code
in which benefits, rights, and privileges are contingent on marital status
or in which marital status is a factor." Seven years later, the GAO
received a similar request from Senator Bill Frist (R-TN), then majority
leader of the U.S. Senate. The GAO responded with the following
summary of its findings, to which it appended a table listing the actual
benefits provided to opposite-sex married couples by U.S. law.*

Dear Senator Frist:

The Defense of Marriage Act (DOMA) provides definitions of
"marriage" and "spouse" that are to be used in construing the meaning
of a federal law and, thus, affect the interpretation of a wide variety of
federal laws in which marital status is a factor. (footnote 1) In 1997, we
issued a report identifying 1,049 federal statutory provisions classified
to the United States Code in which benefits, rights, and privileges are
contingent on marital status or in which marital status is a factor.
(footnote 2) In preparing the 1997 report, we limited our search to laws
enacted prior to September 21, 1996, the date DOMA was signed into
law. Recently, you asked us to update our 1997 compilation.

We have identified 120 statutory provisions involving marital status
that were enacted between September 21, 1996, and December 31, 2003.
During the same period, 31 statutory provisions involving marital
status were repealed or amended in such a way as to eliminate marital
status as a factor. Consequently, as of December 31, 2003, our research
identified a total of 1,138 federal statutory provisions classified to the
United States Code in which marital status is a factor in determining or
receiving benefits, rights, and privileges.

To prepare the updated list, we used the same research methods and
legal databases that we employed in 1997. Accordingly, the same
caveats concerning the completeness of our collection of laws apply to
this updated compilation, as explained more fully in our prior report.
For example, because of the inherent limitations of any global electronic
search and the many ways in which the laws of the United States Code
may deal with marital status, we cannot guarantee that we have

captured every individual law in the United States Code in which marital status figures. However, we believe that the probability is high that the updated list identifies federal programs in the United States Code in which marital status is a factor.

We have organized our research using the same 13 subject categories as the 1997 report. As agreed with your staff, in addition to providing you with a primary table of new statutory provisions involving marital status, we have prepared a second table identifying those provisions in our prior report that subsequently have been repealed or amended in a manner that eliminates marital status as a factor. Finally, in a third table, we have listed those provisions identified in our 1997 report that have since been relocated to a different section of the United States Code. We have also attached a brief summary of the 13 research categories; a full description of each category is set forth in the 1997 report.

We plan no further distribution of this report until 30 days after the date of this letter. At that time, we will send copies of this letter to interested congressional committees. The letter will also be available on GAO's home page at http://www.gao.gov.

[Footnote 1: The Defense of Marriage Act defines "marriage" as "a legal union between one man and one woman as husband and wife"; it defines "spouse" as referring "only to a person of the opposite sex who is a husband or a wife." The Act requires that these definitions apply "[i]n determining the meaning of any Act of Congress, or of any ruling, regulation, or interpretation of the various administrative bureaus and agencies of the United States." 1 U.S.C. § 7.

Footnote 2: U.S. General Accounting Office, Defense of Marriage Act, GAO/OGC-97-16 (Washington, D.C.: January 31, 1997).]

Source: United States General Accounting Office, http://www.gao.gov/new.items/d04353r.pdf, January 23, 2004)

Adoption by Same-Sex Couples (2009)

The United States and the individual states thereof are by no means the only nation in the world where same-sex adoption is an issue of debate. Not surprisingly, however, the issues involved in this debate tend to be similar no matter where it takes place. In July 2009, the Standing Committee on Law and Justice of the New South Wales (Australia) Legislative Council issued a report on its extended study of same-sex adoption. The committee recommended that the state's Adoption Act 2000 be amended to permit same-sex adoption, while adding language that would not require faith-based agencies to participate in such adoptions. Some key points from that report follow.

[From the Chair's Forward:]

The Committee has determined that the Adoption Act 2000 should be amended to allow same-sex couples to adopt, but that an exemption from the application of the Anti-Discrimination Act 1977 be created for faith-based adoption agencies. The Committee has concluded that reform to allow same-sex couples to adopt in NSW will protect children's rights and help to ensure children's best interests. It will do so by providing the security of legal recognition for existing parent-child relationships, by broadening the pool of potential applicants from which the most appropriate parents for any individual child are selected, and by enabling children currently fostered by same-sex couples to have that relationship permanently secured where appropriate. Such reform will also address discrimination against same-sex couples and their children, and address anomalous inconsistencies in their present treatment under the law.

[The report itself consists of six chapters: "Introduction," "Background," "Best Interests of the Child," "Research on Family Form and Family Functioning," "Human Rights and Legal Issues," and "Exemptions." The core of the committee's reasoning about its final decision occurs in Chapter 3, a section of which is quoted here. Footnotes are omitted from the selection.]

3.118 Some members of the Committee share the views expressed by many during the inquiry that the best interests of children are met in the context of a family comprised of a mother and a father in a permanent, preferably married relationship, where children can experience on a daily basis the fundamental complementarity of motherhood and fatherhood. These members consider that mothers and fathers bring unique qualities to their parenting roles, both of which are essential to optimal child development. These members agree with numerous participants that the state has a duty of care to ensure that children are adopted into families that will provide "optimal care", believing strongly that same-sex parenting denies children such care, to their detriment in the short and longer term. Correspondingly, these members consider that the Government has a responsibility to adoptive children and to broader society to maintain the status quo and prevent adoption by same-sex couples.

3.119 The majority of Committee members, however, consider that the gender of parents is not a significant determinant of children's wellbeing, and that as such, the sexual orientation of prospective parents is of no material relevance to the best interests of adoptive children. Nor do the majority consider that the sexuality of gay and lesbian people precludes them from being fit and proper parents, or that children in same-sex families necessarily have insufficient access to both male and female role models. The majority of Committee members are persuaded by the argument that an adoptive child's best interests are determined in the context of an assessment of the individual child's needs and the individual parents' capacity to meet those needs. Same-sex parents should be able to be assessed on exactly the same basis as other prospective parents.

3.120 The majority note that if legally eligible to adopt, gay and lesbian people will, like all prospective parents, be subject to a rigorous assessment process by accredited adoption agencies to determine their suitability to adopt; they will also be subject to the preferences of relinquishing parents; and they must ultimately satisfy a court that they can fulfil the best interests of the child concerned. The majority of Committee members are confident in the rigour of the adoption system to continue to ensure that only those who would make fit and proper parents go on to adopt.

3.121 In addition, the majority of Committee members are persuaded by a number of other arguments examined in this chapter that adoption by same-sex couples is in the best interests of the child. It is highly desirable to broaden the pool of adoptive parents in order to increase the likelihood of the best match between individual child and prospective parent. Also, the permanency that is so desirable for many children in out-of-home care would be facilitated by enabling same-sex couples to adopt their foster children.

3.122 The majority of Committee members are also mindful that the views of children and young people either expressed directly to the Committee, or reported to us, suggest that most are supportive of adoption by same-sex couples. Other Committee members believe that the evidence from children to the inquiry was limited and should not be used to assert a generalised position by children in NSW towards adoption by same-sex couples.

3.123 The Committee members who form the majority are conscious that the views presented in this chapter were quite clearly delineated along religious versus secular lines. They uphold the right of church-based organisations to voice their beliefs with a view to influencing policy, and acknowledge the validity of those views. At the same time, it is their view that the more secular views presented in this chapter, which accept parenting by gay and lesbian people as valid and support adoption by same-sex couples as being in the interests of children, are more aligned with prevailing standards and community aspirations about parenting, the welfare of children and the inclusiveness of society. Other Committee members reject the argument that the debate about adoption by same-sex couples is a religious versus secular contest. Many of the participants in the inquiry who expressed belief-based views also articulated reason-based arguments as to why they opposed adoption by same-sex couples. For many of these participants the key issue is the importance of a child having the opportunity to be raised by a mother and a father in a permanent, preferably married relationship, a view to which a number of people subscribe, not just theists or those of religious persuasion.

3.124 Finally, the majority of Committee members also observe that the focus of many participants' evidence, as captured in this chapter, was on the adoption of unknown young infants. It is clear that a larger number of other children stand to benefit from adoption: first, (generally older) children who as a result of abuse and/or neglect are in foster care; and second, children who are already parented by gay and lesbian people but whose parental relationship with their non-biological parent is not legally recognised. This divergence in the evidence becomes more apparent in subsequent chapters. For now, the majority of the Committee suggest that there may be a certain protectiveness felt towards young infants relinquished for adoption that obscures the broader picture of adoption generally and adoption by same-sex couples in particular.

3.125 The majority of Committee members conclude that the best interests of the child in the adoption context will be served by decisions based on the individual needs of the child and the particular capacities of the parents, without regard to the sexual orientation of the parents.

Source: Standing Committee on Law and Justice, "Adoption by Same-sex Couples," http://www.parliament.nsw.gov.au/Prod/parlment/committee.nsf/0/c81be8593a9fec64ca2575ed000e043f/$FILE/090703%20Final%20Compiled%20-%20Adoption%20report.pdf

European Parliament Resolution of 14 January 2009 on the Situation of Fundamental Rights in the European Union 2004–8 (2009)

Same-sex marriage has been a topic of discussion for some time within the European Union and the European Parliament. The most recent action by the parliament was a resolution adopted on January 14, 2009, covering a number of human and civil rights issues, among them the treatment of same-sex couples. The relevant sections of that resolution are reprinted here.

Sexual orientation

71. Takes the view that discriminatory comments against homosexuals by religious, social and political leaders fuel hatred and violence, and calls on the relevant governing bodies to condemn them;

72. In this regard, wholeheartedly endorses the French initiative, which is supported by all the Member States, for the universal decriminalisation of homosexuality, as in 91 countries homosexuality is still a criminal offence, and in some cases even a capital offence;

73. Welcomes the publication of the first thematic report by the Agency, drawn up at Parliament's request, on "homophobia and discrimination on grounds of sexual orientation in the EU [European Union] Member States" and asks the Member States and EU institutions to urgently follow the Agency's recommendations or state their reasons for not doing so;

74. Reminds all Member States that, in line with ECtHR [European Court of Human Rights] case-law, freedom of assembly may be exercised even if the opinions of those exercising that right go against the majority, and that, accordingly, a discriminatory ban on marches and any failure to meet the requirement to give appropriate protection to those taking part breach the principles guaranteed by the ECtHR, by Article 6 of the EU Treaty on common EU values and principles, and by the Charter;

75. Calls on those Member States who have adopted legislation on same-sex partnerships to recognise provisions with similar effects adopted by other Member States; calls on those Member States to propose guidelines for mutual recognition of existing legislation between Member States in order to guarantee that the right of free movement within the European Union for same-sex couples applies under conditions equal to those applicable to heterosexual couples;

76. Urges the Commission to submit proposals ensuring that Member States apply the principle of mutual recognition for homosexual couples, whether they are married or living in a registered civil partnership, in particular when they are exercising their right to free movement under EU law;

77. Calls on those Member States who have not yet done so, and in application of the principle of equality, to take legislative action to overcome the discrimination experienced by some couples on the grounds of their sexual orientation;

78. Calls on the Commission to make sure that Member States grant asylum to persons fleeing from persecution on the grounds of their sexual orientation in their country of origin, to take initiatives at the bilateral and multilateral level to stop the persecutions of persons on the basis of their sexual orientation, and to launch a study on the situation of trans-sexual people in the Member States and candidate countries, with regard inter alia to the risk of harassment and violence.

Source: European Parliament Resolution of 14 January 2009 on the Situation of Fundamental Rights in the European Union 2004–2008 [2007/2145(INI)], http://www.europarl.europa.eu/sides/getDoc.do ?type=TA&reference=P6-TA-2009-0019&language=EN

Court Cases

E. B. v. France, Application No. 43546/02 (2008)

The legal status of same-sex adoptions in the United States is still a matter of considerable disagreement and dispute. From at least a theoretical standpoint, such is no longer the case in Europe. In January 2008, the Grand Chamber of the European Court of Human Rights ruled that a series of decisions by local governmental units in France on this topic had violated Articles 8 and 14 of the European Convention on Human Rights (ECHR). The case was brought by a 45-year-old primary school teacher, designated as "E. B." in the case, who was in a long-term relationship with another woman and was seeking to adopt a young child. Her application to adopt was denied at both local and regional levels by relevant authorities. Denial was allegedly based on two objections, the lack of a paternal figure in the household and the ambiguity of E. B.'s partner with regard to the adoption.

The Grand Chamber found, by a vote of 11 to 6, in favor of the applicant, E. G. The decision was based on the court's conclusion that the state objections by local and regional French authorities were not, in fact, the real reason for denying E. B.'s application. Instead, it found that her homosexuality was the primary, and probably sole, reason for the denial. And, since discrimination on the basis of sexual orientation is prohibited by the ECHR, the governmental units were deemed to have violated the articles named in the complaint. Key parts of the court's decision are as follows. Omitted citations are designated by ellipses (. . .).

82. With regard to the judicial phase, the Nancy Administrative Court of Appeal noted that the decision was based on two grounds: the lack of a paternal referent and the ambivalence of the commitment of each member of the household. It added that the documents in the file and the conclusions reached after examining the application showed that the applicant's lifestyle did not provide the requisite safeguards for adopting a child, but disputed that the president of the council for the département had refused authorisation on the basis of a position of principle regarding her choice of lifestyle, namely, her homosexuality. . . .

83. Subsequently, the Conseil d'Etat held that the two grounds on which the applicant had been refused authorisation to adopt were in keeping with the statutory provisions. It also held that the reference to the applicant's "lifestyle" could be explained by the documents in the file submitted to the tribunals of fact, which showed that the applicant was,

at the time of her application, in a stable homosexual relationship, but that this could not be construed as a decision based on a position of principle regarding her sexual orientation or as any form of discrimination. . . .

84. The Court therefore notes that the administrative courts went to some lengths to rule that although regard had been had to the applicant's sexual orientation, it had not been the basis for the decision in question and had not been considered from a hostile position of principle.

85. However, in the Court's opinion the fact that the applicant's homosexuality featured to such an extent in the reasoning of the domestic authorities is significant. Besides their considerations regarding the applicant's "lifestyle", they above all confirmed the decision of the president of the council for the département. The Court points out that the latter reached his decision in the light of the opinion given by the adoption board whose various members had expressed themselves individually in writing, mainly recommending, with reasons in support of that recommendation, that the application be refused on the basis of the two grounds in question. It observes that the manner in which certain opinions were expressed was indeed revealing in that the applicant's homosexuality was a determining factor. In particular, the Court notes that in his opinion of 12 October 1998 the psychologist from the children's welfare service recommended that authorisation be refused, referring to, among other things, an "unusual attitude [on the part of the applicant] to men in that men are rejected." . . .

. . .

88. Thus, notwithstanding the precautions taken by the Nancy Administrative Court of Appeal, and subsequently by the Conseil d'Etat, to justify taking account of the applicant's "lifestyle", the inescapable conclusion is that her sexual orientation was consistently at the centre of deliberations in her regard and omnipresent at every stage of the administrative and judicial proceedings.

. . .

90. The applicant therefore suffered a difference in treatment. Regard must be had to the aim behind that difference in treatment and, if the aim was legitimate, to whether the different treatment was justified.

91. The Court reiterates that, for the purposes of Article 14, a difference in treatment is discriminatory if it has no objective and reasonable justification, which means that it does not pursue a "legitimate aim" or that there is no "reasonable proportionality between the means employed and the aim sought to be realized." . . . Where sexual orientation is in issue, there is a need for particularly convincing and weighty reasons to justify a difference in treatment regarding rights falling within Article 8. . . .

92. In that connection the Court observes that the Convention is a living instrument, to be interpreted in the light of present-day conditions. . . .

93. In the Court's opinion, if the reasons advanced for such a difference in treatment were based solely on considerations regarding the applicant's sexual orientation this would amount to discrimination under the Convention. . . .

94. The Court points out that French law allows single persons to adopt a child. . . . thereby opening up the possibility of adoption by a single homosexual, which is not disputed. Against the background of the domestic legal provisions, it considers that the reasons put forward by the Government cannot be regarded as particularly convincing and weighty such as to justify refusing to grant the applicant authorisation.

95. The Court notes, lastly, that the relevant provisions of the Civil Code are silent as to the necessity of a referent of the other sex, which would not, in any event, be dependent on the sexual orientation of the adoptive single parent. In this case, moreover, the applicant presented, in the terms of the judgment of the Conseil d'Etat, "undoubted personal qualities and an aptitude for bringing up children", which were assuredly in the child's best interests, a key notion in the relevant international instruments. . . .

96. Having regard to the foregoing, the Court cannot but observe that, in rejecting the applicant's application for authorisation to adopt, the domestic authorities made a distinction based on considerations regarding her sexual orientation, a distinction which is not acceptable under the Convention. . . .

. . .

98. There has accordingly been a breach of Article 14 of the Convention taken in conjunction with Article 8.

Source: Case of E. B. v. France (Application no. 43546/02), http://cmiskp .echr.coe.int/tkp197/view.asp?item=2&portal=hbkm&action=html &highlight=She%20%7C%20has%20%7C%20been%20%7C%20a%20 %7C%20nursery%20%7C%20school%20%7C%20teacher&sessionid =38351901&skin=hudoc-en

Goodridge v. Department of Public Health, 440 Mass. 309 (2003)

Probably the most significant judicial decision dealing with same-sex marriage in the United States is an opinion issued by the Massachusetts Supreme Judicial Court on November 18, 2003. In that decision, the court ruled that the prohibition of same-sex marriage in Massachusetts

*was illegal under the state's constitution. It gave the state legislature
180 days to rectify its current ban on same-sex marriage. Some important sections of the majority opinion and of three individual dissents
are reprinted here. Omitted citations are designated by ellipses (. . .).*

[From the majority opinion:]

Marriage is a vital social institution. The exclusive commitment of two
individuals to each other nurtures love and mutual support; it brings
stability to our society. For those who choose to marry, and for their
children, marriage provides an abundance of legal, financial, and social
benefits. In return it imposes weighty legal, financial, and social
obligations. The question before us is whether, consistent with the
Massachusetts Constitution, the Commonwealth may deny the
protections, benefits, and obligations conferred by civil marriage to two
individuals of the same sex who wish to marry. We conclude that it may
not. The Massachusetts Constitution affirms the dignity and equality of
all individuals. It forbids the creation of second class citizens. In
reaching our conclusion we have given full deference to the arguments
made by the Commonwealth. But it has failed to identify any
constitutionally adequate reason for denying civil marriage to same-sex
couples.

We are mindful that our decision marks a change in the history of our
marriage law. Many people hold deep-seated religious, moral, and
ethical convictions that marriage should be limited to the union of one
man and one woman, and that homosexual conduct is immoral. Many
hold equally strong religious, moral, and ethical convictions that same-
sex couples are entitled to be married, and that homosexual persons
should be treated no differently than their heterosexual neighbors.
Neither view answers the question before us. Our concern is with the
Massachusetts Constitution as a charter of governance for every person
properly within its reach. "Our obligation is to define the liberty of all,
not to mandate our own moral code." . . .

Whether the Commonwealth may use its formidable regulatory
authority to bar same-sex couples from civil marriage is a question not
previously addressed by a Massachusetts appellate court. . . . It is a
question the United States Supreme Court left open as a matter of
Federal law in Lawrence, supra at 2484, where it was not an issue.
There, the Court affirmed that the core concept of common human
dignity protected by the Fourteenth Amendment to the United States
Constitution precludes government intrusion into the deeply personal
realms of consensual adult expressions of intimacy and one's choice of
an intimate partner. The Court also reaffirmed the central role that
decisions whether to marry or have children bear in shaping one's

identity. . . . The Massachusetts Constitution is, if anything, more protective of individual liberty and equality than the Federal Constitution; it may demand broader protection for fundamental rights; and it is less tolerant of government intrusion into the protected spheres of private life.

Barred access to the protections, benefits, and obligations of civil marriage, a person who enters into an intimate, exclusive union with another of the same sex is arbitrarily deprived of membership in one of our community's most rewarding and cherished institutions. That exclusion is incompatible with the constitutional principles of respect for individual autonomy and equality under law.

[From dissent by Justice Cordy:]

The court's opinion concludes that the Department of Public Health has failed to identify any "constitutionally adequate reason" for limiting civil marriage to opposite-sex unions, and that there is no "reasonable relationship" between a disqualification of same-sex couples who wish to enter into a civil marriage and the protection of public health, safety, or general welfare. Consequently, it holds that the marriage statute cannot withstand scrutiny under the Massachusetts Constitution. Because I find these conclusions to be unsupportable in light of the nature of the rights and regulations at issue, the presumption of constitutional validity and significant deference afforded to legislative enactments, and the "undesirability of the judiciary substituting its notions of correct policy for that of a popularly elected Legislature" responsible for making such policy, . . . , I respectfully dissent. Although it may be desirable for many reasons to extend to same-sex couples the benefits and burdens of civil marriage (and the plaintiffs have made a powerfully reasoned case for that extension), that decision must be made by the Legislature, not the court.

. . .

[After a review of the evidence presented to the court during this case, Cordy continues:]

Taking all of this available information into account, the Legislature could rationally conclude that a family environment with married opposite-sex parents remains the optimal social structure in which to bear children, and that the raising of children by same-sex couples, who by definition cannot be the two sole biological parents of a child and cannot provide children with a parental authority figure of each gender, . . . presents an alternative structure for child rearing that has not yet proved itself beyond reasonable scientific dispute to be as optimal as the biologically based marriage norm. . . . Working from the assumption that a recognition of same-sex marriages will increase the number of children experiencing this alternative, the Legislature could conceivably conclude that declining to recognize same-sex marriages remains prudent until empirical questions about its impact on the upbringing of children are resolved. . . .

[From dissent by Justice Spina:]

What is at stake in this case is not the unequal treatment of individuals or whether individual rights have been impermissibly burdened, but the power of the Legislature to effectuate social change without interference from the courts, pursuant to art. 30 of the Massachusetts Declaration of Rights. . . . The power to regulate marriage lies with the Legislature, not with the judiciary. . . . Today, the court has transformed its role as protector of individual rights into the role of creator of rights, and I respectfully dissent.

[From dissent by Justice Sosman:]

In applying the rational basis test to any challenged statutory scheme, the issue is not whether the Legislature's rationale behind that scheme is persuasive to us, but only whether it satisfies a minimal threshold of rationality. Today, rather than apply that test, the court announces that, because it is persuaded that there are no differences between same-sex and opposite-sex couples, the Legislature has no rational basis for treating them differently with respect to the granting of marriage licenses. . . . Reduced to its essence, the court's opinion concludes that, because same-sex couples are now raising children, and withholding the benefits of civil marriage from their union makes it harder for them to raise those children, the State must therefore provide the benefits of civil marriage to same-sex couples just as it does to opposite-sex couples. Of course, many people are raising children outside the confines of traditional marriage, and, by definition, those children are being deprived of the various benefits that would flow if they were being raised in a household with married parents. That does not mean that the Legislature must accord the full benefits of marital status on every household raising children. Rather, the Legislature need only have some rational basis for concluding that, at present, those alternate family structures have not yet been conclusively shown to be the equivalent of the marital family structure that has established itself as a successful one over a period of centuries. People are of course at liberty to raise their children in various family structures, as long as they are not literally harming their children by doing so. . . . That does not mean that the State is required to provide identical forms of encouragement, endorsement, and support to all of the infinite variety of household structures that a free society permits.

. . .

More importantly, it is not our confidence in the lack of adverse consequences that is at issue, or even whether that confidence is justifiable. The issue is whether it is rational to reserve judgment on whether this change can be made at this time without damaging the institution of marriage or adversely affecting the critical role it has played in our society. Absent consensus on the issue (which obviously does not exist), or unanimity amongst scientists studying the issue (which also does not exist), or a more prolonged period of observation of this new family structure (which has not yet been possible), it is rational for the Legislature to postpone any redefinition of marriage that would include same-sex couples until such time as it is certain that that redefinition will not have unintended and undesirable social consequences. Through the political process, the people may decide when the benefits of extending civil marriage to same-sex couples have been shown to outweigh whatever risks—be they palpable or ephemeral—are involved. However minimal the risks of that redefinition of marriage may seem to us from our vantage point, it is not up to us to decide what risks society must run, and it is inappropriate for us to arrogate that power to ourselves merely because we are confident that "it is the right thing to do."

Source: Hillary Goodridge & Others vs. Department of Public Health & Another, 440 Mass. 309, http://masscases.com/cases/sjc/440/440mass 309.html, 312–13, 357–58, 362, 363–64, 388, 350

Lewis v. Harris, 908 A.2d 196 (2006)

As of early 2010, a number of state and federal courts have handed down opinions about the legality of same-sex marriage, with decisions ranging rather widely across the spectrum. In 2006, the New Jersey Supreme Court issued a decision in a case in which seven same-sex couples had sued the state to have it issue them marriage licenses. The court decided unanimously that withholding marriage licenses from same-sex couples violated the state constitution, and the state legislature was required to change state law or to provide some legal entity equivalent to marriage within 180 days of the court's ruling. Perhaps the most interesting feature of the ruling was that three of the seven justices dissented from the majority view, not, as one might expect, because they disagreed with the decision, but because they thought it did not go far enough. That is, they saw no reason, having given its reasoning in the case, the court did not simply require that the state begin to issue marriage licenses to same-sex couples. (In response to the court decision, the state legislature created civil unions as equivalent to marriage in the state.)

[From the court's syllabus for the case:]

HELD: Denying committed same-sex couples the financial and social benefits and privileges given to their married heterosexual counterparts bears no substantial relationship to a legitimate governmental purpose. The Court holds that under the equal protection guarantee of Article I, Paragraph 1 of the New Jersey Constitution, committed same-sex couples must be afforded on equal terms the same rights and benefits enjoyed by opposite-sex couples under the civil marriage statutes. The name to be given to the statutory scheme that provides full rights and benefits to same-sex couples, whether marriage or some other term, is a matter left to the democratic process.

[The court then outlines the reasons for its decision. Page references are to the actual decision.]

1. As this case presents no factual dispute, the Court addresses solely questions of law. The Court perceives plaintiffs' equal protection claim to have two components: whether committed same-sex couples have a constitutional right to the benefits and privileges afforded to married heterosexual couples, and, if so, whether they have a constitutional right to have their relationship recognized by the name of marriage. (pp. 19–21)

2. In attempting to discern the substantive rights that are "fundamental" under Article I, Paragraph 1, of the State Constitution, the Court has followed the general standard adopted by the United States Supreme Court in construing the Due Process Clause of the Fourteenth Amendment. First, the asserted fundamental liberty interest must be clearly identified. In this case, the identified right is the right of same-sex couples to marry. Second, the liberty interest in same-sex marriage must be objectively and deeply rooted in the traditions, history, and conscience of the people of this State. (pp. 21–25)

3. New Jersey's marriage laws, which were first enacted in 1912, limit marriage to heterosexual couples. The recently enacted Domestic Partnership Act explicitly acknowledges that same-sex couples cannot marry. Although today there is a national debate over whether same-sex marriages should be authorized by the states, the framers of the 1947 New Jersey Constitution could not have imagined that the liberty right protected by Article I, Paragraph 1 embraced same-sex marriage. (pp. 25–28)

4. Times and attitudes have changed. There has been a developing understanding that discrimination against gays and lesbians is no longer acceptable in this State. On the federal level, the United States Supreme Court has struck down laws that have unconstitutionally targeted gays and lesbians for disparate treatment.

Although plaintiffs rely on the federal cases to support the argument that they have a fundamental right to marry under our State Constitution, those cases fall far short of establishing a fundamental right to same-sex marriage "deeply rooted in the traditions, history, and conscience of the people of this State." Despite the rich diversity of this State, the tolerance and goodness of its people, and the many recent advances made by gays and lesbians toward achieving social acceptance and equality under the law, the Court cannot find that the right to same-sex marriage is a fundamental right under our constitution. (pp. 28–33)

5. The Court has construed the expansive language of Article I, Paragraph 1 to embrace the fundamental guarantee of equal protection, thereby requiring the Court to determine whether the State's marriage laws permissibly distinguish between same-sex and heterosexual couples. The test the Court has applied to equal protection claims is a flexible one that includes three factors: the nature of the right at stake, the extent to which the challenged statutory scheme restricts that right, and the public need for the statutory restriction. (pp. 34–36)

6. In conducting its equal protection analysis, the Court discerns two distinct issues. The first is whether same-sex couples have the right to the statutory benefits and privileges conferred on heterosexual married couples. Assuming that right, the next issue is whether committed same-sex partners have a constitutional right to define their relationship by the name of marriage. (p. 37)

7. New Jersey's courts and its Legislature have been at the forefront of combating sexual orientation discrimination and advancing equality of treatment toward gays and lesbians. In 1992, through an amendment to the Law Against Discrimination (LAD), New Jersey became the fifth state to prohibit discrimination on the basis of "affectional or sexual orientation." In making sexual orientation a protected category, the Legislature committed New Jersey to the goal of eradicating discrimination against gays and lesbians. In 2004, the Legislature added "domestic partnership status" to the categories protected by the LAD. (pp. 37–40)

8. Discrimination on the basis of sexual orientation is also outlawed in our criminal law and public contracts law. The Legislature, moreover, created the New Jersey Human Relations Council to promote educational programs aimed at reducing bias and bias-related acts, identifying sexual orientation as a protected category. In 2004, the Legislature passed the Domestic Partnership Act, which confers certain benefits and rights on same-sex partners who enter into a partnership under the Act. (pp. 40–42)

9. The Domestic Partnership Act has failed to bridge the inequality gap between committed same-sex couples and married

opposite-sex couples. Significantly, the economic and financial inequities that are borne by same-sex domestic partners are also borne by their children. Further, even though same-sex couples are provided fewer benefits and rights by the Act, they are subject to more stringent requirements to enter into a domestic partnership than opposite-sex couples entering a marriage. (pp. 43–48)

10. At this point, the Court does not consider whether committed same-sex couples should be allowed to marry, but only whether those couples are entitled to the same rights and benefits afforded to married heterosexual couples. Cast in that light, the issue is not about the transformation of the traditional definition of marriage, but about the unequal dispensation of benefits and privileges to one of two similarly situated classes of people. (p. 48)

11. The State does not argue that limiting marriage to the union of a man and a woman is needed to encourage procreation or to create the optimal living environment for children. Other than sustaining the traditional definition of marriage, which is not implicated in this discussion, the State has not articulated any legitimate public need for depriving committed same-sex couples of the host of benefits and privileges that are afforded to married heterosexual couples. There is, on the one hand, no rational basis for giving gays and lesbians full civil rights as individuals while, on the other hand, giving them an incomplete set of rights when they enter into committed same-sex relationships. To the extent that families are strengthened by encouraging monogamous relationships, whether heterosexual or homosexual, the Court cannot discern a public need that would justify the legal disabilities that now afflict same-sex domestic partnerships. (pp. 48–51)

12. In arguing to uphold the system of disparate treatment that disfavors same-sex couples, the State offers as a justification the interest in uniformity with other states' laws. Our current laws concerning same-sex couples are more in line with those of Vermont, Massachusetts, and Connecticut than the majority of other states. Equality of treatment is a dominant theme of our laws and a central guarantee of our State Constitution. This is fitting for a state with so diverse a population. Article I, Paragraph 1 protects not only the rights of the majority but also the rights of the disfavored and the disadvantaged; they too are promised a fair opportunity for "pursuing and obtaining safety and happiness." (pp. 51–56)

13. The equal protection requirement of Article I, Paragraph 1 leaves the Legislature with two apparent options. The Legislature could

simply amend the marriage statutes to include same-sex couples, or it could create a separate statutory structure, such as a civil union. Because this State has no experience with a civil union construct, the Court will not speculate that identical schemes offering equal rights and benefits would create a distinction that would offend Article I, Paragraph 1, and will not presume that a difference in name is of constitutional magnitude. New language is developing to describe new social and familial relationships, and in time will find a place in our common vocabulary. However the Legislature may act, same-sex couples will be free to call their relationships by the name they choose and to sanctify their relationships in religious ceremonies in houses of worship. (pp. 57–63)

14. In the last two centuries, the institution of marriage has reflected society's changing social mores and values. Legislatures, along with courts, have played a major role in ushering marriage into the modern era of equality of partners. The great engine for social change in this country has always been the democratic process. Although courts can ensure equal treatment, they cannot guarantee social acceptance, which must come through the evolving ethos of a maturing society. Plaintiffs' quest does not end here. They must now appeal to their fellow citizens whose voices are heard through their popularly elected representatives. (pp. 63–64)

15. To bring the State into compliance with Article I, Paragraph 1 so that plaintiffs can exercise their full constitutional rights, the Legislature must either amend the marriage statutes or enact an appropriate statutory structure within 180 days of the date of this decision. (p. 65)

[Chief Justice Deborah T. Poritz concurred with and dissented to the majority opinion. The core of her argument is as follows. (Notes and citations are omitted and indicated by asterisks, ***.)]

I concur with the determination of the majority that "denying the rights and benefits to committed same-sex couples that are statutorily given to their heterosexual counterparts violates the equal protection guarantee of Article I, Paragraph 1 of the New Jersey Constitution *** . I can find no principled basis, however, on which to distinguish those rights and benefits from the right to the title of marriage, and therefore dissent from the majority's opinion insofar as it declines to recognize that right among all of the other rights and benefits that will be available to same-sex couples in the future.

I dissent also from the majority's conclusion that there is no fundamental due process right to same-sex marriage "encompassed within the concept of liberty guaranteed by Article I, Paragraph 1.

*** The majority acknowledges, as it must, that there is a universally accepted fundamental right to marriage "deeply rooted" in the "traditions, history, and conscience of the people." *** Yet, by asking whether there is a right to same-sex marriage, the Court avoids the more difficult questions of personal dignity and autonomy raised by this case. Under the majority opinion, it appears that persons who exercise their individual liberty interest to choose same-sex partners can be denied the fundamental right to participate in a state-sanctioned civil marriage. I would hold that plaintiffs' due process rights are violated when the State so burdens their liberty interests.

Source: Syllabus. http://lawlibrary.rutgers.edu/courts/wordperfect/ supreme/A-68-05.DOC

In re: Gill **(2006)**

Four states—Arkansas, Florida, Mississippi, and Utah—ban some form of same-sex adoption. The oldest of these bans is Florida's law, passed in 1977, largely as a result of a campaign against same-sex rights led by entertainer Anita Bryant. In July 2006, a Florida man, Martin Gill, and his partner filed adoption papers for two boys whom they had been foster-parenting since December 2004. In November 2008, Miami Circuit Court judge Cindy Lederman ruled in favor of Gill and his partner, declaring that the state's adoption law for same-sex couples was unconstitutional. Judge Lederman's ruling was appealed by the state to the Fourth District Court of Appeals in Miami. Whatever the decision in that appeal, most observers expect that the case will eventually be referred to and decided by the Florida Supreme Court.

[In explaining her decision in this case, Judge Lederman reviews the state's three major arguments against allowing same-sex adoption and offers her response to these three points. Citations are indicated by asterisks (***) and omitted.]

    i.   Promoting the well-being of children

The Department argues Fla. Stat. §63.042(3) is rationally related to Florida's interest by protecting children from the undesirable realities of the homosexual lifestyle. However, as thoroughly summarized in the Findings of Fact section of this Final Judgment, the foregoing is, frankly, false. ***

Obviously, in order to be considered rationally related to a governmental interest, the distinctions between individuals may not be based on unsubstantiated assumptions. *** Based on the statistics, there are no set of facts for which such a stated interest can be reasonably conceived of to justify the legislation. *** Fortunate for the Department, the government has no obligation to produce evidence to sustain the rationality of the statutory classification. *** Here, the two witnesses proffered by the Department failed to offer any reasonable, credible evidence to substantiate their beliefs or to justify the legislation. Viewing the statute from this point of view clearly renders it "illogical to the point of irrationality." *** Any exclusion that would declassify an entire group of people based on identical factors is clearly "both discriminatory and overbroad." *** Interestingly, in distinguishing Cleburne, the Lofton court posited that homosexuals were not similarly situated as heterosexuals, citing a 1987 New Hampshire Supreme Court decision holding that a similar statute was rationally related. However, in 1999, the New Hampshire legislature removed its prohibition of adoption and foster parenting by homosexuals. *** Nevertheless, here, the evidence proves quite the contrary; homosexuals are no more susceptible to mental health or psychological disorders, substance or alcohol abuse or relationship instability than their heterosexual counterparts. Accordingly, such governmental interest does not justify the legislation.

ii. Social Stigmatization/Necessity of dual gender homes

The Department next claims that best interests of children are served by placing them in an adoptive home which minimizes the social stigmatization they may experience. Again applying rational basis review, this Court rejects the Department's attempt to justify the statute by reference to a supposed dark cloud hovering over homes of homosexuals and their children. Neither the judiciary, nor the legislature are experts in psychology, psychiatry or child development. As such, we must rely on the professionals in those areas to provide an assessment of the relevant science. Since, the adoption of the statute in 1977, Cox in 1993, Amer in 1997 or even Lofton in 2004, the amount and quality of the relevant research and literature is robust. As expressed by the Florida Supreme Court in Cox, the legislature should revisit this issue in light of the research that has taken place in the last fifteen years. In this regard, the professionals and the major associations now agree there is a well established and accepted consensus in the field that there is no optimal gender combination of parents. As such, the statute is no longer rationally related to serve this interest.

iii. Morality

The Department's final rationale is that §63.042(3) rationally relates to Florida's legitimate moral interest to promote public morality. However, public morality per se, disconnected from any separate legitimate interest, is not a legitimate government interest to justify unequal treatment. *** promoting public morals, in and of itself, does not rescue the statute from constitutional infirmity. Under the rational basis test, a classification can only be upheld if it "bears a reasonable relationship to a permissive legislative objective and is not discriminatory, arbitrary, or oppressive." ***

Nevertheless, a public morality interest is inapplicable in the adoption context. Electing to parent and assume full responsibility for a child not one's own is one of the most noble decisions made in a lifetime; it is respected by many, considered by some, made by few and approved for fewer still. Here Petitioner qualifies for approval as an adoptive parent in all respects but one; his sexual orientation. The Department's position is that homosexuality is immoral. Yet, homosexuals may be lawful foster parents in Florida and care for our most fragile children who have been abused, neglected and abandoned. As such, the exclusion forbidding homosexuals to adopt children does not further the public morality interest it seeks to combat. Based on this scenario, there can be no rationally related public morality interest differentiating in the State's support of a homosexual's long-term foster care relationship with a child and a denial of their legal relationship through adoption. Consequently, there is no "morality" interest with regard to one group of individuals permitted to form the visage of a family in one context but prohibited in another. The contradiction between the adoption and foster care statutes defeats the public morality argument and is thus not rationally related to serving a governmental interest. ***

iv. Conclusion

This Court finds Fla. Stat. §63.042(3) violates the Petitioner and the Children's equal protection rights guaranteed by Article I, § 2 of the Florida Constitution without satisfying a rational basis. Moreover, the statutory exclusion defeats a child's right to permanency as provided by federal and state law pursuant to the Adoption and Safe Families Act of 1997.

Sources: In the Matter of the Adoption of John Doe and James Doe, http://reports.jud11.flcourts.org/Judicial_Orders/REDACTED%20Gill%20Final%20Judgement%20of%20Adoption.pdf

Varnum v. Brien, 763 N.W.2D 862 (IOWA 2009)

As of early 2010, the most recent case establishing the right of same-sex couples to marry was decided in Iowa in April 2009. In that case, a group of 12 plaintiffs who were refused marriage licenses in Polk County sued the state claiming that the action was discriminatory under the Iowa state constitution. In a unanimous opinion, the state Supreme Court agreed with the plaintiffs. Some important sections of that decision are provided here. Omitted citations are designated by ellipses (. . .).

[The court begins with a review of the tripartite structure of American government, including that of the state of Iowa. It sets out its responsibilities under that system of government.]

A statute inconsistent with the Iowa Constitution must be declared void, even though it may be supported by strong and deep-seated traditional beliefs and popular opinion. . . . As Chief Justice John Marshall wrote over two centuries ago, "It is a proposition too plain to be contested, that the constitution controls any legislative act repugnant to it. . . ." . . . It is also well established that courts must, under all circumstances, protect the supremacy of the constitution as a means of protecting our republican form of government and our freedoms. As was observed by Justice Robert H. Jackson decades ago in reference to the United States Constitution, the very purpose of limiting the power of the elected branches of government by constitutional provisions like the Equal Protection Clause is "to withdraw certain subjects from the vicissitudes of political controversy, to place them beyond the reach of majorities and officials and to establish them as legal principles to be applied by the courts." . . .

The same principle applies to the provisions of the Iowa Constitution that limit government power. The idea that courts, free from the political influences in the other two branches of government, are better suited to protect individual rights was recognized at the time our Iowa Constitution was formed. . . .

In fulfilling this mandate under the Iowa Constitution, we look to the past and to precedent. We look backwards, not because citizens' rights are constrained to those previously recognized, but because historical constitutional principles provide the framework to define our future as we confront the challenges of today.

Our responsibility, however, is to protect constitutional rights of individuals from legislative enactments that have denied those rights, even when the rights have not yet been broadly accepted, were at one time unimagined, or challenge a deeply ingrained practice or law viewed to be impervious to the passage of time. The framers of the Iowa Constitution knew, as did the drafters of the United States Constitution, that "times can blind us to certain truths and later generations can see that laws once thought necessary and proper in fact serve only to oppress," and as our constitution "endures, persons in every generation can invoke its principles in their own search for greater freedom" and equality. . . .

[Having clarified its role in the debate over same-sex marriage, the court then reviews in great detail all aspects of the arguments for and against this institution. First, it determines that the Iowa constitution requires that all state laws be equally applied to all individuals:]

In other words, to truly ensure equality before the law, the equal protection guarantee requires that laws treat all those who are similarly situated with respect to the purposes of the law alike.

[Next, the court determines that homosexual couples are situated in precisely the same way as heterosexual couples with regard to the state's marriage laws:]

Therefore, with respect to the subject and purposes of Iowa's marriage laws, we find that the plaintiffs are similarly situated compared to heterosexual persons. Plaintiffs are in committed and loving relationships, many raising families, just like heterosexual couples. Moreover, official recognition of their status provides an institutional basis for defining their fundamental relational rights and responsibilities, just as it does for heterosexual couples. Society benefits, for example, from providing same-sex couples a stable framework within which to raise their children and the power to make health care and end-of-life decisions for loved ones, just as it does when that framework is provided for opposite-sex couples.

In short, for purposes of Iowa's marriage laws, which are designed to bring a sense of order to the legal relationships of committed couples and their families in myriad ways, plaintiffs are similarly situated in every important respect, but for their sexual orientation.

[Based on this line of reasoning, the court finally concludes that:]

In the final analysis, we give respect to the views of all Iowans on the issue of same-sex marriage—religious or otherwise—by giving respect to our constitutional principles. These principles require that the state recognize both opposite-sex and same-sex civil marriage. Religious doctrine and views contrary to this principle of law are unaffected, and people can continue to associate with the religion that best reflects their views. A religious denomination can still define marriage as a union between a man and a woman, and a marriage ceremony performed by a minister, priest, rabbi, or other person ordained or designated as a leader of the person's religious faith does not lose its meaning as a sacrament or other religious institution. The sanctity of all religious marriages celebrated in the future will have the same meaning as those celebrated in the past. The only difference is civil marriage will now take on a new meaning that reflects a more complete understanding of equal protection of the law. This result is what our constitution requires.

J. Constitutional Infirmity. We are firmly convinced the exclusion of gay and lesbian people from the institution of civil marriage does not substantially further any important governmental objective. The legislature has excluded a historically disfavored class of persons from a supremely important civil institution without a constitutionally sufficient justification. There is no material fact, genuinely in dispute, that can affect this determination. We have a constitutional duty to ensure equal protection of the law. Faithfulness to that duty requires us to hold Iowa's marriage statute, Iowa Code section 595.2, violates the Iowa Constitution. To decide otherwise would be an abdication of our constitutional duty. If gay and lesbian people must submit to different treatment without an exceedingly persuasive justification, they are deprived of the benefits of the principle of equal protection upon which the rule of law is founded. Iowa Code section 595.2 denies gay and lesbian people the equal protection of the law promised by the Iowa Constitution.

Source: In the Supreme Court of Iowa, No. 07–1499, http:// www.iowacourts.gov/Supreme_Court/Recent_Opinions/20090403/ 07-1499.pdf?search=07%2D1499#_1, pp. 13–15, 27, 28–29, 66–67

Kutil and Hess v. Blake, WL 1579493 (2009)

The legal status of same-sex adoption in the United States might be characterized as being somewhat uncertainty and probably in a state of flux. Some states have laws specifically prohibiting adoption of children by same-sex couples; other states permit same-sex adoption under some circumstances, but not others; and other states have no laws at all or laws that are at least somewhat ambiguous. As a consequence, the status of same-sex adoptions depends to some extent on case law established by decisions made by state courts. These decisions, like the laws themselves, tend to vary from very permissive to highly restrictive. The case of Kutil and Hess v. Blake *illustrates some of the fundamental issues faced by courts confronted with the issue as to whether same-sex couples are qualified to adoption children.*

[Background: A child identified only as B. G. C. was born on December 8, 2007. She tested positive for cocaine and oxycodone at birth and, as required by West Virginia law, was immediately placed in the foster home of a lesbian couple, Kathryn Kutil and Cheryl Hess. The child's legal guardian, appointed by Fayette County Circuit Court judge Paul M. Blake Jr., objected to this placement, and filed a petition to have the baby removed to a "traditional home." The court denied this petition with the following reasoning.]

C. Summary

Central to our deliberation in this case is the reason or motivation underlying Respondent's decision to remove a child from her foster care home. The motion to remove the child was not supported by any allegation that B. G. C. was receiving improper or unwise care and management in her foster home, or that she was being subjected to any other legally recognized undesirable condition or influence. W.Va. Code § 49-2-12 (1970) (Repl. Vol. 2004); see also W.Va. Code § 49-2-14 (2002) (Repl. Vol. 2004) (criteria and procedure for removal of child from foster home). Likewise, no evidence supporting a legal reason for removing the child was presented at the hearings. As a matter of fact, the court was never presented with any actual evaluation of the home or evidence of the quality of the relationship B. G. C. had with Petitioners. Moreover, Respondent deferred hearing testimony from Petitioners' witnesses regarding their parenting abilities. Nevertheless, there also was no indication that Petitioners provided B. G. C. with anything other than a loving and nurturing home. As Respondent observed from the bench at the November 21 hearing, "there has been absolutely no allegation that these women have not cared for [B. G. C.] or the other kids and, in fact, all of the evidence indicates that they have done very well and have provided very well for the children." Without any information that the foster care placement with Petitioners was not proceeding well, there was no legal reason for the court to remove B. G. C. from the only home she has known.

It is more than apparent that the only reason why Petitioners were being replaced as foster care providers was to promote the adoption of B. G. C. by what Respondent called in his November 12, 2008, order a "traditionally defined family, that is, a family consisting of both a mother and a father." It was only by addressing issues he anticipated would develop and believed would be problems at a later point in this case that Respondent was even able to reach the subject of this conclusion. The conclusion itself thus represents a blurring of legal principles applicable to abuse and neglect and adoption. Moreover, even if our current statutes, rules and regulations could somehow be read to support the adoption preference proposed by Respondent, such a newfound principle would need to be harmonized with established law. Under our current law which encourages adoption by qualified foster parents, one of the Petitioners seeking to adopt B. G. C. individually would at the very least need to be considered if not favored in the selection of the prospective adoptive home. (See footnote 22)

In the present case, all indications thus far are that B. G. C. has formed a close emotional bond and nurturing relationship with her foster parents, which can not be trivialized or ignored. State ex rel. Treadway v. McCoy; In re Jonathan G. As such, it serves as a classic example of a case in which the permanency plan for adoption should move quickly to the desired result of a permanent home for B. G. C. One of the Petitioners who has already adopted a child (See footnote 23) and appreciates the tremendous responsibility adoption entails, has recently expressed the desire to adopt B. G. C. Clearly, that Petitioner should not be excluded from consideration for the reason stated by Respondent. These factors all should serve to facilitate the selection process, which needs to be completed as expeditiously as possible in order to further the best interests of B. G. C. and in recognition and support of the parenting investment which has been made.

IV. Conclusion

For the reasons stated in this opinion, the writ of prohibition sought by Petitioners is granted.

Source: In the Supreme Court of Appeals of West Virginia, January 2009 Term, No. 34618, http://www.state.wv.us/wvsca/docs/spring09/ 34618.htm

Order on Intervenor's Plea to the Jurisdiction (2009)

The increasingly complicated patchwork of laws in the United States with regard to same-sex relationships (marriage, civil unions, domestic partnerships, etc.) has almost inevitably begun to lead to complex legal questions when two or more states are involved in a legal dispute. As an example, in 2009 two men who were legally married in Massachu-setts in 2006 and then moved to Texas, filed for divorce in January 2009. The legal issue is complex in this case because same-sex marriage is spe-cifically prohibited by Section 32a of Article I of the Bill of Rights of the Texas constitution (see below). In October 2009, district court judge Tena Callahan not only ruled that her court had jurisdiction to hear the divorce case, but that Texas state law and Section 32a of the Texas constitution violated the U.S. Constitution. At the time of this writing (early 2010), the consequences of this ruling—verification that laws against same-sex marriage in Texas are invalid—had not fully been explored. The judge's ruling on this issue is reproduced here.

ORDER ON INTERVENOR'S PLEA TO THE JURISDICTION

On the limited issue of whether this Court has jurisdiction to divorce parties who have legally married in another jurisdiction and who otherwise meet the residency and other prerequisites required to file for a divorce in Dallas County, Texas:

The Court FINDS that Article 1, Section 32(a) of the Texas Constitution violates the right to equal protection and therefore violates the 14th Amendment of the United States Constitution,

The Court FINDS that Texas Family Code Section 6.204 violates the right to equal. protection and therefore violates the 14th Amendment of the United States Constitution.

Accordingly, the Court FINDS that it has jurisdiction to hear a suit for divorce filed by persons legally married. in another jurisdiction and who meet the residency and other prerequisites required to file for divorce in Dallas County, Texas, and

IT IS THEREFORE ORDERED" that Intervenor's Plea to the Jurisdiction is denied and that the Intervention filed by the Office of the Attorney General is hereby stricken. SIGNED: October I, 2009.

Cause No. DF-09-1074. In the Matter of the Marriage of J. B. and H. B. http://pdfserver.amlaw.com/tx/intervenor.pdf.

[The two documents to which the order refers are as follows:]

Sec. 32. MARRIAGE. (a) Marriage in this state shall consist only of the union of one man and one woman.

Source: Texas Constitution.http://www.statutes.legis.state.tx.us/Docs/CN/htm/CN.1.htm#1.32

Sec. 6.204. RECOGNITION OF SAME-SEX MARRIAGE OR CIVIL UNION. (a) In this section, "civil union" means any relationship status other than marriage that:

(1)   is intended as an alternative to marriage or applies primarily to cohabitating persons; and

(2)   grants to the parties of the relationship legal protections, benefits, or responsibilities granted to the spouses of a marriage.

(b) A marriage between persons of the same sex or a civil union is contrary to the public policy of this state and is void in this state.

(c) The state or an agency or political subdivision of the state may not give effect to a:

(1) public act, record, or judicial proceeding that creates, recognizes, or validates a marriage between persons of the same sex or a civil union in this state or in any other jurisdiction; or

(2) right or claim to any legal protection, benefit, or responsibility asserted as a result of a marriage between persons of the same sex or a civil union in this state or in any other jurisdiction.

Source: Family Code. Title 1. The Marriage Relationship. Subtitle C. Dissolution of Marriage. Chapter 6. Suit for Dissolution of Marriage. Subchapter A. Grounds for Divorce and Defenses, http://www.statutes .legis.state.tx.us/Docs/FA/htm/FA.6.htm#6.204

Data and Statistics

Table 6.1: Same-Sex Marriages in Massachusetts (2009)

As the first state in the union to legalize same-sex marriage, Massachusetts has the most complete set of data on the number of such ceremonies performed thus far. The table below summarizes unpublished data on same-sex marriages in the commonwealth.

TABLE 6.1
Same-Sex Marriages in Massachusetts (2009)

| Year | Male-to-Female Marriages | Same-Sex Marriages | |
		Male-to-Male	Female-to-Female
2004[a]	27,196 (81.6%)	2,176 (6.4%)	3,945 (11.6%)
2005	37,447 (94.8%)	736 (1.9%)	1,324 (3.4%)
2006	36,550 (96.2%)	543 (1.5%)	899 (2.5%)
2007	36,373 (96.0%)	591 (1.6%)	933 (2.5%)
2008[b]	33,382 (93.9%)	856 (2.4%)	1,282 (3.6%)

[a]May 17 through December 31, 2004.
[b]2008 data are provisional; they include 23 cases with missing gender information.
Percentages may not add to 100% because of rounding.
Source: Massachusetts Registry of Vital Records and Statistics; unpublished data provided by e-mail to author, November 30, 2009.

Table 6.2: Number of Same-Sex Couples in Legally Recognized Relationships (2009)

Data on the number of same-sex couples in legally recognized relationships (marriage, civil union, domestic partnership, etc.) in countries around the world is incomplete. Some nations that recognize such relationships do not collect data on the numbers of couple enrolled in them, and other nations conduct only incomplete surveys. The table below summarizes some of the most recent data available from selected countries worldwide on this topic.

TABLE 6.2
Number of Couples in Legally Recognized Relationships in Selected Countries

Country	2000	2001	2002	2003	2004	2005	2006	2007	2008
Canada[a]							7,465		
Denmark[b]	308	347	303	320	333	394	400	425	441
Netherlands[c]	1,600							1,976	2,019
New Zealand[d]						157	348	320	325
Norway[e]	154	185	183	204	192	192	227		
United Kingdom[f]						1,953	16,195	8,728	7,169
England						1,790	14,383	7,635	6,276
Wales						67	560	294	282
Scotland						84	1,047	688	525
Northern Ireland						12	116	111	86

[a]*Source:* Statistics Canada. Table 2: Distribution of Couples by Conjugal Status, Canada, 2001 and 2006. http://www12.statcan.ca/census-recensement/2006/as-sa/97-553/table/t2eng.cfm.
[b]*Source:* Statistics Denmark. Entered Registered Partnerships by Sex, Age of Youngest Person and Age of Oldest Person. http://www.statbank.dk/statbank5a/SelectVarVal/Define.asp?Maintable=IREG1&PLanguage=1.
[c]*Source:* Centraal Bureau voor de Statistiek. Marriages and Partnership Registrations; Key Figures. http://statline.cbs.nl/StatWeb/publication/?VW=T&DM=SLEN&PA=37772eng.
[d]*Source:* Statistics New Zealand. Provisional Civil Unions and Marriages. http://www.stats.govt.nz/methods_and_services/access-data/tables/civil-unions-marriages-provisional.aspx.
[e]*Source:* Statistics Norway. Table 98: Partnerships Contracted, by Age of the Oldest Partner (1993–2006). http://www.ssb.no/english/yearbook/tab/tab-098.html.
[f]*Source:* Office for National Statistics. Table 1: Number of Civil Partnerships and Average Age of Civil Partners by Country of Formation and Sex, 2005–2008. http://www.statistics.gov.uk/StatBase/Expodata/Spreadsheets/D9873.xls.

Table 6.3: Same-Sex and Opposite-Sex Marriage Data from the Netherlands (2009)

Critics of same-sex marriage sometimes argue that the practice should not be given legal approval because it would have devastating effects on traditional opposite-sex marriages. Although the specifics of this argument are not always clearly stated, one presumes that it implies that, were same-sex couples given the right to marry, opposite-sex couples would be less likely to marry or would divorce more commonly. Since the practice of giving approval for any kind of legal same-sex relationship isrelatively new, there are few data against which to test this hypothesis. Probably the most complete set of data comes from Denmark, the first nation in the world to give legal approval to same-sex relationships, in the form of *registreret partnerskab*, or registered partnerships. These partnerships are identical to opposite-sex marriages except for three modest exceptions. The data below show trends in traditional, opposite-sex marriages, and same-sex registered partnerships in Denmark from 1989 to 2008.

TABLE 6.3
Marriage and Divorce Rates in Denmark, 1989–2008

	1989	1990	1991	1992	1993	1994	1995	1996	1997	1998
Marriages (per 10,000)	60	61	60	62	61	68	66	68	65	66
Divorces (total)	15,152	13,731	12,655	12,981	12,971	13,709	12,976	12,776	12,774	13,141

	1999	2000	2001	2002	2003	2004	2005	2006	2007	2008
Marriages (per 10,000)	67	72	68	69	65	70	67	67	67	68
Divorces (total)	13,537	14,381	14,597	15,304	15,763	15,774	15,300	14,343	14,066	14,695

Source: Statistics Denmark. Summary Vital Statistics. http://www.statbank.dk/statbank5a/SelectVarVal/Define.asp ?Maintable=HISB3&PLanguage=1.

Table 6.4: Same-Sex and Opposite-Sex Marriage Data from Belgium (2009)

A second country from which data are available about the effects of same-sex marriage on opposite-sex marriage is Belgium, which is the second nation in the world (after the Netherlands) to legalize same-sex marriage. Data for the number of same-sex and opposite-sex marriages and divorces are provided here.

TABLE 6.4
Same-Sex and Opposite-Sex Marriage Data from Belgium (2009)

	2003	2004	2005	2006	2007	2008
Marriages, Opposite-Sex	41,777	43,296	43,141	44,813	45,561	45,613
Marriages, Same-Sex	793	954	1,170	1,238	1,719	n/a
Divorces	31,355	31,405	30,840	29,189	30,081	35,366

Sources: Marriages: http://statbel.fgov.be/fr/binaries/31171_fr_tcm326-77711.xls; same-sex marriages: http://statbel.fgov.be/fr/statistiques/chiffres/population/mariage_divorce_cohabitation/cohabitation/index.jsp; divorces: http://statbel.fgov.be/fr/statistiques/chiffres/population/mariage_divorce_cohabitation/divorces/index.jsp.

Table 6.5: Divorce Rates by States, 2004–2007 (2009)

Same-sex marriages are such a recent phenomenon that data on their potential effects on traditional marriage are not yet available. Based on critics' argument that same-sex marriage is a threat to traditional marriage, however, preliminary data are available for national studies of divorce rates in the 50 states and District of Columbia. If critics' argument is correct, one might expect to see divorce rates beginning to rise in states where same-sex marriage is legal. As of early 2010, only one state, Massachusetts, provides sufficient data to permit some assessment of that claim. As the following data show, however, Massachusetts continues to have the lowest divorce rate of any state in the union for which data are available. It may, of course, still be too soon to see the effect of same-sex marriage on divorce rates.

TABLE 6.5
Divorce Rates by States, 2004–2007

State	2004	2005	2006	2007
AL	4.9	4.9	5.0	4.6
AK	4.3	4.3	4.2	4.2
AZ	4.2	4.1	3.9	3.9
AR	6.1	6.0	5.9	5.9
CA	—	—	—	—
CO	4.4	4.4	4.4	4.4
CT	3.1	3.0	3.1	3.2
DE	3.7	3.9	3.8	3.7

(continued)

TABLE 6.5
Divorce Rates by States, 2004–2007 *(continued)*

State	2004	2005	2006	2007
DC	1.9	2.1	2.1	1.7
FL	4.8	4.6	4.8	4.6
GA	—	—	—	—
HI	—	—	—	—
ID	5.0	5.0	5.0	4.9
IL	2.6	2.5	2.5	2.6
IN	—	—	—	—
IA	2.8	2.8	2.7	2.6
KS	3.3	3.1	3.1	3.4
KY	4.9	4.6	5.0	4.7
LA	—	—	—	—
ME	4.3	4.1	4.2	4.3
MD	3.2	3.1	3.0	3.0
MA	2.2	2.2	2.3	2.3
MI	3.4	3.4	3.5	3.4
MN	2.8	—	—	—
MS	4.5	4.4	4.8	4.5
MO	3.8	3.6	3.8	3.8
MT	3.8	4.5	4.4	4.1
NE	3.4	3.3	3.4	3.5
NV	6.4	7.5	6.8	6.5
NH	3.9	3.8	4.0	3.8
NJ	3.0	2.9	3.0	3.0
NM	4.6	4.6	4.3	4.3
NY	3.0	2.8	3.1	2.9
NC	4.2	4.1	4.0	4.0
ND	3.1	3.0	3.1	3.0
OH	3.6	3.5	3.5	3.4
OK	4.9	5.6	5.3	5.2
OR	4.1	4.1	4.0	3.9
PA	3.0	2.3	2.8	2.9
RI	3.0	2.9	3.0	2.8
SC	3.2	2.9	3.0	3.0
SD	3.1	2.8	3.2	3.1
TN	4.9	4.7	4.6	4.3
TX	3.6	3.3	3.4	3.3
UT	4.1	4.0	3.9	3.6
VT	3.9	3.6	3.8	3.6
VA	3.9	4.0	4.0	3.8
WA	4.3	4.3	4.1	4.0
WV	5.0	5.1	5.0	5.1
WI	3.0	2.9	3.0	2.9
WY	5.2	5.3	5.2	5.0

Source: National Center for Health Statistics. "Divorce Rates by State: 1990, 1995, and 1999–2007." http://www.cdc.gov/nchs/data/nvss/Divorce%20Rates%2090%2095%20and%209907.pdf.

7

Organizations

The issues of same-sex marriage and same-sex adoption are now very contentious issues in the United States and several nations around the world. A number of organizations are engaged in promoting one viewpoint or another about these two issues. On the one hand, gay and lesbian civil rights groups have been especially active in pushing for legalization of same-sex marriage, as are a number of groups traditionally interested in human and civil rights. On the other hand, the most vociferous objections to same-sex marriage and same-sex adoption have come from religious groups, including not only those of the Christian faith, but also those from other faiths, especially those in Muslim countries. This chapter provides information on a number of these groups who are lobbying both for and against same-sex marriage and same-sex adoption, as well as some organizations who attempt to take a more neutral stance on the issue. The chapter is divided into three main sections: those that favor same-sex marriage, those that oppose same-sex marriage, and those that are interested in the issue of marriage, but neutral on the question of same-sex marriage. Within each section, groups are then listed alphabetically.

Organizations in Favor of Same-Sex Marriage

American Civil Liberties Union (ACLU)
URL: http://www.aclu.org/

The American Civil Liberties Union was founded in 1920 for the purpose of working for the protection of the civil rights of all Americans. The ACLU is arguably the best known, most highly respected, and most successful of all organizations associated with civil rights issues in the United States. Its current areas of concern include the rights of disabled people, free speech, prisoners' rights, reproductive freedom, the rights of the poor, voting rights, and women's rights. In the area of gay and lesbian rights, the organization has led or participated in a number of legal actions, including a lawsuit against the University of Pittsburgh over benefits for gay and lesbian employees, a lawsuit in Texas against the state's sodomy laws, domestic partner benefits for the lesbian survivor of the 9/11 attack, and a number of legal actions involving adoption rights of lesbians and gay men. Most of the ACLU's current activities on behalf of lesbians and gay men are conducted through the organization's Lesbian Gay Bisexual Transgender Project.

Publications: *Too High a Price: The Case Against Restricting Gay Parenting; Transgender People and the Law: Frequently Asked Questions; Why We're Asking Courts and Legislatures for Transgender Equality; The Rights of Lesbian, Gay, Bisexual and Transgendered People; Where We Are 2003: The Annual Report of the ACLU's Nationwide Work on LGBT Rights and HIV/AIDS.*

API Equality
URL: http://www.apiequality.org/

API Equality was founded in 2004 as the Asian Pacific American Coalition for Equality (APACE) in order to work for marriage equality for all individuals of Asian and Pacific Island heritage. It later changed its name to Asian Equality and eventually to API Equality. API Equality is an ad hoc coalition of more than 50 Asian and Pacific Island organizations cooperating in the effort to attain equal civil rights in marriage for Americans of Asian and Pacific Island heritage. The organization has been especially active in efforts to obtain legalization of same-sex marriage in California, where it filed an amicus curiae brief in the 2006 *Marriage Cases* heard before the state supreme court and in the later statewide election dealing with same-sex marriage.

Publications: None.

Children of Lesbians and Gays Everywhere (COLAGE)
URL: http://www.colage.org/

Children of Lesbians and Gays Everywhere grew out of a 1998 national conference of the Gay and Lesbian Parents Coalition International (now the Family Equality Council), at which sessions were arranged for children of same-sex parents as well as for parents themselves. Some of the children attendees at the conference eventually decided to form a more formal organization of their own, which they named Just for Us. At its annual conference in 1993, Just for Us decided to change the organization's name to its current name of Children of Lesbians and Gays Everywhere. COLAGE opened its first national office in San Francisco in 1995 and hired its first paid director two years later. The organization now has five paid full-time staff members, as well as fellows, interns, volunteers, and part-time employees. Much of the organization's work is carried out through its 41 chapters in 26 states, the District of Columbia, Canada, England, and Sweden.

Publications: *Just for Us* newsletter; free posters about parents of lesbian, gay, bisexual, and transgendered (LGBT) persons.

Egale Canada
URL: http://www.egale.ca/

Egale Canada is Canada's premier organization working to obtain equal rights for LGBT persons. It has members in every province and territory, and its board of directors includes one male and one female member from every such district. Egale Canada has been involved in every important legal action in Canada aimed at providing civil and legal equality of all citizens, regardless of their sexual orientation. Members of the organization have also testified before parliament on a number of times on issues of interest to LGBT persons, such as tax policy, immigration, same-sex marriage and divorce, child custody and adoption, and school safety for LGBT youth.

Publications: *INFO Egale* (quarterly newsletter); *Egale Update* (monthly report); *The Year in Review* (annual report).

Equality Federation (EF)
URL: http://www.equalityfederation.org/

The Equality Federation was formed in 2006 to work for the advancement of equal civil rights for LGBT persons. The organization focuses its efforts on state and local projects rather than primarily on the federal level. It provides resources and leadership training for state and local groups in the pursuit of these goals. One of its most useful projects is the annual "State of the States" report, which summarizes and analyzes a host of information about the finances, organization, activities, and personnel of state and local LGBT organizations. EF's Web site also provides an interactive map that allows access to equal rights organizations in 40 of the 50 states. As of early 2010, the organization's campaigns of special interest concerned support for passage of the Employment Non-Discrimination Act (ENDA) pending in the U.S. Congress, promotion of benefits for domestic partners of federal employees, support for health care reform legislation (an issue of concern for gay men and lesbians as much as it is for nongays and nonlesbians), and support for the Reuniting Families Act, also pending in the Congress.

Publications: Occasional online reports on lesbian, gay, bisexual, and transgender issues.

Families Like Ours (FLO)
URL: http://www.familieslikeours.org/

Families Like Ours is an organization of adoptive and foster parents offering assistance to other couples who wish to become adoptive or foster parents. FLO focuses its efforts primarily, but not exclusively, on gay and lesbian couples. It offers advice, counseling, and mentoring for couples, from the time they begin to consider fostering or adopting, until that process has been completed. The organization provides a comprehensive guide to adoption and fostering in its publication "Adoption 101: A Family Guide," available on its Web site. In 2009, the organization was named nonprofit of the year by the Greater Seattle Business Association for its work in reducing barriers to adoption by qualified couples.

Publications: *Families Like Ours* (monthly newsletter); *Adoption 101: A Family Guide* (online publication); *Becoming a Foster Parent* (online publication).

Family Equality Council (FEC)
URL: http://www.familyequality.org/

Founded originally as the Gay Fathers Coalition in 1979, this organization later changed its name to Gay and Lesbian Parents

Coalition International in 1986 and to its current name in 2007. FEC is a national nonprofit organization that works to gain equality not only for same-sex couples, but also for other nontraditional families, such as single-parent families and families of mixed race whose needs may be ignored by society at large. Family Equality Council operates OUTspoken, a national speakers bureau that provides speakers on family equality for a wide range of groups and events. As of early 2010, more than one thousand men and women from 39 states, the District of Columbia, one U.S. territory, and three foreign countries have volunteered to participate in the OUTspoken program.

Publications: *52 Ways to Be OUTspoken; Family Discussions about Political Attacks on Our Families; Talking to Children about Our Families; Interactive Tool: The Rainbow Report Card;* and many other brochures available online.

Freedom to Marry
URL: http://www.freedomtomarry.org/

Freedom to Marry was founded by civil rights attorney and activist Evan Wolfson for the purpose of promoting the rights of all Americans to marry, regardless of their sexual orientation. Through its Voices of Equality program, it draws on a diverse group of prominent Americans who speak out on equality of marriage rights. The group includes individuals such as Rocky Anderson, mayor of Salt Lake City; Christine Chavez, political director of the United Farm Workers of America; Dakota Fine, Washington, DC, activist; Kim Gandy, president of the National Organization for Women; Congressman John Lewis; and Reverend William G. Sinkford, president of the Unitarian Universalist Association.

Publications: *Why Marriage Matters America, Equality, and Gay People's Right to Marry* (book); *Candidates' Guide on How to Support Marriage Equality and Get Elected* (online publication); *Marriage Makes a Word of Difference* (online publication); *The Freedom to Marry: Why Non-Gay People Care and What We Can Do About It* (online publication); *For Richer, for Poorer: The Freedom to Marry as a Matter of Economic Justice* (online publication); *What Is Freedom to Marry?* (online publication); *The Time Is Now to Fight for the Freedom to Marry* (online publication); *Stand Up for Our Constitution* (online publication).

Gay and Lesbian Advocates and Defenders (GLAD)
URL: http://www.glad.org/

GLAD is one of the oldest gay and lesbian rights organizations in the nation, having been formed in 1978 to fight for an end to discrimination based on sexual orientation, HIV status, and gender identity. Some of the issues about which GLAD has litigated in the past are civil rights, crime and law enforcement, employment, family issues, health care, marriage and civil unions, public accommodations, transgender issues, and gay and lesbian youth and students. GLAD's current work includes five major campaigns: the Civil Rights Project, AIDS Law Project, Transgender Rights Project, New England Marriage Campaign, and DOMA Section 3 Challenge. The New England Marriage Campaign has as its goal the legalization of same-sex marriage for all six New England states by the year 2012.

Publications: Legal publications such as *A Legal Q & A for Kids of Trans Parents; Transgender Students' Use of Bathrooms and Locker Rooms; Maine: Joint Adoption Practice and Procedure; New Hampshire Civil Unions; Legal Issues for Non-MA Couples Who Married in MA; Marriage Guide for RI Couples; Rights of LGBTQ Youth in RI; Rights of LGBTQ Youth in ME.*

Gill Foundation
URL: http://www.gillfoundation.org/

The Gill Foundation was established in 1994 by Coloradan Tim Gill in response to a rancorous campaign to limit the rights of gay men and lesbians in that state. Founder of the software company Quark, Inc., Gill was financially able to provide a solid basis for the foundation. Since its creation, the foundation has awarded more than $120 million to support programs and organizations working to ensure equal civil rights for lesbians and gay men in the United States. Much of the foundation's work is currently carried out through two programs, OutGiving and the Democracy Project. OutGiving is an effort to increase philanthropic giving to gay and lesbian organizations, while the Democracy Project is a program to increase the efficient operation of more than 400 groups in the United States working for gay and lesbian rights. One of the major areas of concern to the Gill Foundation is the support for efforts to achieve equal treatment for lesbians and gay men in the field of personal relationships, such as same-sex marriage, domestic partnerships, and civil unions.

Publications: Annual Reports (available online).

Human Rights Campaign (HRC)
URL: http://www.hrc.org/

The Human Rights Campaign was founded in 1980 to work for the civil rights of all gay men and lesbians in the United States. The organization currently claims 700,000 members and calls itself the largest organization of its kind in the country. The organization's Center for the Study of Equality works to improve the general understanding of gay and lesbian issues. HRC has published a number of reports on various aspects of the gay and lesbian rights movement, such as "Transgender Inclusion in the Workplace," "Family Matters," "Equality from State to State: Gay, Lesbian, Bisexual and Transgender Americans and State Legislation," and "Small Business Basics." One of the HRC's current campaigns is its Millions for Marriage Petition, an effort to obtain more than a million signatures for a petition to be sent to the U.S. Congress in support of same-sex marriage. The organization also provides information about the current status of same-sex marriage and other arrangements, such as domestic partnerships and civil unions, on its Web site.

Publications: *Resource Guide to Coming Out; A Straight Guide to GLBT Americans; Coming Out for African Americans; Guía de Recursos Para Salir del Clóset; Coming Out As Transgender; Living Openly in Your Place of Worship; Buying for Equality 2008; Corporate Equality Index 2008; Healthcare Equality Index 2008.*

Human Rights Watch (HRW)
URL: http://hrw.org/

For many years, Human Rights Watch has included issues of lesbian, gay, bisexual, and transgender rights as one of its primary fields of concern. Each year, it reviews and comments on progress and problems with regard to these issues in various countries around the world. HRW activities span the globe; in 2008 alone, for example, it investigated cases of human rights violation involving lesbians, gay men, bisexuals, and transgendered people in Colombia, Egypt, Gambia, Jamaica, Kyrgyzstan,

Morocco, Nigeria, Turkey, Uganda, and the United States. The organization's Web site contains links to organizations working for LGBT rights in more than 100 countries around the world.

Publications (selection only): *Courting History: The Landmark International Criminal Court's First Years; Still Waiting: Bringing Justice for War Crimes, Crimes against Humanity, and Genocide in Bosnia and Herzegovina's Cantonal and District Courts; My Rights, and My Right to Know: Lack of Access to Therapeutic Abortion in Peru; "As If I Am Not Human": Abuses against Asian Domestic Workers in Saudi Arabia; China's Forbidden Zones: Shutting the Media out of Tibet and Other "Sensitive" Stories; United Kingdom: Briefing on the Counter-Terrorism Bill 2008; Preempting Justice: Counterterrorism Laws and Procedures in France; "As If They Fell from the Sky": Counterinsurgency, Rights Violations, and Rampant Impunity in Ingushetia; Neighbors In Need: Zimbabweans Seeking Refuge in South Africa; "We Need a Law for Liberation": Gender, Sexuality, and Human Rights in a Changing Turkey; "We Have the Upper Hand": Freedom of Assembly in Russia and the Human Rights of Lesbian, Gay, Bisexual, and Transgender People; Restrictions on AIDS Activists in China.*

Immigration Equality (IE)
URL: http://www.immigrationequality.org/

Immigration Equality claims a membership of over ten thousand lesbians, gay men, bisexuals, and transgendered and HIV-positive people throughout the United States. The organization was formed in 1994 to work for changes in U.S. immigration law that would allow such individuals to sponsor their partners for immigration benefits, which is not possible under current immigration law. IE works for the passage of the Uniting American Families Act of 2009 to achieve this goal. IE currently focuses its efforts in five major areas: binational couples, asylum for individuals who may be persecuted for their sexual orientation, transgender issues, HIV issues, and detection for immigrants.

Publications: "Family, Unvalued"; "LGBT/HIV Asylum Manual"; "LGBT Immigration Basics"; "HIV Immigration Basics" (Web publications); also available online are archival copies of the organization's earlier newsletters and brochures on specific topics.

International Gay and Lesbian Human Rights Commission (IGLHRC)
URL: http://www.iglhrc.org/cgi-bin/iowa/home/index.html

The International Gay and Lesbian Human Rights Commission is a New York–based nonprofit corporation whose purpose it is to work for the civil rights of gay men and lesbians in all nations of the world. IGLHRC coordinates its efforts with other social organizations and agencies throughout the world, conducts an active program of education about issues of human sexuality, and provides rapid responses to human rights violations related to issues of sexuality throughout the world. The organization's work is currently organized under six major topics: Africa, Asia, Asylum Documentation, Eastern Europe and Central Asia, HIV/AIDS, and Latin America and Caribbean. IGLHRC is an excellent source of information on the status of same-sex marriage, civil unions, and domestic and registered partnerships in most countries of the world. Its reports can be found in the Press Room and Take Action sections of its Web sites.

Publications: Numerous newsletters, annual reports, facts sheets, statements, public presentations, and other resource materials.

International Lesbian and Gay Association (ILGA)
URL: http://www.ilga.org/

The International Lesbian and Gay Association was founded in 1978 to work for achieving equal rights for gay men and lesbians (and now bisexuals and transgendered persons) in all countries throughout the world. Today, it consists of more than 600 member organizations in 90 countries, ranging from small local groups to national organizations with thousands of members. ILGA holds an annual conference and a number of regional conferences. It has produced a number of reports on the status of LGBT people in various countries and regions of the world, as well as on specific topics, such as HIV/AIDS disease, homophobia, same-sex marriage, the worldwide legal status of same-sex relationships, workplace discrimination, and hate music. ILGA's News section on its Web sites contains useful information on the status of same-sex marriage in nations around the world. In a recent posting, the section had articles on same-sex marriage and other types of unions in the United States, Nepal, South Africa, Malawi, Mexico, Australia, and Russia.

Publications: See reports listed above.

Lambda Legal
URL: http://www.lambdalegal.org/

Lambda Legal is an organization devoted to achieving equal rights for LGBT persons by litigating cases, promoting public education programs, and advocating for appropriate public policy decisions. The organization has a national office in New York City and regional offices in Los Angeles, Dallas, Chicago, and Atlanta. Lambda Legal has been involved on some level or another in almost every major court case related to LGBT issues since its founding in 1973.

Publications: *Of Counsel; Of Counsel on Campus* (newsletters); *eNews* (online newsletter).

Log Cabin Republicans
URL: http://online.logcabin.org/

Log Cabin Republicans is an organization of gay and lesbian Republicans working to transform the Republican Party on issues of concern to them from inside the party. The organization maintains a full-time staff at its national headquarters in Washington, DC, and at its western field office in Sacramento, California, and has 44 chapters in 30 states. Log Cabin Republicans described themselves as "loyal Republicans" who subscribe to traditional party values, such as a strong national defense, individual liberty, individual responsibility, and a free-market economy. Although the organization is in agreement with most tenets and policies of the Republic Party, it holds very different views on some issues related to same-sex relationships. For example, it supports the right of same-sex couples to marry and to adopt children. In 2009, for example, the group strongly criticized President Barack Obama for failing to work for the repeal of the federal Defense of Marriage Act and for removing the current "don't ask, don't tell" policy for gay men and lesbians in the U.S. military.

Publication: *Inclusion Wins* (electronic newsletter).

Marriage Equality USA (MEUSA)
URL: http://www.marriageequality.org/

Marriage Equality USA was officially formed on Valentine's Day and National Freedom to Marry Day, February 12, 1998. The organization was created by a small group of gay and lesbian activists who believed that individuals of the same sex had the same right to marry as did any other American citizen. The organization has expanded to include chapters in Arizona, California, Florida, Indiana, Iowa, New Hampshire, Ohio, and Pennsylvania. MEUSA works with local groups to push for legislation legalizing same-sex marriage, and partners with plaintiffs in court cases challenging the limitation of marriage to opposite-sex couples. It sponsors a Same-Sex Wedding Expo in New York City at which gay and nongay vendors provide information about their services for same-sex weddings and other commitment ceremonies.

Publications: The MEUSA online shop carries a number of print and nonprint resources produced by other agencies, such as "Freedom to Marry" (DVD), "Tying the Knot" (DVD), *Why You Should Give a Damn about Gay Marriage* (book), "The Gay Marriage Thing" (DVD), and "Saving Marriage" (DVD).

National Center for Lesbian Rights (NCLR)
URL: http://www.nclrights.org/

The National Center for Lesbian Rights was founded in 1977 by lesbian attorneys Roberta Achtenberg and Donna Hitchens to work for the rights of LGBT persons. Each year the center provides legal services for about five thousand seniors, youth, immigrants, athletes, and other LGBT persons. The organization is also active in public advocacy and educational programs dealing with LBGT issues. It has been involved in all of the important court cases involving same-sex marriage and same-sex adoption heard in the United States.

Publications: Press releases, news announcements, and other media resources online.

National Gay and Lesbian Task Force (NGLTF)
URL: http://www.thetaskforce.org/

The National Gay and Lesbian Task Force focuses on a number of issues of special interest to gay men, lesbians, bisexuals, and transgendered people, including elections and politics, issues of aging, nondiscrimination, parenting and families, hate crimes, and HIV/AIDS. In addition to its national office in Washington, DC, it maintains regional offices in Cambridge, Massachusetts; Miami; New York City; Los Angeles; and Minneapolis. The NGLTF Policy Institute conducts research and issues periodic reports, issues maps, and fact sheets on a variety of topics related to the civil rights of LGBT people. The Task Force has issued a number of reports on same-sex marriage, civil unions, and domestic partnerships, and has been actively involved in state campaigns for the legalization of same-sex marriage and adoption and in opposition to proposed laws defining marriage strictly in heterosexual terms.

Publications: *Opening the Door to the Inclusion of Transgender People: The Nine Keys to Making Lesbian, Gay, Bisexual and Transgender Organizations Fully Transgender-Inclusive* (report); *Living in the Margins: A National Survey of Lesbian, Gay, Bisexual and Transgender Asian and Pacific Islander Americans* (report); *Same-Sex Marriage Initiatives and Lesbian, Gay and Bisexual Voters in the 2006 Elections* (report); *Policy Priorities in the Lesbian, Gay, Bisexual and Transgender Community* (report).

National Lesbian and Gay Law Association (NLGLA)
URL: http://www.lgbtbar.org/

The National Lesbian and Gay Law Association was founded at the 1987 March on Washington for lesbian and gay rights. Within two years, the new organization had adopted a set of by-laws, held its first Lavender Law conference in San Francisco, and added 239 paid members to its roles. In 1992, NLGLA became an official affiliate of the American Bar Association (ABA). Its current activities in promoting equal treatment of all persons regardless of sexual orientation are carried out in cooperation with the ABA's Section on Individual Rights and Responsibilities and its Committee on Sexual Orientation and Gender Identity.

Publications: Monthly electronic newsletter.

National Organization for Women (NOW)
URL: http://www.now.org/

The National Organization for Women was founded in 1966 by a group of 28 women led by Betty Friedan as a mechanism by which they could work for the civil rights of women. The organization now claims a membership of more than half a million contributing members in five hundred chapters in all 50 states and the District of Columbia. It lists its six top priorities as of 2010 as abortion rights and reproductive issues, violence against women, constitutional equality, promoting diversity and ending racism, lesbian rights, and economic justice. NOW also lists 21 other important issues in which it is interested, including family and family law, marriage equality, immigration, women-friendly workplace, and young feminist programs. The organization devotes an extended Web page on the topic of same-sex marriage that includes talking points on the issue, NOW conference resolutions, fact sheets, and updated information on the status of same-sex marriage nationally and in various states.

Publications: Clothing, gifts, bumper stickers, buttons, and DVDs ("Hollywood's Smoke and Mirrors" and "Redefining Liberation").

New Family Social (NFS)
URL: http://www.newfamilysocial.co.uk/

New Family Social is an English agency organized to provide information about and support for same-sex couples who wish to adopt. The organization was formed in 2007, two years after same-sex adoption became legal in the United Kingdom. The purpose of the organization is to provide assistance for same-sex couples who are thinking about adopting a child, are in the process of adopting a child, or who have already adopted a child and have questions or need support in these procedures. The NFS Web site provides useful information on the basics of same-sex adoption, links to a number of same-sex adoption agencies and organizations in the United Kingdom, a page for sharing information and experiences, and access to the organization's library.

Publications: None.

Our Family Coalition (OFC)
URL: http://www.ourfamily.org/

Our Family Coalition is based in the San Francisco Bay area and consists of about 750 same-sex couples and their families, educators, caregivers, children, youth, and others. The wide variety of programs offered by the group includes social events, school advocacy programs, peer support groups, parent educational programs, social justice campaigns, training sessions for medical and social service agencies, and fiscal assistance programs. OFC's Web site provides links to a number of relevant state and national organizations interested in same-sex adoption and families.

Publications: *Our Family Coalition Newsletter; Best of the Gay* (family resource guide); handouts and reports, such as "Our Families—Attributes of Gay Area LGBTQ Families" and "Quick Facts"; posters on "Family Values"; and program materials for educational workshops.

Parents, Families & Friends of Lesbians & Gays (PFLAG)
URL: http://community.pflag.org/

Parents, Families & Friends of Lesbians & Gays is a nonprofit organization of more than 200,000 members and supporters with over five hundred chapters in the United States. It operates out of a national office in Washington, DC, and 13 regional offices. PFLAG has six strategic goals that focus on building an organization strong enough to carry out its objectives: creating a world in which young people can grow up without fear of violence or discrimination; ending the isolation of gay men, lesbians, bisexuals, and transgendered people; working for the inclusion of people of all gender orientations in all religious faiths; eliminating prejudice and discrimination in the workplace; and achieving full civil rights and equality for all gay men, lesbians, bisexuals, and transgendered persons. PFLAG issued its first statement in support of equality in marriage in 2000 and has continued to work for marriage equality ever since. Most recently it was involved in the writing of three briefs for presentation to the New York state senate in its consideration of the legalization of same-sex marriage in the state. The organization has also spoken out in support of and worked for the adoption of rules recognizing equal rights for adoption by same-sex couples.

Publications: The PFLAG Web site lists a number of press releases, "tools for journalists," "hot topics," and articles about PFLAG in the news.

Stonewall
URL: http://www.stonewall.org.uk/

Stonewall is a British organization formed in 1989 in response to the adoption of Section 28 of the Local Government Act, prohibiting the "promotion of homosexuality" in schools. A number of gay men and lesbians were outraged at the stigmatizing of same-sex relationships and decided to create an organization that would work toward overturning this legislation and promoting equal rights of lesbians and gay men in the United Kingdom. Since 1989, the organization has been extraordinarily successful, contributing to changes in the nation's age-of-consent laws, elimination of the ban against gay men and lesbians' serving in the military, passage of same-sex adoption legislation, the repeal of Section 28 (in 2003), nondiscrimination in economic transactions (the Equality Act of 2007), and recent passage of domestic partnership legislation. Stonewall currently has offices in England, Scotland, and Wales. The organization is an invaluable source of information about the status of same-sex civil partnerships in the United Kingdom. The "At Home" section of its Web site includes a number of articles on the battle over approval of civil partnerships and the current status of that entity in the United Kingdom.

Publications: Ebulletin (online newsletter); numerous press releases.

Stonewall Democrats
URL: http://www.stonewalldemocrats.org/

Stonewall Democrats is a political organization affiliated with the national Democratic Party founded by Representative Barney Frank (D-MA) in 1998. The organization's name is taken from the famous Stonewall riots of 1969 that mark the beginning of the modern gay and lesbian rights movement. A number of independent gay and lesbian Democratic groups existed throughout the United States prior to 1998, but Frank saw the potential of unifying the efforts of all those groups in a national organization. Today there are nearly one hundred affiliates in virtually every state of the union and the District of Columbia. Members of these local clubs are involved in a variety of activities typical of traditional political organizations, including envelope stuffing, door-to-door solicitations, telephone calling, get-out-the-vote campaigns, and running for office. Stonewall Democrats are involved in essentially all political issues of interest to gay men and lesbians, including the U.S. military "don't ask, don't tell" discharge policy; equality in housing and employment; the 2009–10 health care bill; and the advancement of same-sex marriage, civil unions, and domestic partnerships in the United States.

Publications: Press releases at "Newsroom" page of Web site.

Unid@s, the National Latina/o Lesbian, Gay, Bisexual & Transgender Human Rights Organization
URL: http://www.unidoslgbt.org/

Unid@s, the National Latina/o Lesbian, Gay, Bisexual & Transgender Human Rights Organization, was founded in 2007 as a replacement for an earlier Latino organization, National Latina/o Lesbian Gay, Bisexual, and Transgender Organization, often known as LLEGÓ, which disbanded in 2004. At the time of its founding, Unid@s also consolidated with the National Latino/a Coalition for Justice, an organization working for marriage equality among people of all sexual orientations. In its early phases, Unid@s is developing plans to become a multi-issue organization with strong emphasis on local activism on issues of concern to lesbian, gay, bisexual, and transgendered Latina/os.

Publications: Online news at Web site.

Williams Institute at the University of California at Los Angeles School of Law
URL: http://www.law.ucla.edu/williamsinstitute/home.html

The Williams Institute is a national think tank concerned with legal aspects of issues of interest to lesbians, gay men, bisexuals, and transgendered persons. The institute carries out its objectives by conducting research; authoring public policy studies and law review articles; providing amicus curiae briefs for important court cases; offering expert testimony at legislative hearings; and training lawyers, judges, and other members of the legal protection as well as the general public. In 2006, the institute absorbed the Institute for Gay and Lesbian Strategic Studies, another think tank with objectives similar to those of the Williams Institute. Same-sex marriage and similar unions are among the primary topics of interest for researchers at the Williams Institute. Some reports they have produced include *Same-Sex Couples and the Gay, Lesbian, Bisexual Population: New Estimates from the American Community Survey; Federal Estate Tax Disadvantages for Same-Sex Couples; Same-Sex Spouses and Unmarried Partners in the American Community Survey, 2008;* and *The Impact of Inequalities for Same-Sex Partners in Employer-Sponsored Retirement Plans.*

Publications: *The Dukeminier Awards Best Sexual Orientation and Gender Identity Law Review Articles of 2008* (monthly journal; date changes annually); *Adoption and Foster Care by Gay and Lesbian Parents in the United States* (report); *The Impact of Extending Marriage to Same-Sex Couples on the New Jersey Budget* (report; similar reports available for California, Iowa, Oregon, New Mexico, Maryland, and other states); *Unequal Taxes on Equal Benefits: The Taxation of Domestic Partner Benefits* (report).

Organizations Opposed to Same-Sex Marriage

Alliance Defense Fund (ADF)
URL: http://www.alliancedefensefund.org/main/default.aspx
The Alliance Defense Fund was formed in 1994 by a group of 35 ministers who were concerned about the loss of religious freedom in the United States. The organization's work is currently organized under three major issues topics: sanctity of life (right-to-life issues), traditional family (same-sex marriage issues), and religious freedom (actions against expression of religious beliefs). The organization has been active in providing funding, legal advice, and leadership training in campaigns against same-sex marriage, civil unions, and domestic partnerships in many states. Some of the Fund's work is carried out through subsidiary and affiliate organizations, such as the Community Defense Council (formerly the National Family Legal Foundation), the Corporate Research Council, and DOMA Watch, described as "your legal source for Defense of Marriage Act information."

Publications: Videos and audio clips available online at Web site.

Alliance for Marriage (AFM)
URL: http://www.allianceformarriage.org/

Alliance for Marriage is a 501(c)(3) nonprofit organization working to promote the traditional marriage pattern between one man and one woman. It focuses on efforts to educate the general public, the media, elected officials, and civil society leaders with regard to the benefits of traditional marriage for adults, children, and the society at large. Its current fields of interest are promotion of adoption among heterosexual families, reducing the number of fatherless families, encouragement of stay-at-home parents, improving tax benefits for traditional families, and welfare reform.

Publications: *Not Married to the Job* (report); numerous news clippings, articles, and articles online at Web site.

American Center for Law and Justice (ACLJ)
URL: http://www.aclj.org/

The American Center for Law and Justice was founded in 1990 to work for the constitutional and religious freedom of all Americans. Today, ACLJ has extended its interests to other parts of the world and provides expertise in American Constitutional law, European Union law, and human rights law. It has been active in opposing the extension of marriage and marriage rights to same-sex couples. Attorneys for ACLJ have worked on a number of state cases involving same-sex marriage, have testified before the U.S. Congress on the Federal Marriage Amendment, and have issued a number of press releases and fact sheets on the subject of same-sex marriage.

Publications: Numerous online resources at Web site, including sections on "ACLJ Commentaries"; "ACLJ Spotlight"; "In the Courts"; "In the News"; "On the Issues"; "Trial Notebook"; "Washington Report"; and "Litigation Report."

American Family Association (AFA)
URL: http://action.afa.net/

The American Family Association is a nonprofit 501(c3) organization founded in 1977 by Donald E. Wildmon, a minister at the First United Methodist Church in Southaven, Mississippi. The organization was originally called the National Federation for Decency, but was given its new name in 1988. The purpose of the organization is to promote an agenda that is based on a literal reading of the Bible as a guide to all social and political action in the United States. Its work focuses on preservation of marriage and the family, promotion of decency and morality, working for the sanctity of human life, and ensuring the integrity of the public media. One of its major campaigns is the effort to ensure that same-sex marriage is not legalized. Over the past few years, it has made available online a petition to be delivered to the U.S. Congress listing the names of individuals who support their position in this regard (NoGayMarriage.com).

Publications: *American Family Association Journal; AFA Action Alert* (newsletter); books, pamphlets, audio programs, video programs, electronic resources, such as "It's Not Gay" (DVD); "How to Take Back America Conference" (DVDs); and "The Lost and Found Family" (DVD).

Christian Coalition of America (CC)
URL: http://www.cc.org/

The Christian Coalition of America was founded in 1989 in order to provide a stronger voice for conservative Christians in the American political system. For many years, it was a powerful voice in shaping the policies of the Republican Party, although its influence appears to have waned considerably in the last decade. Although it claims to speak for more than two million Americans, some evidence suggests that its current active membership is closer to about thirty thousand individuals. Among the issues in which CC is currently most interested are the election and appointment of more conservative judges; ensuring the accessibility of the Internet for groups of all political persuasions, including the Christian Coalition; protecting religious programming on television; preventing approval of the federal government for stem cell research; and advancement of the Federal Marriage Amendment, which prohibits same-sex marriage.

Publications: *Washington Weekly Review* (newsletter); numerous press releases; OneNewsNow.com (online news releases).

Church of Jesus Christ of Latter-day Saints (Mormon Church)
URL: http://www.lds.org/ldsorg/

Although almost all Christian denominations are opposed to same-sex marriage and to many other features of the lesbian and gay rights movement, the Church of Jesus Christ of Latter-day Saints (LDS) has been especially active politically in working against these issues. During the November 2008 initiative on Proposition 8, for example, the church was the largest single financial donor to the "Yes on 8" (supporting a constitutional ban on same-sex marriage in the state of California) campaign, donating more than $5 million for the campaign. According to one proponent of the ban, the church also provided between 80 and 90 percent of the volunteers who walked door-to-door during the campaign. The church's Web site contains much more information on its stand on same-sex marriage and related issues.

Publications: A very large selection of books, booklets, pamphlets, and other reading materials, as well as electronic publications on a variety of topics; a number of regular magazines, including *Ensign*, a general publication for adults; *New Era*, a similar publication for youth; *Friend*, a magazine for children; *Liahona*, a publication intended for international readers; and *Church News*, a weekly publication.

Concerned Women for America (CWA)
URL: http://www.cwfa.org/

Concerned Women for America was founded in 1979 by Beverly LaHaye, whose husband, Timothy, was one of the founders of the Christian Coalition. Mrs. LaHaye established the organization in response to pronouncements and activities of the National Organization for Women that, she felt, did not reflect the views of many women in America. Today, CWA's activities focus on six major areas: family (one-man, one-woman marriages), sanctity of life (antiabortion), education (support of private schooling), pornography, religious liberty, and national sovereignty.

Publications: "What Your Teacher Didn't Tell You about Abstinence"; "How to Lobby From Your Home"; "Political Guidelines for Churches and Pastors"; "Pro-Life Action Guide"; "A Painful Choice: Abortion's Link to Breast Cancer"; "Why Children Need Fathers: Five Critical Trends"; "The Grab for Power: A Chronology of the National Education Association" (pamphlets and brochures; available online at Web site).

Ethics & Religious Liberty Commission (ERLC) of the Southern Baptist Convention
URL: http://erlc.com/

The Ethics & Religious Liberty Commission is the public policy arm of the Southern Baptist Convention. Its mission is to address social and ethical issues of interest to Southern Baptists and to consider their implications on public policy at all levels of government, from local city halls to the U.S. Congress. The overarching topics in which ERLC is interested are faith, family, life, citizenship, and science, with emphasis on a number of more specific issues, such as apologetics, pastoral integrity, children, marriage, pop culture, abortion, bioethics, birth control, stem cell research, capital punishment, immigration, race relations, war, cloning, and homosexuality. The commission has taken strong stands against same-sex marriage and related legal institutions. In May 2005, it published the Nashville Declaration on "Same-Sex Marriage," which states that the "Baptist Faith and Mission" states unequivocally that "[m]arriage is the uniting of one man and one woman in covenant commitment for a lifetime." The commission has organized and promoted a number of specific actions in opposition to the approval of same-sex unions. In May 2006, for example, the ERLC asked Baptist churches across the nation to observe Marriage Protection Sunday on June 4 of that year, suggesting that pastors preach on the topic and that church members write their senators asking them to support the Marriage Protection Amendment then being considered.

Publications: Articles on a number of topics of interest to ERLC, as well as feeds and podcasts of the commission's regular radio broadcasts.

Family Research Council (FRC)
URL: http://www.frc.org/

The Family Research Council was founded in 1983 to promote the traditional family and traditional marriage. It pursues its work through a number of venues, including books, pamphlets, and other kinds of publications; testimony before a variety of legislative bodies; analysis and review of legal and policy documents with the potential for impacting marriage and the family; and appearances in public debates and discussions.

Publications: Press releases, op-eds, and blog available online at Web site.

Focus on the Family
URL: http://www.focusonthefamily.com/

Focus on the Family is a Christian organization that attempts to follow biblical principles in nurturing and defending the (heterosexual) family. It generally tends to oppose any definition of the family other than one consisting of one man, one woman, and one or more children. The guiding principles under which the organization operates is the preeminence of an evangelical interpretation of the Bible, the importance of a permanent marriage between one man and one woman, the value of children to a family, the sanctity of human life, the importance of social responsibility, and the confirmation of clearly defined male and female roles in a family.

Publications: *Citizen* magazine; the organization's primary news and issue analysis outlet is the Web site CitizenLink at http://www.citizenlink.org/citizenmag/.

Heritage Foundation
URL: http://www.heritage.org/

The Heritage Foundation is a conservative think tank founded in 1973 to work for a strong national defense, individual freedom, limited government, traditional American values, and the advancement of free enterprise. The organization does research on and takes positions on a vast number of issues on both the domestic and international level. Some of the domestic issues with which it is currently concerned are American political thought, crime, the economy, education, energy and the environment, family and marriage, the federal budget and spending, government reform of health care, immigration, labor, and regulation. It has taken a strong stance against same-sex marriage, arguing that it leads to the breakdown of traditional families and that "when marriages break down, communities break down." In November 2009, the foundation issued a report suggesting that same-sex marriage was one of the nation's current "dirty dozen" policies that was undermining civil society in the United States.

Publications: Commentaries, news releases, and updates on "hot" topics available online at Web site.

Institute for Marriage and Public Policy (IMAPP)
URL: http://www.marriagedebate.com/

The Institute for Marriage and Public Policy is a nonprofit, nonpartisan organization that works to promote discussion on important issues relating to marriage, with the overall goal of strengthening that institution in American society. IMAPP focuses on issues such as adoption, divorce reform, same-sex marriage, tax policy, and unwed pregnancies.

Publications: Articles, policy briefs, community brochures, and model legislation available online at Web site.

Liberty Counsel
URL: http://www.lc.org/

Liberty Counsel was founded in 1989 to provide free legal assistance to individuals and organizations in defense of Christian religious liberty, the sanctity of human life, and the protection of traditional (i.e., opposite-sex) marriage. The organization is closely affiliated with Liberty University, in Lynchburg, Virginia, founded by Jerry Falwell to promote Christian values in the process of providing opportunities in higher education. Some notable cases in which the organization has been involved include representing the placement of a Ten Commandments monument on public grounds in Tennessee, the limits of protests permitted at public abortion clinics, and the use of public facilities to conduct Bible study classes in a public school. Liberty Counsel has assisted organizations in efforts to prevent same-sex marriage from becoming law and in promoting so-called "defense of marriage" legislation and constitutional amendments.

Publications: "The Liberator" (monthly newsletter); frequent news releases on special topics, such as "Game Over for ACLU's War Against Santa Rosa County Students," "Pediatricians Set the Facts Straight about Sexual Orientation and Gender Confusion," "Personhood Amendment Qualified for Mississippi's November 2011 Ballot," "Homeland Security Raid of Religious Tracts Violates Fourth Amendment," and "Liberty University Files Lawsuit Against the Government Takeover of Healthcare."

Marriage Law Project (MLP)
URL: http://www.marriagewatch.org/

The Marriage Law Project is a program of the Interdisciplinary Program in Law and Religion of Columbus School of Law at the Catholic University of America in Washington, DC. It works to reaffirm the traditional view of marriage as being between one man and one woman by carrying out research, publishing helpful information, sponsoring conferences, offering pro bono legal advice, taking part in important legal cases, and advising policy makers.

Publications: Headline news; "hot topics"; and background information on many topics available online at Web site.

National Organization for Marriage (NOM)
URL: http://www.nationformarriage.org/

The National Organization for Marriage is a 501(c)(4) nonprofit organization founded in 2007 for the purpose of working against the legalization of same-sex marriage and comparable relationships and for the protection of religious organizations that oppose such arrangements. The president of NOM is also president of the Institute for Marriage and Public Policy (see above). NOM works to provide a national resource for the many groups working against same-sex marriage throughout the nation by developing political messages, building a database of supporters, providing political intelligence for state and local groups, and building a financial infrastructure for the support of anti-gay-marriage activities. Its online Advocacy Center provides an opportunity for supporters to become actively involved in state issues, which, as of early 2010, included campaigns in Delaware, Iowa, New Jersey, New York, Rhode Island, the District of Columbia, and the 23rd New York House of Representatives district, as well as ongoing support for the Defense of Marriage Act.

Publications: Online press releases.

Renew America
URL: http://www.renewamerica.com

Renew America is an organization founded in 2002 by Alan Keyes to promote the concept that Americans must return to the principles enunciated by the Founding Fathers in the Declaration of Independence and the Constitution if it is to survive as a nation. The organization claims to be nonpartisan and nondenominational, although its Web site takes a very strong evangelical Christian stand in support of its efforts. Its Web page on "Positions and Policies" talks at length about the importance and meaning of being converted to Jesus Christ. Although the organization has apparently taken no official stance on same-sex marriage, it has published a number of articles opposing the legalization of such marriages on its "Columns" page at http://www.renewamerica.com/columns.php.

Publications: None.

Stand4Marriage
URL: http://www.stand4marriagedc.com/

Stand4Marriage is a coalition of organizations and private citizens in the District of Colombia who are opposed to the District council's decision to grant same-sex marriage rights to citizens of the District. The organization was founded by a group of mostly religious leaders, including Bishop Harry Jackson; Robert King, an Advisory Neighborhood Commissioner; Reverend Dale Wafer; Bishop James Silver; Reverend Anthony Evans; Reverend Melvin Dupree; Elder Howard Butler; and Reverend Walter Fauntroy. In September 2009, the group filed an initiative petition with the District Board of Elections, requesting that a public vote be held on the District council's actions in approving same-sex marriage. In its statement of principles, the group explains that it is committed to "the good of marriage as the union of one husband with one wife."

Publications: None.

Traditional Values Coalition
URL: http://www.traditionalvalues.org/

The Traditional Values Coalition was founded in 1980 by Louis P. Sheldon to "empower people of faith through knowledge." The organization currently claims to speak for more than forty-three thousand churches from virtually every Christian denomination and every racial and socioeconomic status. Among the issues of primary concern to the Coalition are same-sex marriage, abortion rights, rights of transgendered persons, abstinence in sex education, and anti-Christian bigotry.

Publications: *50-State Survey of Marriage Protection Amendments; A Gender Identity Disorder Goes Mainstream; A Report on the San Diego 'Gay Pride' Parade and Festival in San Diego, July 29, 2006; Abstinence and Fidelity in Marriage Are Keys to Global AIDS Battle* (special reports); press releases, action alerts, editorials, church bulletin inserts available online at Website.

United States Conference of Catholic Bishops (USCCB)
URL: http://www.usccb.org/

The United States Conference of Catholic Bishops traces its history to 1917 when the hierarchy of the Roman Catholic church in the

United States established the National Catholic War Council to provide a mechanism by which Catholics could provide funds for the war and offer personnel services for men and women serving in the military. That effort evolved over time into other types of agencies that allowed Catholics to pursue lay activities consistent with their religious beliefs, including the National Welfare Council in 1919 and the National Welfare Conference in 1922. The current organization was established in 1966 as two separate organizations, the National Conference of Catholic Bishops and the United States Catholic Conference, which were merged into the USCCB in 2001. The conference has consistently been one of the strongest opponents of same-sex marriages in the United States. It bases its position on the belief that marriage is not a civil institution, but a religious tradition created by God that cannot be changed by human actions. The organization has been at the forefront of state campaigns over same-sex marriage and is generally credited with being primarily responsible for the defeat of the same-sex initiatives in Maine and New York State in 2009. It has also stated its opposition to any form of immigration reform legislation that includes equal protection for lesbians and gay men.

Publications: Many books, brochures, pamphlets, prayer cards, DVDs, and videos dealing with topics such as leadership, life and human dignity, liturgy and prayer, marriage and family, migration and refuge services, official teachings, religious education, and social justice issues. Examples include *Marriage: Love and Life in the Divine Plan; Between Man and Woman: Questions and Answers about Marriage and Same-Sex Unions; Ministry to Persons with a Homosexual Inclination: Guidelines for Pastoral Care;* and *Putting Children and Families First: A Challenge for Our Church, Nation, and World.*

Organizations with an Interest in Marriage, but Who Are Neutral about Same-Sex Marriage

Alternatives to Marriage Project (AMP)
URL: http://www.unmarried.org/

The Alternatives to Marriage Project is a 501(c)(3) nonprofit organization formed to meet the needs of individuals, couples, and groups who are not in opposite-sex marriages. Its target audience includes people who are single, who choose not to marry, who are not allowed legally to marry, or who choose to live together before marriage. The organization was founded in 1998 by Marshall Miller and Dorian Solot, a couple who have been in a committed, long-term, unmarried relationship. AMP works not only to provide information and support for unmarried individuals, but also to educate the general public about the nature of unmarried relationships and the validation that people in such circumstances deserve. Among the specific issues with which the organization is currently concerned are health care, housing, adoption, federal income tax policy, immigration, welfare issues, and voting opportunities.

Publications: "Alternatives to Marriage Project Update" (newsletter).

American Association for Marriage and Family Therapy (AAMFT)
URL: http://www.aamft.org/

The American Association for Marriage and Family Therapy was founded in 1942 as the professional organization of marriage and family therapists. The association currently claims to have twenty-four thousand members worldwide. Its purpose is to promote scholarly research in the field of marriage and family therapy, to educate the general public about important issues in these fields, and to ensure that an adequate number of well-trained practitioners is available to meet the public's need for aid and assistance. The organization sponsors a national training conference, publishes material dealing with issues in the field, and produces a variety of multimedia products for practitioners in marriage and family therapy.

Publications: *Journal of Marital and Family Therapy; Family Therapy Magazine; Clinical Updates for Family Therapists: Research and Treatment Approaches for Issues Affecting Today's Families* (reports); *Family Therapy Effectiveness* (book); and numerous other books, brochures, reports, monographs, and DVDs.

National Marriage Project (NMP)
URL: http://www.virginia.edu/marriageproject/

The National Marriage Project was founded at Rutgers University in 1997. In the summer of 2009, the program was moved to the

University of Virginia, which now serves as its sponsor. The project is a nonpartisan, nonsectarian, interdisciplinary program whose purpose it is to conduct research and analysis on the status of marriage in the United States. It also focuses on the social and cultural forces that act on marriage and strategies for improving the stability and quality of marriage in this country. The three primary areas of research at NMP currently are organized under the rubrics of "The Foundations of Marital Quality and Stability," "The State of Our Unions," and "Religion and Marriage among African Americans and Latinos."

Publications: A variety of books, monographs, journal articles, and annual and special reports, such as "Life without Children," "Cohabitation, Marriage, and Child Wellbeing," "The State of Our Unions," and "Making a Love Connection: Teen Relationships, Pregnancy, and Marriage."

8

Resources

The issues of same-sex marriage are relatively new topics of debate in the United States and a number of countries around the world. Still, these debates have inspired a flood of books, articles, reports, commentaries, editorials, and other expressions of opinion. This chapter provides annotated reviews of some of the most important of those documents. The resources listed here are divided into two major sections, print and nonprint items, the latter primarily Web sites on the Internet. Within each of these major sections, items are further subdivided according to the primary subject with which an book, article, or Web site deals: history, gay and lesbian rights issues in general, arguments in favor of same-sex marriage, arguments in opposition to same-sex marriage, and general articles dealing with the topic of same-sex marriage. Finally, resources are subdivided further by format, books or articles in the case of print materials, and Internet sources in the case of nonprint sources.

Print

History
Books
Boswell, John. *Same-Sex Unions in Premodern Europe*. New York: Vintage Books, 1995.

Boswell's exhaustive study of the literature of medieval Europe provides convincing evidence that same-sex unions, especially within religious communities, were widespread and widely accepted by both the church and the lay public.

Coontz, Stephanie. *Marriage, a History: From Obedience to Intimacy, or How Love Conquered Marriage*. New York: Viking Adult, 2005.

Discussions of same-sex marriage today are almost universally framed within a meaning of traditional marriage that is not, in fact, traditional at all. Coontz reviews the history of the evolution of marriage, showing how it has changed in form and meaning over the centuries so that it is difficult to talk with any specificity at all about a concept such as "traditional marriage."

Gozemba, Patricia A., and Karen Kahn. *Courting Equality: A Documentary History of America's First Legal Same-Sex Marriages*. Boston: Beacon Press, 2007.

This richly illustrated volume provides a superb historical background of the history behind the first legalization of same-sex marriages in the United States.

Herdt, Gilbert H. *Ritualized Homosexuality in Melanesia*. Berkeley: University of California Press, 1993.

The eight essays in this book present a strikingly original view of the role of homosexual behavior in Melanesia, with substantial evidence of the practice of unions between two individuals of the same sex.

Hinsch, Bret. *Passions of the Cut Sleeve: The Male Homosexual Tradition in China*. Berkeley: University of California Press, 1992.

This book reviews the evidence available about the long tradition of same-sex relationships in China, with some discussion of formalized relationships between two individuals of the same sex.

Jordan, Mark D. *Blessing Same-Sex Unions: The Perils of Queer Romance and the Confusions of Christian Marriage*. Chicago: University of Chicago Press, 2005.

The author provides an exhaustive review of Christian doctrine and tradition with regard to same-sex relationships and concludes that marriage of any kind was strongly opposed by the early church, so that same-sex marriage was not that much of an issue. He considers the significance of this history and theological background for the modern-day debate over same-sex marriage.

Merin, Yuval. *Equality for Same-Sex Couples: The Legal Recognition of Gay Partnerships in Europe and the United States*. Chicago: University of Chicago Press, 2002.

The author provides one of the very few detailed descriptions and analysis of the evolution of legalized same-sex relationships in nations around the world. The information is now somewhat dated because of the rapid rate at which this situation has changed, but the historical perspective provided by the book is valuable.

Neill, James. *The Origins and Role of Same-Sex Relations in Human Societies*. Jefferson, NC: McFarland & Company, 2009.

The author suggests that the dominant traditional idea that all unions between individuals is heterosexual may be incomplete or false in many instances. He reviews the evidence for various types of same-sex unions in ancient Greece, Rome, early Christian societies, Japan, China, and Islam.

Vanita, Ruth. *Love's Rite: Same-Sex Marriage in India and the West*. New York: Palgrave Macmillan, 2005.

The author provides an extensive review not only of the current status of same-sex relationships in India today, but also of the long traditions with respect to same-sex relationships in the Indian subcontinent.

Vanita, Ruth, and Saleem Kidwai, eds. *Same-Sex Love in India: Readings from Literature and History*. New York: Palgrave Macmillan, 2001.

The book provides a rich and extensive collection of articles about same-sex love and same-sex relationships going back to classic Indian history.

Articles
Eskridge, William N. "A History of Same-Sex Marriage." *Virginia Law Review* 79 (7, October 1993): 1419–1513.

The author provides an extensive review of the history of various types of same-sex unions in a variety of cultures throughout human history. This article is one of the most valuable resources on the topic.

Forbes, Jack D. "What Is Marriage? A Native American View." *Wind Speaker* 22 (2, May 1, 2004): 27. Also available online at http://westgatehouse.com/art161.html.

The author is professor emeritus of Native American Studies at the University of California at Davis. He takes note of the fact that the current debate over same-sex marriage often refers to the "American tradition" about legal relationships, but that this term is a misnomer, since the real "American tradition" is that which comes from Native American culture. In that regard, "marriage" has traditionally had a much more complex and inclusive meaning than that currently used by opponents of same-sex marriage.

Goldberg, Suzanne B. "A Historical Guide to the Future of Marriage for Same-Sex Couples." *Columbia Journal of Gender and Law* 15 (1, January 2006): 249–54.

The author notes that opponents of same-sex marriage today commonly call upon the precedent of the long history of "traditional marriage." She argues that these "superficial references" will "not suffice" to deal with the complex question as to the historical nature of legal relationships between two individuals, whether of the same or opposite sex.

Gay and Lesbian Civil Rights Issues
Books
Adam, Barry D. *The Rise of a Gay and Lesbian Movement*, revised edition. Boston: Twayne Publishers, 1995.

Adam's book is especially strong in its coverage of the international gay and lesbian rights movement. He does a thorough job of reviewing the early movements in Germany and the United States, along with the reactions that developed to those movements. But he also provides sketches of changes taking place in Canada, Mexico, Europe, and other parts of the world.

Alsenas, Linas. *Gay America: Struggle for Equality*. New York: Amulet Books, 2008.

The author provides a review of some of the most important events in the history of the gay and lesbian rights movement in the United States from the Colonial period to the present day.

Bullough, Vern, ed. *Before Stonewall: Activists for Gay and Lesbian Rights in Historical Context*. New York: Harrington Park Press, 2002.

This collection of articles tells the story of the gay and lesbian movement in the United States and other countries from its earliest beginnings through biographical sketches of some of the most important individuals involved in the movement.

D'Emilio, John. *Sexual Politics, Sexual Communities: The Making of a Homosexual Minority in the United States, 1940–1970*. Chicago: University of Chicago Press, 1983.

Many people think that the modern gay and lesbian civil rights movement began with the Stonewall riots of 1969. D'Emilio shows, however, that a small but vigorous movement existed at least two decades before Stonewall. He presents an interesting and thoroughly researched review of the origins of the Mattachine Society, the Daughters of Bilitis, and other early gay and lesbian groups.

Duberman, Martin. *About Time: Exploring the Gay Past*, revised and expanded edition, 1991.

Distinguished Professor of History Emeritus at Lehman College and the Graduate School of the City University of New York, Duberman is one of the finest writers on gay topics in the world. This volume collects a number of his own essays with a selection of historical writings dating to 1826. See especially Part Two of the book, containing essays dealing with the gay liberation and gay rights movement.

Duberman, Martin. *Stonewall*. New York: Dutton, 1993.

In this book, Duberman describes and analyzes the events that occurred on June 27 and 28, 1969, during the Stonewall riots in New York City. He uses stories of the lives of four gay men and two lesbians to tell his tale.

Duberman, Martin, Martha Vincus, and George Chauncey Jr., eds. *Hidden from History: Reclaiming the Gay and Lesbian Past*. New York: New American Library, 1989.

This collection of essays surveys the history of homosexual behavior from the ancient world to the late twentieth century. Major sections of the book deal with preindustrial societies, the nineteenth century, the early twentieth century, and World War II and the postwar era. The book provides an excellent background for the modern gay liberation gay rights movements.

Dugan, Kimberly B. *The Struggle over Gay, Lesbian, and Bisexual Rights: Facing Off in Cincinnati.* New York: Routledge, 2005.

Dugan offers a detailed analysis of the 1993 vote in Cincinnati, Ohio, over the legal status of gay men and lesbians as a protected minority. In that election, voters overwhelmingly adopted an ordinance prohibiting the city from extending protection in housing, employment, and public accommodation to gays and lesbians.

Eisenbach, David. *Gay Power: An American Revolution.* Cambridge, MA: De Capo Books, 2006.

Eisenbach discusses changes that took place in New York City over the past half century to illustrate the growth and development of the gay and lesbian rights movement. He bases his book on a number of interviews with men and women involved in that movement as well as on archival materials from the period.

Endean, Steve. *Bringing Lesbian and Gay Rights into the Mainstream: Twenty Years of Progress.* Edited by Vicki L. Eaklor. New York: Harrington Park Press, 2006.

Endean was involved in the gay and lesbian rights movement for more than two decades. His memoir provides a comprehensive and powerful review of changes that have taken place in the movement during that period of time.

Eskridge, William N., Jr. *Dishonorable Passions: Sodomy Laws in America, 1861–2003.* New York: Viking Press, 2008.

The debate over gay and lesbian rights has a long history in the United States, dating back to Colonial days. In this book, Eskridge focuses on the issue of antisodomy laws, finally resolved by the U.S. Supreme Court in its 2003 decision in *Lawrence v. Texas.*

Fejes, Fred. *Gay Rights and Moral Panic: The Origins of America's Debate on Homosexuality.* New York: Palgrave Macmillan, 2008.

Some of the seminal battles over gay and lesbian rights took place in the late 1970s, especially in Dade County and Miami, Florida; St. Paul, Minnesota; Eugene, Oregon; and Wichita, Kansas. This book discusses and analyzes these battles and considers their influence on the national discussion about legal issues related to homosexual behavior.

Fetner, Tina. *How the Religious Right Shaped Lesbian and Gay Activism*. Minneapolis: University of Minnesota Press, 2008.

Most people probably think of religious groups and gay and lesbian civil rights groups as political adversaries and, to a very considerable extent, they are. At the same time, the actions and positions taken by both groups also shape the philosophies and strategies of the other group. Fetner's book provides a fascinating analysis of the symbiotic relationship between these two political forces.

Gallo, Marcia M. *Different Daughters: A History of the Daughters of Bilitis and the Rise of the Lesbian Rights Movement*. Berkeley, CA: Seal Press, 2006.

The author discusses the formation and activities of the earliest lesbian rights movement in the United States, the Daughters of Bilitis.

Marcus, Eric. *Making Gay History: The Half-Century Fight for Lesbian and Gay Equal Rights*. New York: Harper Perennial, 2002.

This review of the history of the gay and lesbian rights movements is divided into seven chronological periods, pre-1950, 1950–61, 1961–68, 1986–73, 1973–81, 1981–92, and 1992–2001. The author relies on a large number of interviews with gay men, lesbians, and nongay and nonlesbians who had a part in the movement during each period.

Mucciaroni, Gary. *Same Sex, Different Politics: Success and Failure in the Struggles over Gay Rights*. Chicago: University of Chicago Press, 2008.

The battle over equal rights for lesbians and gay men has taken place in a number of different fields: military service, civil rights, hate crimes, marriage, and adoption, to mention some of the most important. The gay and lesbian rights movement has had different degrees of success in each of these fields. The author attempts to analyze the reason for these differing levels of accomplishment.

Smith, Miriam. *Political Institutions and Lesbian and Gay Rights in the United States and Canada.* New York: Routledge, 2009.

This book is part of the Routledge Studies in North American Politics. It examines the ways in which political institutions in the United States and Canada have responded to the calls for civil rights for gay men and lesbians in quite different ways. She extends her analysis to a discussion of the varying ways in which Canadian and U.S. institutions are dealing with the issues of same-sex marriage and adoption.

Weeks, Jeffrey. *Coming Out: Homosexual Politics in Britain, from the Nineteenth Century to the Present.* London: Quartet Books, 1977.

Although somewhat dated, no better history of the gay political movement in Great Britain exists than this work. Weeks is one of the finest thinkers about gay issues in the world. His book provides not only factual information, but a thoughtful analysis of the changes that occurred from the beginning of the nineteenth century to the late 1970s.

Williams, Walter L., and Yolanda Retter, eds. *Gay and Lesbian Rights in the United States: A Documentary History.* Westport, CT: Greenwood Press, 2003.

This invaluable reference book contains a variety of documents dealing with all aspects of the gay and lesbian rights movement dating from the Colonial period to the present day. Among the documents cited are court cases, personal opinion pieces, and laws.

Articles
Bond, Julian, et al. "Is Gay Rights a Civil Rights Issue?" *Ebony* 59 (9, July 2004): 142–46.

Representatives of the black community from politics, religion, and the arts explain their reasons for replying to this question in the affirmative, in the negative, and, in one case, with both a "yes" and a "no."

Carter, David. "What Made Stonewall Different." *The Gay & Lesbian Review* 16 (4, July–August 2009): 11–14.

The author writes about the series of riots in New York City in 1969 that in some ways marked the beginning of the modern gay and lesbian civil rights movement. He sets the scene as to the status of gay men and lesbians at the time, and explains the significance of the cultural revolution that began as a result of the riots.

Feldblum, Chai. "Gay Rights and the Rehnquist Court." *Gay and Lesbian Review Worldwide* 8 (1, January–February 2001): 11–14.

The author reviews in some detail the treatment of cases involving gay and lesbian rights decided by the U.S. Supreme Court during the tenure of Chief Justice William Rehnquist. These decisions reflect attitudes toward demands by gay men and lesbians for equal rights by the nation's highest court and some prevailing social and moral attitudes on the subject in the larger population.

Freeman, Susan Kathleen. "Forging Gay Identities: Organizing Sexuality in San Francisco, 1950–1994." *Journal of the History of Sexuality* 12 (4, October 2003): 637–41.

Freeman outlines the transformation of the gay and lesbian civil rights movements in the second half of the twentieth century, from an effort to gain personal recognition, to a "liberation" movement designed to allow individuals to pursue their own sexuality, to a political movement striving for civil rights.

Leland, John. "Shades of Gay: With AIDS No Longer an All-Consuming Crisis, the Battle for Tolerance Has Moved to Schools, Churches, Offices and the Frontiers of Family Life." *Newsweek* 135 (March 20, 2000): 46–49.

The movement for gay and lesbian civil rights was largely stalled during the worst years of the HIV/AIDS epidemic. Now that the epidemic is coming under control, lesbians and gay men are once more turning to their demands for equal treatment under the law, a trend that Leland reviews in this article.

Raimondo, Justin. "A Gay Man Decries 'Gay Rights.'" *American Enterprise* 11 (2, March 2000): 44–45.

The author provides a brief review of the origin and evolution of the gay and lesbian civil rights movement and notes how the objectives of that movement have changed significantly.

He explains why he is troubled by the movement's move toward a more authoritarian bent, especially with the push for same-sex marriage and similar "rights."

Reports

Egan, Patrick J., Murray S. Edelman, and Kenneth Sherrill. *Findings from the Hunter College Poll of Lesbians, Gays and Bisexuals: New Discoveries about Identity, Political Attitudes, and Civic Engagement.* New York: Hunter College, 2008.

The study reported here consists of findings from 25-minute interviews with 768 lesbians, gay men, and bisexuals (LGBs). Among the study's findings are that LGBs tend to be more liberal and more politically active than non-LGBs. Political issues of highest priority tend to be elimination of workplace discrimination, provision for federal partner benefits, and laws against hate crimes. Same-sex marriage is an issue of greater concern among younger LBGs than it is among the older colleagues.

Human Rights Campaign Foundation. *Equality from State to State: Gay, Lesbian, Bisexual and Transgender Americans and State Legislation.* Washington, DC: Human Rights Campaign Foundation, December 2007.

This annual report summarizes the status of state legislation on topics such as same-sex marriage, child adoption, hate crimes, and nondiscrimination in housing and employment.

Human Rights Watch. *Family, Unvalued Discrimination, Denial, and the Fate of Binational Same-Sex Couples under U.S. Law.* URL: http://hrw.org/reports/2006/us0506/. Posted May 2006.

This report describes the legal status of same-sex couples in the United States in which one member of the couple is not an American citizen. The study finds that such couples have essentially no rights under existing laws.

Human Rights Watch. *Hatred in the Hallways: Violence and Discrimination Against Lesbian, Gay, Bisexual, and Transgender Students in U.S. Schools.* URL: http://www.hrw.org/reports/2001/uslgbt/toc.htm. Posted May 2001.

Researchers conclude from their extensive study of American schools that gay, lesbian, bisexual, and transgendered children face constant physical and emotional threats in their daily lives from their peers. They say that the U.S. government has demonstrated an "abject failure" to deal with this problem.

Arguments in Favor of Same-Sex Marriage
Books
Babst, Gordon A., Emily R. Bill, and Jason Pierceson, eds. *Moral Argument, Religion, and Same-Sex Marriage: Advancing the Public Good*. Lanham, MD: Rowman and Littlefield, 2009.

The papers that make up this book argue, in general, that the tide has shifted in the moral debate over same-sex marriage, and that supporters of that institution have begun to have the stronger position. As one of the editors has written on the Internet, "[I]t is unlikely that supporters of same-sex marriage will ever again be on the defensive."

Gerstmann, Evan. *Same-Sex Marriage and the Constitution*, 2nd edition. New York: Cambridge University Press, 2008.

Gerstmann argues that the U.S. Constitution provides a fundamental right of marriage in the United States, a right that includes marriage between two people of the same sex. He asks why that right, which now extends to almost all classes of people who are otherwise marginalized in our society, has still not been expanded to include gay men and lesbians.

Greenwood, David Valdes. *Homo Domesticus: Notes from a Same-Sex Marriage*. Cambridge, MA: Da Capo Press, 2007.

The author discusses the process of meeting his future husband, falling in love, getting married, adopting children, and living a reasonably normal married life together, except that the couple described is a same-sex couple. The book presents a very different view of same-sex marriage from the carefully reasoned arguments and polemics more commonly found on bookstore shelves.

Kotulski, Davina. *Why You Should Give a Damn about Gay Marriage*. Los Angeles: Advocate Books, 2004.

This book is directed in a significant sense to members of the gay and lesbian community who may themselves not be very convinced about the importance of legalizing same-sex marriage.

The author discuses the more than one thousand ways in which opposite-sex married couples enjoy civil benefits that are not available to their same-sex counterparts. She argues that achieving civil equality will come about only when members of the gay and lesbian community become more aggressive in their efforts to achieve marriage rights currently available only to the heterosexuals.

Myers, David G., and Letha Dawson Scanzoni. *What God Has Joined Together?: A Christian Case for Gay Marriage.* New York: HarperSanFrancisco, 2005.

The authors present an analysis from the standpoint of Christian theology in support of same-sex marriage, pointing out the Jesus had nothing to say about same-sex relationships, and the Bible also has no comment on long-term, committed relationships between two people of the same sex. They also present arguments that same-sex marriages can be in the best interest of families and of children in such relationships.

Polikoff, Nancy D. *Beyond (Straight and Gay) Marriage: Valuing All Families under the Law.* Boston: Beacon Press, 2009.

Polikoff argues that events have overtaken the traditional meaning of marriage, and that society now must find ways to adjust to new types of relationships between men and women including same-sex marriages and unmarried partnerships. She points out a number of areas in which the validation of such relationships is needed, such as workers' compensation death benefits, Social Security, probate, adoption and health care issues.

Rauch, Jonathan. *Gay Marriage: Why It Is Good for Gays, Good for Straights, and Good for America.* New York: Times Books/Henry Holt and Company, 2004.

Rauch argues that current efforts to provide "separate-but-equal" arrangements for same-sex couples (such as domestic partnerships) can only harm the traditional institution of heterosexual marriage itself as well as the best interests of same-sex couples.

Wolfson, Evan. *Why Marriage Matters: America, Equality, and Gay People's Right to Marry.* New York: Simon & Schuster, 2005.

Attorney Wolfson defends the right of same-sex couples to marry as a matter of civil rights, one that he calls "one of the first important civil rights campaigns of the 21st century." The book has been discussed widely and is one of the most important works on same-sex marriage in the United States.

Articles

Becker, Mary. "Family Law in the Secular State and Restrictions on Same-Sex Marriage: Two Are Better Than One." *University of Illinois Law Review* 2001: 1 (Winter 2001): 1–56.

Becker acknowledges that marriage has been regarded as a one-man, one-woman institution for thousands of years. She then examines the aspects of marriage that are so essential to society and decides that those benefits can also be achieved by any loving relationship between two individuals, whether they are of the same or opposite sex.

Brown, Stephen. "Naturalized Virtue Ethics and Same-Sex Love." *Philosophy in the Contemporary World* 13 (2006): 41–47.

The author, assistant professor of philosophy at Briar Cliff University, argues that any action or institution that helps humans achieve their fullest potential is a good and worthy action or institution. Since same-sex marriage achieves that objective for gay men and lesbian, he asserts, same-sex marriage is a moral good.

Brunk, Doug. "Delegates Endorse Same-Sex Adoption." *Family Practice News* 32 (21, November 2002): 1–2.

At its annual meeting, the Congress of Delegates of the American Academy of Family Physicians voted to endorse a policy supporting legislation that promotes adoption by same-sex parents. This article provides a brief summary of that action.

Burt, Robert A. "Overruling *Dred Scott:* The Case for Same-Sex Marriage." *Widener Law Journal* 17 (2007): 73–95.

Burt reviews in some detail the famous case of *Dred Scott v. Sanford* of 1857, when the U.S. Supreme Court ruled that African Americans had no rights as American citizens and, in fact, could not even be citizens. He compares the judicial mentality behind that decision with that of courts that today deny the right of same-sex couples to legally marry and asserts that such action is as dehumanizing as was the *Dred Scott* decision.

Chartier, Gary. "Natural Law, Same-Sex Marriage, and the Politics of Virtue." *UCLA Law Review* 48 (2001): 1593–1632.

The author reviews efforts by philosophers who espouse a new and somewhat modified version of the philosophical view known as "natural law" ("new natural law") and the ways that philosophy is used to justify opposition to same-sex marriage. He attempts to show that their arguments are not convincing and that, in fact, "new natural law" can be used to support the concept of same-sex marriage. For comparison, also see Eric Reid, below.

Committee on Psychosocial Aspects of Child and Family Health. American Academy of Pediatrics. "Coparent or Second-Parent Adoption by Same-Sex Parents." *Pediatrics* 109 (2, February 2002): 339–40.

A special committee of the American Academy of Pediatrics appointed to study same-sex adoptions recommends that pediatricians support legislative and legal efforts to recognize such adoptions.

Gay Parent Magazine.

This magazine was established in 1998. It carries articles and advertisements of interest to same-sex parents. Contact information is as follows:

P.O. Box 750852

Forest Hills, NY 11375-0852

(718) 380-1780

e-mail: gayparentmag@gmail.com

ISSN 1545-6714

Katz, Pamela S. "The Case for Legal Recognition of Same-Sex Marriage." *Journal of Law & Policy* 8 (1999):61–106.

Katz argues for same-sex marriage on the basis of two legal principles: due process law and discrimination based on gender and/or sexual orientation. She says that there is no legitimate reason for suspecting that the existence of same-sex marriages will represent a threat to the stability of society.

Silverman, Jennifer. "Chapter Forum Retains Policy: Adoption by Same-Sex Parents." *Pediatric News* 36 (10, October 2002): 2.

Chapter representatives of the American Academy of Pediatrics voted to retain a previously adopted policy in support of adoption by same-sex couples, with a new proviso that the issue be reassessed in the light of any new scientific evidence that becomes available.

Volokh, Eugene. "Same-Sex Marriage and Slippery Slopes." *Hofstra Law Review* 33 (2005): 1155–1201.

Critics of same-sex marriage often offer the "slippery-slope" argument: such relationships may be without harm at the moment, but they may lead to serious problems at some time in the future. Volokh analyzes the logic of this argument and concludes that it is inappropriately used to argue against same-sex marriages. He also reviews a number of reasons that same-sex marriages are good not only for the individuals involved, but also for society as a whole.

Arguments Opposed to Same-Sex Marriage
Books
Dobson, James. *Marriage Under Fire: Why We Must Win This Battle.* Sisters, OR: Multnomah Books, 2004.

Dobson suggests that gay men and lesbian have been working for years to "utterly destroy the family." In this book, he explains why same-sex marriages will destroy conventional marriages, lead to a large increase in divorces, and cause irreparable harm to children.

Kennedy, D. James, and Jerry Newcombe. *What's Wrong with Same-Sex Marriage?* Wheaton, IL: Crossway Books, 2004.

The authors review the recent spread of same-sex marriage in the United States and point out the threat this trend poses to traditional marriage. They explain that marriage was established by God, and that no human institution has the right to change the way in which marriage is established or how it functions.

Lutzer, Erwin W. *The Truth about Same Sex Marriage: 6 Things You Need to Know about What's Really at Stake.* Chicago: Moody Publishers, 2004.

Lutzer, the pastor of the Moody Church in Chicago, Illinois, argues that same-sex marriage is a "deep and dangerous threat" to modern society, and the church has an obligation to speak out, "in love and in truth," against the spread of this practice. He refers extensively to and bases his arguments on biblical pronouncements about the nature of marriage that are fundamental to Christian doctrine.

Sprigg, Peter. *Outrage: How Gay Activists and Liberal Judges Are Trashing Democracy to Redefine Marriage*. Washington, DC: Regnery Press, 2004.

The author suggests that the American public is not aware of the fact that homosexuals are attempting to redefine one of the oldest traditions in human society, opposite-sex marriage. In this book, he takes on a number of tasks related to this frightening possibility, explaining why same-sex marriage is not a civil right, the "shocking medical and scientific data" about homosexual behavior, the threat that same-sex marriage poses to children, and why a constitutional amendment is necessary to prevent liberal judges and the homosexual community from overthrowing the traditional definition of marriage.

Stanton, Glenn T., and Bill Maier. *Marriage on Trial: The Case Against Same-Sex Marriage and Parenting*. Downers Grove, IL: InterVarsity Press, 2004.

The authors suggest that "nature is very narrow in its definition of marriage," and that same-sex marriages are a serious threat to the community as a whole and to the next generation. They argue that no society that has permitted arrangements other than opposite-sex marriage have ever been able to survive.

Staver, Mathew D. *Same-Sex Marriage: Putting Every Household at Risk*. Nashville, TN: B&H Publishing Group, 2004.

The author argues that the institution of marriage was established by God and that it is intended only for opposite-sex couples. In this book, he explains how same-sex marriages are a threat to all heterosexual marriages and to the children of those marriages, and he explains "what parents need to know" about same-sex attraction and the development of gender identity.

TFP Committee on American Issues. *Defending a Higher Law: Why We Must Resist Same-Sex "Marriage" and the Homosexual Movement*.

Spring Grove, PA: American Society for the Defense of Tradition, Family and Property, 2004.

The TFP Committee on American Issues explains that it is writing this book to defeat the homosexual community in a battle for the nation's soul. Its goal in the book is to refute doctrinal and factual errors advanced by the homosexual minority, to explore its agenda, and to reveal its tactics in the battle to defeat those who believe in morality in the nation.

Articles

Coolidge, David Orgon, and William C. Duncan. "Reaffirming Marriage: A Presidential Priority." *Harvard Journal of Law & Public Policy* 24 (Spring 2001): 623–51.

The authors present arguments for maintaining the definition of a marriage as a union between one man and one woman, explain how some activists are trying to break down that traditional definition through civil unions and same-sex marriages, and propose actions by the incoming administration of George W. Bush to retain and enforce the traditional definition of marriage.

Duncan, William C. "Avoidance Strategy: Same-Sex Marriage Litigation and the Federal Courts." *Campbell Law Review* 29 (2006): 29–46.

The author points out that advocates for same-sex marriage nearly always bring suit in state, and not federal, courts. He suggests that the reason for this pattern is that the U.S. Constitution provides no basis for endorsing same-sex marriage, and he cites a number of past rulings to confirm this view. He argues that the adoption of same-sex marriages nationwide through actions by individual state courts will have a "sorry legacy," not only for traditional marriage, but also for the law.

Jurand, Sara Hoffman. "Pennsylvania Nixes Second-Parent Adoptions for Same-Sex Couples." *Trial* 37 (108, February 1, 2001): 108–9.

In two separate rulings, both decided by a six-to-three vote, the Pennsylvania Supreme Court ruled that individuals in a same-sex relationship cannot adopt the biological children of their partners. This article briefly reviews the facts and reasoning in the cases.

Kurtz, Stanley. "Beyond Gay Marriage." *The Weekly Standard* 8 (August 4–11, 2003): 26–33.

Kurtz argues that legalization of same-sex marriage raises some serious questions about the nature of marriage itself that need to be discussed on a broad and open front in American society. He suggests that approval of the practice will lead to a variety of other kinds of nontraditional relationships, such as polygamy and three-person marriages.

MacLeod, Adam J. "The Search for Moral Neutrality in Same-Sex Marriage Decisions." *BYU Journal of Public Law* 23 (2008): 1–59.

The author considers decisions made by three state courts in California, Connecticut, and Massachusetts about same-sex marriage and noted that each claimed to have a moral-neutral basis for their decisions. In fact, he says, "all three courts committed themselves to morally partisan conceptions of marriage." In conclusion, he offers some "morally neutral rational bases" for upholding existing state laws that limit marriage to opposite-sex couples.

Reid, Eric. "Assessing and Responding to Same-Sex 'Marriage' in Light of Natural Law." *Georgetown Journal of Law & Public Policy* 3 (2005): 523–39.

Reid bases his objection to same-sex marriage on one of the fundamental principles of Roman Catholic philosophy, that of natural law. He attempts to show that same-sex marriage represents a profound rejection of that principle and, therefore, must be prevented. For comparison, see Gary Chartier, above.

Republican Policy Committee. "The Threat to Marriage from the Courts." URL: http://rpc.senate.gov/releases/2003/jd072903.pdf. Accessed on April 14, 2010.

In this press release, the Republican Policy Committee argues that courts cannot be trusted to make fair and rational decisions about the same-sex issue and that an amendment to the U.S. Constitution is the only certain way to preserve traditional marriage in the United States.

Sommerville, Margaret. "Children's Human Rights and Unlinking Child-Parent Biological Bonds with Adoption, Same-Sex Marriage and New Reproductive Technologies." *Journal of Family Studies* 13 (2, November 2007): 179–201.

The author argues that "the most fundamental human right of every person is the right to be born from natural human origins that have not been tampered with by anyone else," and that new policies and technologies, including same-sex adoption, violate that right. She sees these policies and technologies as having some of the worst consequences for children that can be imagined and suggests that, should same-sex marriage continue to become more popular, legislation be adopted to prevent children from losing this most basic of human rights.

Wilkins, Richard G. "The Constitutionality of Legal Preferences for Heterosexual Marriage." *Regent University Law Review* 16 (2003–4):121–37.

Wilkins suggests that the traditional definition of marriage as being between one man and one woman is under attack from a number of forces, same-sex unions being one. He asks if "the various legal preferences conferred on traditional marriage [must] be extended to alternative partnership arrangements?" and decides that the answer is "no." He offers both constitutional and social reasons for reaching this decision.

General Reviews of Same-Sex Marriage and Adoption

Books

Andryszewski, Tricia. *Same-Sex Marriage: Moral Wrong or Civil Right?* Breckenridge, CO: Twenty First Century Books, 2007.

The author attempts to present a balanced view of same-sex marriage for young adult readers. She opens with a review of the gay and lesbian rights movement in the United States, and then talks about political developments in the 1990s, the adoption of same-sex marriage in Massachusetts, and some features of gay and lesbian family life.

Badgett, M. V. Lee. *When Gay People Get Married: What Happens When Societies Legalize Same-Sex Marriage*. New York: New York University Press, 2009.

The vast majority of the books and articles written about same-sex marriage express philosophical or theological positions on the topic. One important question worthy of consideration is what the scientific evidence is about locations where same-sex marriage has been legalized. Such data are difficult to come by because few such nations or states exist. Badgett chooses the Netherlands, where same-sex marriage has been legal since 2001, to carry out her sociological study of the effects of the practice on the society as a whole. Her analysis is very important for the ongoing debate over legalization of same-sex unions in the United States.

Baird, Robert M., and Stuart E. Rosenbaum, eds. *Same-Sex Marriage: The Moral And Legal Debate.* Amherst, NY: Prometheus Books, 2004.

The articles in this book are divided into three sections. The first section deals specifically with the decision by the Massachusetts Supreme Judicial Court requiring the state to issue marriage licenses to same-sex couples. The second section deals with emotional issues raised by the possibility of same-sex marriages. The third section offers philosophical arguments for and against same-sex marriage.

Brewer, Paul R. *Value War: Public Opinion and the Politics of Gay Rights.* Lanham, MD: Rowman and Littlefield, 2007.

The author argues that surveys of public opinion about same-sex marriage and those who are actually involved in the battle over this issue have a reciprocal relationship with each other, each side influencing the thoughts and actions of the others. He provides data and analysis to support this view and shows how it affects the long-term development of the debate over civil rights for gay men and lesbians, including same-sex marriage and adoption.

Chauncey, George. *Why Marriage?: The History Shaping Today's Debate over Gay Equality.* New York: Basic Books, 2005.

The author places the current controversy over same-sex marriage within the context of the historical development of antigay attitudes in the United States (beginning primarily in the mid-twentieth century) and pressures brought to bear on the gay and lesbian communities as a result of the HIV / AIDS crisis in the United States.

Hertz, Frederick, and Emily Doskow. *Making It Legal: A Guide to Same-Sex Marriage, Domestic Partnership and Civil Unions.* Berkeley, CA: NOLO, 2009.

This book avoids a discussion of the dispute as to the advisability of same-sex relationship and simply lays out legal principles involved in consummating a legal same-sex marriage, civil union, or domestic partnership. Some of the issues included are prenuptial agreements, wills and trusts, tax consequences, special issues for couples with children, and relationships with stepparents and former partners.

Jordan, Mark D., ed. *Authorizing Marriage?: Canon, Tradition, and Critique in the Blessing of Same-Sex Unions.* Princeton, NJ: Princeton University Press, 2006.

This collection of essays considers the historical and theological literature dealing with same-sex unions and analyzes the relevance of that literature for the modern debate over same-sex marriage.

Laycock, Douglas, ed. *Same-Sex Marriage and Religious Liberty: Emerging Conflicts.* Lanham, MD: Rowman & Littlefield, 2008.

The five chapters in this book provide overviews of specific issues that are likely to arise as the result of the dispute between religious organizations and groups who support the right of same-sex couples to marry and adopt children.

Mezey, Susan. *Gay Families and the Courts: The Quest for Equal Rights.* Lanham, MD: Rowman and Littlefield, 2009.

This book provides a comprehensive and useful overview of the legal status of same-sex marriage and same-sex families.

Pinello, Daniel R. *America's Struggle for Same-Sex Marriage.* New York: Cambridge University Press, 2006.

The author presents an overview of the history of the battle over same-sex marriage from a quite different perspective, that of ordinary people who have been caught up in that struggle, individuals such as county clerks, legislators, judges, activists on both sides of the debates, and same-sex couples who are eager to obtain legal validation of their relationships.

Polikoff, Nancy D. *Beyond (Straight and Gay) Marriage: Valuing All Families under the Law.* Boston: Beacon Press, 2008.

The author argues that the meanings of marriage and family have, for a number of years, been changing, in both the United

States and other parts of the world. She reviews this history and examines the social, economic, political, and legal significance of these changes for many types of families, including those of gay men, lesbians, bisexuals, and transgendered individuals.

Shanley, Mary L. *Making Babies, Making Families: What Matters Most in an Age of Reproductive Technologies, Surrogacy, Adoption, and Same-Sex and Unwed Parents' Rights.* Boston: Beacon Press, 2002.

The author explores all aspects of adoption by other-than-traditional opposite-sex married couples. She devotes chapters to adoption by transracial couples, fathers' rights, surrogate motherhood, lesbian comothers, and other related topics.

Sullivan, Andrew. *Same-Sex Marriage: Pro and Con*, revised and updated edition. New York: Vintage Books, 2004.

The more than six dozen essays that make up this anthology have been taken from a wide variety of sources, from the Bible and other ancient literature to modern-day court decisions, laws, and polemics on both sides of the same-sex marriage debate.

Articles

Allen, Douglas W. "An Economic Assessment of Same-Sex Marriage Laws." *Harvard Journal of Law and Public Policy* 29 (2006): 949–80.

The author argues that the debate over same-sex marriage often omits consideration of the economic issues involved. He points out that such costs could be enormous and, for that reason, society might consider the possibility of having two types of marriage, homosexual marriage and heterosexual marriage. Although not an ideal solution, he believes that the two-marriage model would have fewer harmful economic effects than a one-marriage-for-all model.

Blankenhorn, David, and Jonathan Rauch. "A Reconciliation on Gay Marriage." *New York Times*, February 22, 2009, "Week in Review," 11.

This very interesting op-ed article was written by one opponent and one supporter of same-sex marriage, suggesting a compromise position: civil unions that provide nearly all of the same rights as opposite-sex marriage, which religious organizations can choose to opt out of recognizing in their own functions.

Brooks Devon, and Sheryl Goldberg. "Gay and Lesbian Adoptive and Foster Care Placements: Can They Meet the Needs of Waiting Children?" *Social Work* 46 (2, April 2001): 147–57.

The authors review the demographics of the adoption problem in the United States today, find that there are far more children waiting for adoption than potential adoptive parents, and suggest that laws and regulations be eased to permit same-sex couples to adopt more easily. They review policy implications and changes in practice necessitated by this recommendation.

"Can Anyone Show Just Cause Why These Two Should Not Be Lawfully Joined Together?" *New England Law Review* 38 (2003–4): 487–688.

The 15 articles in this issue deal with a variety of issues relating to same-sex marriage, such as constitutional issues, evolving patterns in the United States and other countries of the world, estate planning for same-sex couples, adoption by same-sex couples, issues for grandparents, and religious issues involved in the approval of same-sex marriages.

"Editors' Symposium: The Meaning of Marriage." *San Diego Law Review* 42 (2005): 821–1149.

This issue consists of 22 articles dealing with almost every conceivable aspect of the so-called Federal Marriage Amendment, a proposed amendment to the U.S. Constitution defining marriage as the union of one man and one woman. Some issues discussed include the meaning of marriage, the effects of same-sex marriage on children, the amendment and polygamy, and lessons from natural law and tradition.

Franke, Katherine M. "The Politics of Same-Sex Marriage Politics." *Columbia Journal of Gender and Law* 15 (2006): 236–48.

After the decriminalization of same-sex sex practices by the U.S. Supreme Court in *Lawrence v. Texas*, many members of the lesbian and gay community chose to raise the political ante by pushing for same-sex marriage. The author explores the history of this evolution of political goals and some problems that it raises for both the gay and lesbian community and the society at large.

Goldberg, Suzanne B. "A Historical Guide to the Future of Marriage for Same-Sex Couples." *Columbia Journal of Gender and Law* 15 (2006): 249–72.

The author notes that most decisions about same-sex marriage include reference to the history of such relationships, but that those references are flawed for two reasons. First, historical precedence is an insufficient basis on which to make such decisions, and, second, the historical analyses that are made are typically based on inaccurate readings of historical documents.

Hitchings, Emma, and Tracey Sagar. "The Adoption and Children Act 2002: A Level Playing Field for Same-Sex Adopters?" *Child and Family Law Quarterly* 19 (1, June 2007): 60–80.

The United Kingdom's Adoption and Children Act of 2002 permits couples to adopt children whether they are of the same or opposite sex. The authors of this article consider the potential effects of this act on adoptees. They report the results of interviews with a very small sample (five individuals) of social workers with experience in this area, who report that the playing field will probably still not be level for same-sex couples seeking to adopt.

Knauer, Nancy J. "Same-Sex Marriage and Federalism." *Temple Political & Civil Rights Law Review* 17 (2, 2008): 101–22.

The author explores the implications of same-sex marriage for the U.S. tradition of federalism, in which individual states are allowed to carry out experiments on new social, economic, and political systems. Her essay consists of three major parts, the first of which deals with the current status of same-sex marriage in the nation. The second part outlines some of the problems involved with the federalist system in ensuring that the rights of minorities are preserved. The third part explores the human costs to same-sex couples for whom legal recognition is not available.

Koppelman, Andrew. "Interstate Recognition of Same-Sex Marriages and Civil Unions: A Handbook for Judges." *University of Pennsylvania Law Review* 153 (2005): 2143–94.

As legal same-sex arrangements (marriages, civil unions, domestic partnerships, etc.) become more common, the legal question as to whether states must recognize such arrangements from other states becomes more important. Koppelman reviews four kinds of same-sex arrangements, "evasive," "migratory," "visitor," and "extraterritorial" marriages (depending on the relationship of the couple to the state in which they are married), and the legal consequences of each for the question of recognition.

Lipkin, Robert Justin. "The Harm of Same-Sex Marriage: Real or Imagined?" *Widener Law Review* 11 (2005): 277–308.

Conservatives argue that permitting same-sex marriage will harm society, and liberals suggest they cannot imagine how such harm can occur. Lipkin says that conservatives are right, but that the real question is how any harm that may occur is balanced by providing a segment of the population (gay men and lesbians) with a legitimate civil right.

Ryan, Patrick J. "Here's Your 'Traditional Marriage.' " *Gay and Lesbian Review* 16 (6, November–December 2009): 25–27.

The author notes that critics of same-sex marriage often base their appeal on the precedence of "traditional marriage," although the form of marriage practiced in the United States and many other countries today is anything but "traditional." He reviews what the more common forms of relationships among men and women have been throughout human history.

Samar, Vincent J. "Throwing down the International Gauntlet: Same-Sex Marriage as a Human Right." *Cardozo Public Law Policy & Ethics Journal* 6 (2007): 1–55.

The author points out that the spread of same-sex marriage in some European countries, Canada, and South Africa raises a new issue in international law, the obligation of nations to recognize same-sex marriages conducted in other nations, even if they are not conducted in the host nation. He says this issue is only a relatively modest part of a larger issue of the relationship between domestic and international human rights.

"Same-Sex Couples: Defining Marriage in the Twenty-first Century." *Stanford Law and Policy Review* 16 (2005): 1–232.

The eight articles in this special symposium issue deal with legal, religious, economic, and moral issues related to the increasing popularity of same-sex marriages.

Schuman, Ben. "Gods and Gays: Analyzing the Same-Sex Marriage Debate from a Religious Perspective." *Georgetown Law Journal* 98 (1, August 2008): 2103–41.

As the title of this article suggests, the author explores the religious implications of the growing demand for same-sex marriage rights in the United States and analyzes the role of religion versus legal considerations in the debate.

Stewart, Monte Neil. "Judicial Redefinition of Marriage." *Canadian Journal of Family Law* 21 (2004): 11–132.

The author examines four judicial decisions dealing with same-sex marriage, two in the United States and two in Canada, from the standpoint of their judicial quality. He finds that all four decisions were "materially defective" in that they failed to deal adequately with basic issues raised by opponents of same-sex marriage, such as the importance of a couple's being able to reproduce. He concludes that "courts did an unacceptable job with their performance of the very tasks that lie at the heart of judicial responsibility in virtually every case."

Wardle, Lynn D. "A Critical Analysis of Constitutional Claims for Same-Sex Marriage," *Brigham Young University Law Review* 1 (1996): 96–100.

A listing of law review articles dealing with same-sex marriage dating from 1970 to 1975 and from 1990 to 1995. The articles are categorized as in favor of or opposed to same-sex marriage.

Weiser, Jay. "Foreword: The Next Normal: Developments Since Marriage Rights for Same-Sex Couples in New York." *Columbia Journal of Gender and Law* 13 (2004): 48–69.

The author provides a comprehensive and exhaustive introduction to the subject of same-sex marriage, with special focus on circumstances in the state of New York. The article is an introduction to a 2000 report issued by a number of committees of the Association of the Bar of the City of New York, "A Report on

Marriage Rights for Same-Sex Couples in New York," reprinted on pages 70–99 of the same issue of the journal.

Wright, Wade K. "The Tide in Favour of Equality: Same-Sex Marriage in Canada and England and Wales." *International Journal of Law, Policy & the Family* 20 (2006): 249–85.

Wright reviews the trend in favor of same-sex marriage and civil unions on both sides of the Atlantic, some common themes, and some differences between developments in Canada and in the United Kingdom. He considers the possibility that courts in the United Kingdom will follow a path similar to that laid out by Canadian courts in legalizing same-sex marriage.

Reports

The Beckett Fund for Religious Liberty. "Scholars' Conference on Same-Sex Marriage and Religious Liberty." URL: http://www .becketfund.org/index.php/article/494.html. Posted on May 4, 2006.

This report summarizes the proceedings of a conference sponsored by the Beckett Fund on the consequences of the legalization of same-sex marriages on religious freedom. The Web site has links to seven papers presented at that conference, along with the text of three amicus curiae briefs based on the presentations made and filed by the fund in related cases heard by courts in Connecticut, Iowa, and Maryland.

Brodzinsky, David M., and the staff of the Evan B. Donaldson Adoption Institute. *Adoption by Lesbians and Gays: A National Survey of Adoption Agency Policies, Practices, and Attitudes.* New York: Evan B. Donaldson Adoption Institute. URL: http://www .adoptioninstitute.org/whowe/Lesbian%20and%20Gay%20 Adoption%20Report_final.doc (October 29, 2003).

Researchers report on a study of policies and practices of 307 private and public adoption agencies in all 50 states and the District of Columbia. The study shows that, in general, adoption agencies are increasingly willing to place children with same-sex couples. About two of five responding agencies have already placed children with couples known to be gay or lesbian, and 60 percent of respondents indicate a willingness to accept applications for adoptions from same-sex couples.

Gates, Gary J., M. V. Lee Badgett, Jennifer Ehrle Macomber, and Kate Chambers. *Adoption and Foster Care by Gay and Lesbian Parents in the United States*. URL: http://www.urban.org/UploadedPDF/411437_Adoption_Foster_Care.pdf. Posted March 2007.

The four researchers from the Williams Institute at the University of California at Los Angeles School of Law and the Urban Institute in Washington, DC, summarize demographic data about an estimated 65,500 children living in families headed by a same-sex couple or a single gay or lesbian parent in the United States, and they compare those data with information about comparable heterosexual families. They point out ways in which same-sex and opposite-sex families are alike and different and conclude that, in general, bans on adoptions by same-sex couples are likely to have more negative than positive results for children, adoptive parents, and the general community.

Nonprint

History
Internet
elephantjournal.com. http://www.elephantjournal.com/2009/02/gregory-hinton-for-daily-camera-march-26-1975-the-first-same-sex-marriage-licenses-in-the-united-states-were-heroically-issued-in-boulder-by-county-clerk-clela-rorex/. Accessed on January 5, 2010.

This article provides a fascinating historical view of one of the earliest events in the history of gay marriage in the United States, when county clerk Clela Rorex issued marriage licenses to a same-sex couple because she could find nothing in state law that prohibited her from doing so.

Frakes, Robert. "Why the Romans Are Important in the Debate about Gay Marriage." http://hnn.us/articles/21319.html. Accessed on February 14, 2010.

The author, professor of history at Clarion University, explains why knowing the history of Roman attitudes about same-sex behavior is relevant to the modern-day debate over same-sex marriage.

Hay, Bob. "A World History of Homosexuality." http://bobhay
.org/u3a/homo_index.html. Accessed on April 12, 2010.

Hay offered this course through the United Kingdom's University
of the Third Age (U3A) in 2006, 2007, and 2008. It is an amazing
collection of lectures on the early and more recent history of
same-sex relationships, including same-sex marriage, in a number
of cultures.

"History of Chinese Homosexuality." http://www.chinadaily
.com.cn/english/doc/2004-04/01/content_319807.htm.
Accessed on January 12, 2010.

This article provides a brief, but very interesting, history of same-
sex relationships, including same-sex marriages, in Chinese
culture.

Igwe, Leo. "Tradition of Same Gender Marriage in Igboland."
Nigerian Tribune. http://revrowlandjidemacaulay.blogspot.com/
2009/06/tradition-of-same-gender-marriage-in.html. Accessed
on March 24, 2010.

The writer discusses a form of same-sex marriage that has existed
in a region of Nigeria in which he was born and raised.

"Love, Marriage, Romance & Women. . . . In Medieval & Celtic
Culture." http://www.dfwx.com/medieval_cult.html. Accessed
on February 17, 2010.

This article provides a very extensive, scholarly, informative, and
sometimes surprising review of the nature of marriage and
relationships during the medieval period.

Religious Tolerance. "Bible Passages Describing Eight Family/
Marriage Types." http://www.religioustolerance.org/mar
_bibl0.htm. Accessed on February 14, 2010.

This Web page offers an antidote to the concept that traditional
marriage is and always has been an arrangement between one
man and one woman.

[United Church of Christ]. "Same-Sex Marriage: A Timeline." http://
www.ucc.org/assets/pdfs/emr9.pdf. Accessed on January 17,
2010.

This resource is of limited value because it covers only a limited period of time (1970–88), but it is still useful because of the detail it provides about events in the first years of the same-sex marriage debate.

Vanita, Rith. "Homosexuality in India: Past and Present." *IIAS Newsletter*, no. 29. http://www.iias.nl/iiasn/29/IIASNL29_10 _Vanita.pdf. Accessed on March 25, 2010.

This article is of considerable importance because it is one of the first scholarly studies of same-sex relationships in historical Indian culture.

Walker, Jonathan P. "Reconsidering Homosexuality and the Bible." http://www.gsafe.org/jonathan_walker.htm. Accessed on February 14, 2010.

The author reviews the evidence that biblical passages cited as condemning same-sex relationships may not be as clear on that point as proponents suggest that they are.

Gay and Lesbian Civil Rights Issues
Internet
About.com. "Gay Life." URL: http://gaylife.about.com/od/ samesexmarriage/Marriage.htm. Accessed on December 13, 2009.

This Internet resource includes articles on a number of issues related to gay and lesbian rights, such as civil unions, domestic partnerships, same-sex marriage, tax issues for same-sex couples, estate planning, a review of gay and lesbian rights in other nations, benefits of legalized marriage, arguments against same-sex marriage, and the Federal Marriage Amendment.

"Affidavit of William Eskridge, Jr." URL: http://www.same sexmarriage.ca/docs/Affidavit%20of%20William%20N%5B1 %5D.%20Eskridge,%20JR.pdf. Accessed on December 11, 2009.

This document summarizes the author's research on the appearance of formal, ritualized, same-sex relationships in a number of societies in various part of the world throughout history.

Dunne, Bruce. "Power and Sexuality in the Middle East." URL: http://www.merip.org/mer/mer206/bruce.htm. Accessed on January 12, 2010.

This article provides a fascinating overview of attitudes toward heterosexual and homosexual relationships in the Islamic nations of the Middle East.

FindLaw. "Gay and Lesbian Rights/Sexual Orientation Discrimination." URL: http://public.findlaw.com/civil-rights/more-civil-rights-topics/gay-lesbian-civil-rights-more/. Accessed on December 13, 2009.

An extraordinary resource on the legal rights of gay men and lesbians, with information on federal, state, and local legislation, corporate policies, hate crimes, civil rights, and many other important topics.

Fitzpatrick, Brian. "Media Ignore Impending Collision: Gay Rights vs. Religious Liberty." URL: http://www.cultureand mediainstitute.org/articles/2008/20080610145004.aspx. Posted on June 10, 2008.

The author presents a somewhat different take on the gay and lesbian rights movement, arguing that it is not really a civil rights movement at all, but, instead, "a war against Western civilization's Judeo-Christian moral order." He discusses the evolution of attitudes toward same-sex relationships in Canada as evidence for this position.

National Center for Lesbian Rights. URL: http://www.nclrights.org/. Accessed on December 13, 2009.

This Web site provides a great deal of information on lesbian civil rights issues in particular, and on gay and lesbian issues in general. Some topics for which information is available are elder law, employment, families and parenting, federal legislation, health care, immigration, marriage, sports, and youth.

[Pinello, Daniel R.] ["Casebook on Sexual Orientation and the Law."] URL: http://www.danpinello.com/Family2.htm. Accessed on July 5, 2008.

This Web site contains information extracted from the author's book *Gay Rights and American Law*. It contains links to about three dozen important appellate cases dealing with same-sex issues such as marriage, property disputes, wills and estates, domestic violence, and legal rights of same-sex partners.

Public Agenda. "Issue Guide: Gay Rights." URL: http://www .publicagenda.org/citizen/issueguides/gay-rights. Accessed on December 13, 2009.

Public Agenda is a highly regarded, impartial source for information on a variety of important political, economic, and social issues. Its Web site provides relevant facts on an issue, a discussion guides, additional resources, existing and proposed legislation, public opinion summaries, and additional resources for understanding the issue.

"Queer Resources Directory." URL: http://www.qrd.org/qrd/. Last updated on April 29, 2009.

This invaluable Web site has links to 25,488 files on virtually every aspect of lesbian, gay, bisexual, and transgendered topics, including same-sex marriage and parenting; gay and lesbian youths; religion; health and safety issues; electronic resources; gay media, culture, and events; international information; business and workplace issues; organizations; and politics and activism.

Robinson, Bruce A. "Homosexuality and Bisexuality: All Viewpoints." Ontario Consultants on Religious Tolerance. URL: http:// www.religioustolerance.org/homosexu.htm. Accessed on December 13, 2009.

This Web site provides a great deal of unbiased information about homosexual and bisexual behavior, with detailed discussions on topics such as the impact of religion on beliefs and attitudes about homosexuality and bisexuality; same-sex unions and civil unions; challenges faces by gay men, lesbians, and bisexuals; hate crimes; reparative therapies; laws affecting gay men, lesbians, and bisexuals; and essays, comments, sermons, and other resources.

SpeakOut.com. "Gay Rights." URL: http://www.speakout.com/ activism/gayrights/. Accessed on December 13, 2009.

This Web site provides basic information on a number of gay-related issues, such as gays and lesbians, in the military, antidiscrimination laws, hate crimes, same-sex marriage, civil unions, and social issues. It also offers links to a number of related Internet sites.

Arguments in Favor of Same-Sex Marriage

Internet

Bidstrup, Scott. "Gay Marriage: The Arguments and the Motives." URL: http://www.bidstrup.com/marriage.htm. Last updated on June 3, 2009.

The author reviews the reasons that people give for opposing same-sex marriage, what he believes are the real reason for their opposition, the agenda that anti-same-sex marriage individuals and organizations are pursuing, and the reasons that same-sex marriage is a civil rights issue.

Cline, Austin. "Arguments for Gay Marriage: Moral and Social Arguments for Gay Marriage." URL: http://atheism.about.com/od/gaymarriage/p/ProGayMarriage.htm. Accessed on April 14, 2010.

Cline starts by acknowledging that most arguments in favor of same-sex marriage focus on the benefits to couples who would benefit from such an arrangement. In this article, however, he points out how same-sex marriage can also benefit many other groups of people, including the children of gay men and lesbians, parents and other relatives of lesbians and gay men, and society in general.

Cyberhiway.com. "The Gay Adoption Mailing List." URL: http://www.cyberhiway.com/aparent/faq.html. Accessed on December 15, 2009.

This Web site is designed to provide information and support for same-sex couples who are considering adoption, are in the process of adopting a child, or who have already adopted a child. Weekly archives of posted messages are available back as far as August 1998.

Deason, Claire B. "An Argument for Same-Sex Marriage." URL: http://digitalcommons.macalester.edu/cgi/viewcontent.cgi?article=1003&context=poli_honors. Accessed on April 14, 2010.

In this honors project at Macalester College, the author attempts to answer the question, "What might a sound legal argument for same sex marriage look like?" In order to do so, she draws on constitutional law, legislative actions, and court cases dealing with same-sex marriage.

Faucette, Judith. "The Constitutional Same Sex Marriage Debate." URL: http://marital-gender-equality.suite101.com/article.cfm/the_constitutional_same_sex_marriage_debate. Accessed on April 14, 2010.

This article summarizes two of the crucial legal issues related to the legalization of same-sex marriage, the right to liberty under the due process clause, and the right to equality under the equal protection clause.

The Gay Christian Network. "What I Believe." URL: http://gaychristian.net/justins_view.php. Accessed on February 14, 2010.

This article, written by a very conservative gay Christian, explains why he thinks that same-sex marriage does not violate the scriptures and, in fact, is probably blessed by God.

Head, Tom. "10 Really Bad Arguments against Same-Sex Marriage." URL: http://civilliberty.about.com/od/gendersexuality/tp/Arguments-Against-Gay-Marriage.htm. Accessed on April 14, 2010.

Head responds, point by point, to 10 arguments offered by James Dobson in his book *Marriage Under Fire* against same-sex marriage.

Head, Tom. "Four Reasons to Support Gay Marriage and Oppose the Federal Marriage Amendment." URL: http://civilliberty.about.com/od/gendersexuality/a/marriageamend.htm. Accessed on December 13, 2009.

The author focuses on the proposed constitutional amendment defining marriage as a contract between two individuals of the opposite sex. He argues that (1) the amendment would not protect heterosexual marriages, (2) the amendment is contrary to the basic principles of American democracy, (3) legalizing same–sex marriage causes no harm to opposite-sex marriage, and

(4) legalizing same-sex marriage acknowledges the legitimacy of same-sex relationships.

Joe.My.God. "New York's Heroes." URL: http://joemygod .blogspot.com/2009/12/new-yorks-heroes.html. Accessed on December 13, 2009.

This Web site contains four videos originally posted on YouTube of speeches made in the New York Senate debate over a bill to grant same-sex couples the right to marry in New York State, a vote held in December 2009. The four speeches were all given by members of the senate, explaining the reasons that they were going to vote in favor of the bill. The bill that was the subject of these speeches failed in the senate.

Liberated Christians. "Serious Study of Leviticus: Has Nothing to Do with Today's Homosexuality." http://www.libchrist.com/ other/homosexual/leviticus.html. Accessed on February 14, 2010.

The author offers a scholarly analysis of the texts in Leviticus that contemporary Christians use to condemn same-sex behaviors and concludes that they do not say what they appear to say about same-sex relationships.

Olson, Theodore B. "The Conservative Case for Gay Marriage." *Newsweek.* http://www.newsweek.com/id/229957. Posted on January 18, 2010.

One of the lead attorneys for the plaintiffs in the case of *Perry v. Schwarzenegger* before the U.S. District Court for the Northern District of California, Olson argues that allowing same-sex couples to marry in the United States is purely a matter of equality and fundamental rights.

Roste, Vaughn. "Ten Reasons Why Christians Should Support Same-Sex Marriage." http://www.samesexmarriage.ca/equality/ ten_reasons.htm. Accessed on April 14, 2010.

The writer, the son of two Lutheran pastors, with a degree in theology, outlines 10 reasons that Christians ought to support same-sex marriage. His reasons tend to emphasize changes that have taken place in the political scene in Canada, as well as in the Christian church itself over recent decades.

Arguments Opposed to Same-Sex Marriage
Internet
Alliance Defense Fund. "The Truth about Same-Sex 'Marriage.' "
URL: http://www.alliancedefensefund.org/userdocs/SameSex
Marriage.pdf. Accessed on December 13, 2009.

This pamphlet outlines the major objections to same-sex marriage
from a group that has been involved in virtually all state and local
campaigns surrounding the right of same-sex couples to marry. It
argues, among other things, that civil unions and domestic partnerships are as much of a risk to traditional marriage as is same-
sex marriage itself, that churches may be required to perform
same-sex marriages if they are legalized, that same-sex marriage
is only a first step in a more comprehensive "homosexual agenda,"
and that legalization of same-sex marriage will mean that children
will have to be taught about homosexuality in public schools.

Blankenhorn, David. "Protecting Marriage to Protect Children."
Los Angeles Times, September 19, 2008. http://articles.latimes
.com/2008/sep/19/opinion/oe-blankenhorn19. Accessed on
April 14, 2010.

The author describes himself as a "liberal Democrat" who is
opposed to same-sex marriage. The basis for his position is that
he believes that children would be harmed by same-sex marriage,
that they should all grow up in a family with one father and one
mother.

Camenker, Brian. "What Same-Sex 'Marriage' Has Done to Massachusetts. It's Far Worse than Most People Realize." http://
www.massresistance.org/docs/marriage/effects_of_ssm.html.
Accessed on January 17, 2010.

Camenker argues that approval of same-sex marriage in Massachusetts has wrecked havoc in many areas, including public
education, public health, domestic violence, business, the legal
profession, government mandates, the media, public demonstrations, and adoption by same-sex couples. He concludes the article
with a consideration of the question as to whether same-sex marriage is really legal in the Commonwealth.

Concerned Women for America. "Top 10 Reasons to Support the
Marriage Affirmation and Protection Amendment." URL: http://

www.cwfa.org/articledisplay.asp?id=5351&department=CFI &categoryid=family. Posted on March 10, 2004.

Concerned Women for America is an evangelical Christian group that works for the introduction of religious principles into political life in the United States. It has taken strong stands against the legalization of same-sex marriage, a position that is explained and defended in this document.

Crouse, Janice Shaw. "Five Myths about Same Sex Marriage." http:// townhall.com/columnists/JaniceShawCrouse/2010/03/09/five _myths_about_same_sex_marriage. Posted on March 9, 2010.

Crouse responds to five traditional arguments in favor of same-sex marriage, such as same-sex marriage does no harm to other individuals, same-sex marriage is a matter of civil rights, and same-sex marriages are just like opposite-sex marriages. As of April 12, 2010, the article had produced over a thousand responses from bloggers to the Web site both in support of and opposed to the article.

Dobson, James. "Marriage Under Fire: Arguments Against Same-Sex Marriage." URL: http://www.citizenlink.org/focusaction/ fofafeatures/A000006871.cfm. Posted in June 2004.

Dobson is founder of the evangelical organization, Focus on the Family, and was its president, when he wrote this article in 2004. It outlines the fundamental argument as to why evangelical Christians object to the legalization of same-sex marriages.

Family Research Council. "InFocus." http://www.frc.org/get.cfm ?i=if03h01. Accessed on April 14, 2010.

The anonymous writer of this Web page offers an extended response to the many reasons that are often suggested for supporting the legalization of same-sex marriage. He concludes that amending the U.S. Constitution may be the only way to be certain that same-sex marriage is not eventually adopted in this country.

Somerville, Margaret A. "The Case against 'Same-Sex Marriage.'" A Brief Submitted to the Standing Committee on Justice and Human Rights [of the Canadian Parliament]. http://www .catholiceducation.org/articles/homosexuality/ho0063.html. Accessed on April 15, 2010.

The author, Samuel Gale Professor of Law and professor in the Faculty of Medicine at McGill University's Centre for Medicine, Ethics, and Law, lays out the arguments for not legalizing same-sex marriage in Canada. The argument proved to be unsuccessful as same-sex marriage was eventually authorized by the parliament in July 2005.

"Testimony of Jay Alan Sekulow, Chief Counsel, the American Center for Law and Justice Before the Judiciary Subcommittee on the Constitution May 13, 2004." http://www.aclj.org/media/pdf/040513_FMAHearingTestimony.pdf. Accessed on February 22, 2010.

In this document, Sekulow very aptly lays out the case against same-sex marriage, presenting arguments against the practice and offering rebuttals to arguments made in favor of same-sex unions.

United States Conference of Catholic Bishops. "How Does Legalizing 'Same-Sex Marriage' Deny the True Nature of Marriage?" http://www.usccb.org/laity/marriage/samesexeng.shtml. Accessed on March 14, 2010.

This document examines three specific claims made in support of legalizing same-sex marriage, arguments that can be made against those positions, and church teachings on each of the three claims. The document concludes that demands for same-sex marriage have arisen out of an increasing tendency to focus on "adult fulfillment," rather than the needs of children.

Ventrella, Jeffrey J. "An Evaluation of Professor Michael Seidman's October 20, 2005 Testimony Regarding the Proposed Federal Marriage Amendment." URL: http://www.alliancedefensefund.org/UserDocs/Testimony_JefferyVentrella.pdf. Accessed on December 13, 2009.

Ventrella is senior vice president of the Alliance Defense Fund, an organization whose purpose it is to defend religious freedom in the United States, and which has taken a leading role in the battle against same-sex marriage. This document is a record of Ventrella's testimony before the U.S. Senate Subcommittee on the Constitution, Civil Rights, and Property Rights of the Judiciary Committee, which was holding hearings on a proposed constitutional amendment to define marriage as being between two members of the opposite sex only.

General Reviews of Same-Sex Marriage
Internet
Axel-Lute, Paul. "Same-Sex Marriage: A Selective Bibliography of the Legal Literature." http://law-library.rutgers.edu/SSM.html. Accessed on April 12, 2010.

This bibliography is an extraordinary achievement, providing a host of useful references on all aspects of same-sex marriage, including articles both supporting and opposing same-sex marriage, polygamy, parenting and children, taxation, defense of marriage legislation, the federal marriage amendment, and international aspects of the topic.

Dvorak, Petula. "Reality Makes Gay Marriage Debate Obsolete." *The Washington Post.* URL: http://www.washingtonpost.com/wp-dyn/content/article/2009/09/03/AR2009090303585.html?hpid=topnews. Posted on September 4. 2009.

The columnist makes the interesting observation that the District of Columbia council's then-current debate over legalizing same-sex marriage in the District is largely irrelevant since same-sex couples have been a real and essential part of the District's life now for many years. (The District council eventually approved the bill legalizing same-sex marriage, by a vote of 11 to 2, on December 1, 2009.)

Eskridge, William N., Darren R. Spedale, and Hans Ytterberg. "Nordic Bliss? Scandinavian Registered Partnerships and the Same-Sex Marriage Debate." Issues in Legal Scholarship. http://asemus.asef.org/go/subsite/ccd/documents/nordicbliss-ytterberg.pdf. Accessed on February 23, 2010.

The authors analyze in considerable detail the information available as to the effects of same-sex marriage in three Scandinavian countries—Denmark, Norway, and Sweden—where it has been legal for at least a few years. They conclude that the institution has so far had no harmful effects on opposite-sex marriage or divorce rates.

FindLaw. Same-Sex Marriage Pros and Cons. http://family.findlaw.com/same-sex-couples/legal-same-sex-marriage.html. Accessed on April 14, 2010.

This Web site provides a number of legal issues with which the same-sex marriage is concerned, including having children, property rights, inheritance and death taxes, immigration, and government benefits.

Forbes, Jack D. "What Is Marriage? A Native American View." http://nas.ucdavis.edu/Forbes/what_is%20Marriage.pdf. Accessed on January 13, 2010.

Forbes suggests that people who speak about "traditional marriage" probably know little or nothing about the topic from the perspective of Native Americans. He outlines some traditions about marriage in the Native American culture.

La Pook, Jon. "Debate: Should Same Sex Marriage Be Legal?" CBS News.com. Posted on March 11, 2010. http://www.cbsnews.com/video/watch/?id=6288663n.

La Pook, CBS News medical correspondent, hosts a debate between Cathy Marino-Thomas, of Marriage Equality New York, and Janice Crouse, of Concerned Women for America, on the pros and cons of legalizing same-sex marriage in the United States.

O'Grair, Scot. "Effects of Same-Sex Unions." http://isocrat.org/science/demog/mar_stats.php#ymde. Accessed on February 23, 2010.

This Web page summarizes the evidence on the effects of same-sex marriage on opposite-sex marriage and divorce patterns in (primarily) Denmark, the Netherlands, Norway, and Sweden. The author concludes that there are no identifiable harmful effects and, perhaps, some positive effects of same-sex marriage in these countries.

PollingReport.com. "Law and Civil Rights." http://www.pollingreport.com/civil.htm. Accessed on February 13, 2010.

This Web site summarizes the results of dozens of public opinion polls about same-sex marriage and same-sex unions in the United States over the past decade or more.

"Same Sex Marriage, Civil Unions and Domestic Partnerships."
http://www.ncsl.org/IssuesResearch/HumanServices/Same
SexMarriage/tabid/16430/Default.aspx. Accessed on January 6,
2010.

The National Conference of State Legislatures provides accurate and up-to-date information on the status of same-sex marriage laws and so-called defense of marriage acts adopted by legislative bodies in all 50 states.

Silver, Nate. "Divorce Rates Higher in States with Gay Marriage
Bans." FiveThirtyEight. http://www.fivethirtyeight.com/2010/
01/divorce-rates-appear-higher-in-states.html. Accessed on
April 12, 2010.

This article provides a very interesting summary of divorce rates in states that have and have not passed bans on same-sex marriage, with the results indicated by the title of the article. The findings produced an extended and extensive series of comments from bloggers to the Web site.

Statistics Canada. "Family Portrait: Continuity and Change in
Canadian Families and Households in 2006, 2006 Census."
http://www.samesexmarriage.ca/docs/FamilyCensus2006.pdf.
Accessed on March 29, 2010.

The Canadian government provides its first extended review of the demographics of same-sex couples in the country since same-sex marriage was legalized in 2005.

United States General Accounting Office. "Defense of Marriage
Act: Update to Prior Report." http://www.gao.gov/new.items/
d04353r.pdf. Accessed on March 15, 2010.

In 1997, the General Accounting Office prepared a report listing provisions in the U.S. Code that gave legally married couples certain benefits that are not available to nonmarried couples. This report updates the 1997 report, resulting in a finding that, as of 2004, there were "a total of 1,138 federal statutory provisions classified to the United States Code in which marital status is a factor in determining or receiving benefits, rights, and privileges."

Glossary

adelphopoiesis A ceremony practiced by a number of early Christian sects in which two individuals, usually men, were joined in marriage-like relationships.

amicus curiae A person or organization that offers information and advice to a court about a legal issue in which the person or organization is not directly involved.

antimiscegenation law A law that prohibits the marriage of two people of different races. Antimiscegnation laws in the United States were considered to be constitutional until 1967.

artificial insemination The introduction of a man's semen into a woman's uterus by some method other than sexual intercourse.

bisexual A term that refers to acts, fantasies, or feelings that involve individuals of either sex. People who call themselves bisexual experience an erotic interest in both men and women, although not necessarily to an equal extent.

civil rights Personal rights guaranteed to all citizens, usually as the result of some defining document, such as the U.S. Constitution.

civil union A legally sanctioned relationship between two individuals of the same or opposite sex who are not otherwise allowed to marry under laws of the state. *See also* **domestic partnership; registered partnership**.

domestic partners Two individuals who are not legally married to each other but who do live together and share their lives together, sometimes in a legally sanctioned relationship known as a civil union, domestic partnership, or registered partnership.

domestic partnership A legally sanctioned relationship between two individuals of the same or opposite sex who are not otherwise allowed to marry under laws of the state. The term is used most commonly in the United States. *See also* **civil union; registered partnership**.

foster care   Placement of a child or young adult in the care of person or family because of some type of disruption in that child or young adult's own personal life, such as the loss of both parents or the inability of parents to properly care for the child or young adult.

full faith and credit clause   Section 1 of the Fourth Amendment to the U.S. Constitution says that all states must accept and honor all legal decisions made by another state. One of the very few situations in which that clause has been ignored in U.S. history has been same-sex marriage, in which nearly all states have decided not to honor same-sex marriages conducted in another state.

gay   A term that has come to be associated with individuals, organizations, acts, events, or other phenomena involving two individuals of the same gender, most commonly, two men.

gay liberation   A movement whose goals it was to free lesbians and gay men from long-standing prejudices, fears, and hatreds of nongays and, in many cases, to make issues of sexuality more open and free for all people whatever their sexual orientation.

gay marriage   A term sometimes used as a synonym for same-sex marriage, especially for purposes of saving space in print publications (as per the current *Associated Press Stylebook*).

gay rights legislation   Any law, executive order, administrative rule, or other legal action that specifically provides for the protection of some civil liberty (such as employment or housing) for lesbians and gay men.

gender   A term that refers to a person's social identity as a man or a women. The concept of gender includes not only one's biological sex (male or female), but also the social constructs created by a culture that tend to be associated with one or the other sex.

heterosexual   Any feeling, fantasy, or act that involves two people of the opposite sex.

homophobia   The irrational fear of gay men and lesbians.

homosexual   A term that should probably best be used as an adjective, referring to any feeling, fantasy, or act that involves two people of the same sex. Historically, the word has also been used to an individual or group of individuals. It is less successful in that context because it tends to define individuals and groups of individuals solely on the basis of their erotic interests.

lesbian   A women whose primary erotic interest involves other women.

marriage   A relationship between two individuals legally recognized by a state or nation that generally includes a number of benefits not available to single individuals or to individuals in a relationship not recognized by the government. Although the term generally refers to an opposite-sex couple, alternative types of marriages have existed throughout history and are available in some nations and states within nations today. (The *Oxford English Dictionary* has accepted the more inclusive definition of the term since 2000.)

mutual adoption   The process by which each member of a couple legally adopts the children of his or her partner. The term usually, but not inevitably, applies to same-sex couples.

next-of-kin   A person who is legally recognized as the closest relative to a person, such as a husband, wife, child, sibling, or same-sex partner (where same-sex relationships are legally recognized).

partner   A term that has become increasingly popular in describing one member of a same-sex couple.

queer   A derogatory word used to describe gay men and lesbians. The term has now been adopted by many gay men and lesbians as an act of defiance against those who would use the term in a disparaging manner.

registered partnership   A legally sanctioned relationship between two individuals of the same or opposite sex who are not otherwise allowed to marry under laws of the state. The term is used most commonly in Europe. *See also* **civil union; domestic partnership**.

second-parent adoption   A process by which the partner of a child's parent legally adopts the child, as in stepparent adoption.

sex   The genetic and biological characteristic of maleness or femaleness, usually characterized by the presence or absence of certain sex organs, such as a penis and a vagina.

sexual orientation   The tendency of a person to be erotically attracted to someone of the same gender, the opposite gender, or both genders. The term *orientation* usually suggests that this tendency is not consciously chosen by a person, but is determined by some genetic or biological factor. *See also* **sexual preference**.

sexual preference   The tendency of a person to be erotically attracted to someone of the same gender, the opposite gender, or both genders. The term *preference* usually suggests that this tendency is consciously selected by a person rather than being the result of a genetic or biological factor.

slippery slope argument   An argument that claims that taking one action inevitably leads to other actions that, in turn, lead to even more actions, so that the significance of the first action is much greater than it might otherwise seem. For example, some people believe that allowing two people of the same sex to become legally married will eventually lead to (1) three-person marriages, (2) marriages between a human and an animal, and/or (3) marriages between nonhuman animals.

spouse   One of the two members of a close relationship, most commonly a legal marriage between a man and a woman, but also applicable to an individual in a long-term opposite-sex or same-sex relationship recognized by a legal entity or not.

spousal benefit   Values that may be passed from one member of a couple to the other member upon the first person's death or incapacity, such as pension income, Social Security payments, or Medicare benefits.

surrogate mother   A woman who agrees to be inseminated with the sperm of a man and carry the fetus thus produced to term, after which the baby is given to some other couple.

traditional marriage   A term commonly used by opponents of same-sex marriage to mean marriage between one man and one woman, although the term is historically inaccurate.

Index

AAMFT. *See* American Association for Marriage and Family Therapy (AAMFT)
About Time: Exploring the Gay Past (Duberman), 231
Achilles, 8
Achtenberg, Roberta, 209
ACLJ. *See* American Center for Law and Justice (ACLJ)
ACLU. *See* American Civil Liberties Union (ACLU)
An Act to End Discrimination in Civil Marriage and Affirm Religious Freedom, 166–67
Adam, Barry D., 230
Adams, Richard, 113
Adams v. Howerton, 113
Adelphopoiesis, 41
ADF. *See* Alliance Defense Fund (ADF)
Adoption
  adult, 135
  mutual, 271
  second-parent, 115, 243, 271. *See also* Same-sex adoption
"Adoption 101: A Family Guide," 202
"The Adoption and Children Act 2002" (Hitchings & Sagar), 250
Adoption and Foster Care by Gay and Lesbian Parents in the United States (Gates et al.), 254
Adoption by Lesbians and Gays (Brodzinsky), 253
Adult adoption, 135
AFA. *See* American Family Association (AFA)
"Affidavit of William Eskridge, Jr.," 256

Afflect, Annie, 114
Afghanistan, 85
AFM. *See* Alliance for Marriage (AFM)
Africa
  laws against same-sex relationships, 85
  same-sex marriage in, 82–84
After the Ball: How America Will Conquer Its Fear and Hatred of Gays in the '90s (Kirk & Madsen), 52
Alabama, divorce rate in, 53
Alabama Marriage Protection Act, 158–59
Alarcn, Hernando de, 6
Alaska
  employment benefits for same-sex couple, 126
  restriction of marriage to man and woman, 118
  same-sex adoption and, 114
Alberta (Canada), 94
Albin, Barry T., 133–34
Alcuin, 38–39
Alice B. Toklas Memorial Democratic Club, 147, 149
Allen, Douglas W., 248
Alliance Defense Fund (ADF), 215, 262
Alliance for Marriage (AFM), 215–16
Alsenas, Linas, 230–31
Alternatives to Marriage Project (AMP), 224–25
American Association for Marriage and Family Therapy (AAMFT), 225
American Center for Law and Justice (ACLJ), 49, 216

American Civil Liberties Union
(ACLU), 55, 199–200
American Family Association (AFA),
216–17
American Indians
marriage traditions, 266
same-sex marriage and, 48–49
same-sex relationships and, 6–7
American Law Institute, 15
American Pediatric Association, 60
American Psychiatric Association, 20
America's Struggle for Same-Sex Marriage
(Pinello), 247
AMP. *See* Alternatives to Marriage
Project (AMP)
Andalusia (Spain), 98
Anderson, Rocky, 203
Andorra, 89, 123
Andryszewski, Tricia, 245
Ann Arbor (Michigan), 20
Antidiscrimination laws, 20–22
Antimiscegenation laws, 51, 112
Antinous, 9
Antisodomy laws, 14–16, 232
APACE. *See* Asian Pacific
American Coalition for Equality
(APACE)
API Equality, 200
Apostolic United Brethren, 48
Aragon (Spain), 88, 98
Argentina
civil unions in, 98–99, 121
inheritance rights for same-sex
couples, 127
public opinion on same-sex
marriage, 101
same-sex marriage in, 102, 130,
131, 132
"An Argument for Same-Sex
Marriage" (Deason), 259–60
"Arguments for Gay Marriage"
(Cline), 259
Arizona, restriction of marriage to man
and woman, 125, 128
Arkansas, divorce rate in, 53
Arkansas Family Council, 163
Arkansas Same-Sex Adoption Law,
162–64
Arkes, Hadley, 55
Arranged marriages, 43

Articles
arguments in favor of same-sex
marriage, 239–41
arguments opposed to same-sex
marriage, 243–45
gay and lesbian civil rights issues,
234–36
general reviews of same-sex
marriage and adoption, 248–53
history of same-sex unions, 229–30
Aruba, 99
Asian Pacific American Coalition for
Equality (APACE), 200
"Assessing and Responding to Same-
Sex 'Marriage' in Light of
Natural Law" (Reid), 244
Asturias (Spain), 88, 98
Australia
de facto relationships in, 97
Domestic Relationship Act, 116
public opinion on same-sex
marriage, 102
restriction of marriage to man
and woman, 122
same-sex marriage in, 131
Australian Capital Territory (ACT), 97
Austria, 89, 130
Authorizing Marriage? (Jordan), 247
"Avoidance Strategy" (Duncan), 243
Axel-Lute, Paul, 265

Babst, Gordon A., 237
Badgett, M. V. Lee, 245–46, 254
Baehr, Ninia, 23
Baehr v. Miike, 23–24
BAGLY. *See* Boston Alliance of Gay,
Lesbian, Bisexual and
Transgendered Youth (BAGLY)
Bahati, David, 85
Baird, Robert M., 246
Baker, Jack (Richard John), 1–2, 22, 112,
149–50
biographical sketch, 134–35
Baker v. Nelson, 1–2, 36, 112, 134
Baldacci, John, 68, 129, 142
Balearic Islands, 98
Barnsley, William, 114
Barr, Bob, 135–36
Barwick, Paul, 113
Basque Country (Spain), 98

Battered Wives (Martin), 149
Bazile, Leon, 51
Beach, Frank A., 3
Becker, Mary, 239
Bedouins, 6
Before Stonewall (Bullough), 231
Belgium
  common-law marriage rights for
    same-sex couples in, 118
  public opinion on same-sex
    marriage, 101
  registered partnerships in, 119
  same-sex adoption in, 125
  same-sex and opposite-sex marriage
    data, 196, 197
  same-sex marriage in, 88, 121
Benefits
  available to married couples, 63,
    168–69, 267
  employment, for same-sex couples,
    116, 123, 126, 127
Benson, Ezra Taft, 151
Berdache, 7, 48
Berkeley (California), domestic
  partnerships in, 114
"Beyond Gay Marriage" (Kurtz), 244
Beyond (Straight and Gay) Marriage
  (Polikoff), 238, 247–48
Bible
  references against same-sex
    relationships, 11, 13, 15, 33–35, 261
  same-sex relationships portrayed in,
    11, 12–13, 256
  types of marriage mentioned, 35
"Bible Passages Describing Eight
  Family/Marriage Types," 255
Bidstrup, Scott, 259
Bill, Emily R., 237
Bishop of Urgell, 123
Blackstone, William, 43, 49, 90
Blake, Paul M., Jr., 191
Blankenhorn, David, 248–49, 262
Blessing Same-Sex Unions (Jordan),
  228–29
Bloomberg, Michael, 123
Blue Earth County (Minnesota), 1, 112
Body of Civil Law (*Corpus Jurus
  Civilis*), 37
Body of Laws and Liberties, 15
Bogues, Leon, 155

Boies, David, 136–37, 153
Bolivia, 87
Bonauto, Mary, 137–38
Bond, Julian, 234
Books
  arguments in favor of same-sex
    marriage, 237–39
  arguments opposed to same-sex
    marriage, 241–43
  gay and lesbian civil rights issues,
    230–34
  general reviews of same-sex
    marriage and adoption, 245–48
  history of same-sex unions, 227–29
Boston Alliance of Gay, Lesbian,
  Bisexual and Transgendered
  Youth (BAGLY), 146
Boston marriage, 44
Boston Women's Fund, 146
Boswell, John E., 9, 38–39, 41, 138–39,
  227–28
Bottoms, Pamela, 117
Bottoms, Sharon, 117
Bottoms, Tyler, 117
Bottoms v. Bottoms, 117
Boulder County (Colorado), 2
Bourassa, Kevin, 120
Bowers v. Hardwick, 16, 114, 121
Bracher, Barbara Kay, 154
Bradley, Vincent, 155
Brewer, Paul R., 246
Bride sale, 42
*Bringing Lesbian and Gay Rights into the
  Mainstream* (Endean), 232
British Columbia, same-sex marriage
  ruling, 121
Brodzinsky, David M., 253
Brooks, Devon, 249
Brother-making, 40
Brown, Stephen, 239
Brunk, Doug, 239
Bryant, Anita, 56, 185
Bryant, Chris, 139–40
Buenos Aires (Argentina), 130, 132
Buggery Law, 14
Bulgaria, 116
Bull, Benjamin, 53
Bullough, Vern, 231
Burt, Robert A., 239
Bush, George W., 122, 153

Bush v. Gore, 137, 153
Butler, Howard, 223
Buturo, James Nsaba, 86
Byron, Lord, 6

Cabeza de Vaca, Alvar Nuñez, 6
California
  antidiscrimination law, 21
  domestic partnership laws, 70, 114
  In re: Marriage Cases, 127. *See also*
    Proposition 8
California Supreme Court
  on procreation and marriage, 57–58
  on same-sex marriage, 62
Callahan, Tena, 192–94
Cambodia, 116
Camenker, Brian, 262
Canada
  court rulings on same-sex unions,
    100, 121
  number of same-sex couples in
    legally recognized relationships,
    94–95, 195
  public opinion on same-sex
    marriage, 101–102
  same-sex marriage in, 58, 93, 94–95,
    120, 123, 124
Canadian Psychological Association, 59
"Can Anyone Show Just Cause Why
    These Two Should Not Be
    Lawfully Joined Together?," 249
Canary Islands, 88, 98
Canon law, prohibition of same-sex
    relationships in, 14, 37
Carter, David, 234–35
"The Case against 'Same-Sex
    Marriage'" (Somerville), 263–64
"Casebook on Sexual Orientation and
    the Law" (Pinello), 257–58
"The Case for Legal Recognition of
    Same-Sex Marriage" (Katz), 240
The Case for Same-Sex Marriage
    (Eskridge), 144
Catalonia (Spain), 88, 98, 118
Catholic Education Resource
    Center, 59
The Catholic Encyclopedia, 38
Catholic University of America,
    Marriage Law Project, 221
Cayman Islands, 87

CC. *See* Christian Coalition
    of America (CC)
Celibacy, 45
Centennial Park group, 48
Center for the Study of Equality, 205
Chambers, Kate, 254
Chang, Kevin S. C., 23–24
"Chapter Forum Retains Policy"
    (Silverman), 240–41
Chartier, Gary, 240
Chauncey, George, Jr., 231, 246
Chavez, Christine, 203
Cherokee Nation, ban on same-sex
    marriage, 49
Chico Enterprise-Record, 147
Child custody, lesbian mothers
    and, 112, 113
Child rearing, marriage and, 58–60
Children of Lesbians and Gays
    Everywhere (COLAGE), 201
"Children's Human Rights and
    Unlinking Child-Parent
    Biological Bonds with
    Adoptions, Same-Sex Marriage
    and New Reproductive
    Technologies" (Sommerville),
    244–45
Chile, 102
China, same-sex relationships in
    ancient, 5, 83, 112, 255
Christian Coalition of America (CC),
    217
Christianity
  attitude toward same-sex
    relationships, 13
  Christian model of marriage, 35–36
  same-sex marriage in Judeo-
    Christian history, 33–36. *See also*
    Bible
*Christianity, Social Tolerance, and
    Homosexuality* (Boswell), 38–39
Church of Jesus Christ in Zion, 48
Church of Jesus Christ of Latter-day
    Saints (Mormons), 217–18
  polygamy and, 46–48
  Proposition 8 and, 150–51, 217–18
Church of the Firstborn in the Fullness
    of Time, 48
CitizenLink, 52
Civil pact of solidarity, 89, 99, 119, 126

"Civil Partnership: A Framework for the Legal Recognition of Same-Sex Couples," 92
Civil Partnership Act, 124
Civil partnerships
  in Europe, 89, 91–93
  in Jersey, 99
  in UK, 122
Civil Partnerships Bill, 91–92
Civil rights. *See* Gay and lesbian civil rights issues
Civil Rights Act of 1964, 18, 20
Civil unions, 70–71, 88, 89, 90
  in Argentina, 98–99
  bans against, 70–71
  chronology of, 119, 122, 123, 125, 126, 127, 128
  constitutional amendments to ban, 87
  in New Zealand, 95
  public opinion on, 71. *See also* Domestic partnerships; Registered partnerships
Claudius, 9
Clergy, same-sex relationships among Roman Catholic, 38–40
Cline, Austin, 259
Clinton, Bill, 3, 25, 65, 117, 152, 157
Coahuila (Mexico), 99, 126
Code of Hammurabi, 4
Coexistence partnerships, 99
Cohabitation unions, 96, 127
COLAGE. *See* Children of Lesbians and Gays Everywhere (COLAGE)
Colombia
  court rulings and same-sex unions, 100
  rights for same-sex couples, 128
  same-sex unions in, 96, 103, 127
Colonizing nations, transfer of attitudes toward same-sex relationships, 85
Colorado
  custody rights of lesbian mothers, 113
  law defining marriage as between man and woman, 2
Colorado Springs (Colorado), 2
Coming Out (Weeks), 234
Commentaries on the Laws of England (Blackstone), 43

Common-law marriage, refusal of divorce for two men involved in, 114
Common-law marriage rights for same-sex couples, 88, 113–14, 115, 117, 118, 119
Community Defense Council, 215
Complex marriage, 46
Concerned Women for America (CWA), 44–45, 218, 262–63, 266
Connecticut
  antidiscrimination law, 21
  civil unions in, 70, 123
  same-sex marriage in, 67, 69, 128
  sodomy law, 15
Connecticut Supreme Court, 69
"The Conservative Case for Gay Marriage" (Olson), 261
Constans, 37, 111
Constantine, 37
Constantius II, 37, 111
Constitutional amendments
  banning civil unions/domestic partnerships, 87
  banning same-sex adoption, 86–87
  limiting marriage to opposite-sex couples, 3, 24, 25, 31, 55, 57, 65, 86–87, 117, 118, 119, 122, 129, 135–36, 157–58, 168, 208
"The Constitutionality of Legal Preferences for Heterosexual Marriage" (Wilkins), 245
"The Constitutional Same Sex Marriage Debate" (Faucette), 260
Coolidge, David Orgon, 243
Coontz, Stephanie, 228
Cooper, Charles J., 31, 140–41
"Coparent or Second-Parent Adoption by Same-Sex Parents" (Committee on Psychosocial Aspects of Child and Family Health), 240
Coquille tribe, recognition of same-sex marriage, 49, 67
Cordy, Robert J., 178
Cornish, Richard, 15
Corporate Research Council, 215
Corpus Jurus Civilis, 37
Corzine, Jon, 134
Costa Rica, 100

Cotler, Irwin, 141
Council of Florence, 36
Council on Religion and the
    Homosexual, 147, 149
Court cases, 174–94
    E. B. v. France, 174–76
    *Goodridge v. Department of Public
        Health*, 121–22, 137, 145, 146,
        176–80
    Kutil and Hess v. Blake, 190–92
    Lewis v. Harris, 180–85
    Order on Intervenor's Plea to the
        Jurisdiction, 192–94
    In re: Gill, 185–87
    on same-sex adoption, 174–76,
        185–87, 190–92
    on same-sex marriage, 119, 121, 123,
        176–85, 188–90, 246
    on same-sex unions, 100, 125
    Varnum v. Brien, 188–90
*Courting Equality: A Documentary
    History of America's First Legal
    Same-Sex Marriages* (Gozemba &
    Kahn), 228
Craig, Larry, 65
Cranney, Jared, 139, 140
Cripps, Stafford, 140
"A Critical Analysis of Constitutional
    Claims for Same-Sex Marriage"
    (Wardle), 252
Croatia, 121
Cross-generational marriage, 48
Crouse, Janice Shaw, 263, 266
Cuba, 113
Custody rights, of gay father, 115
CWA. *See* Concerned Women for
    America (CWA)
Cyprus, 101
Czech Republic, 89, 118, 119, 120, 124

Damon, Dennis, 142
Dancel, Genora, 23
Darden, Buddy, 136
Dare to Discipline (Dobson), 143
Data and statistics
    divorce rates by U.S. state, 197–98
    marriage and divorce rates in
        Denmark, 196
    same-sex and opposite-sex marriage
        data from Belgium, 196, 197

same-sex and opposite-sex marriage
    data from Netherlands, 195–96
same-sex couples in legally
    recognized relationships, 195
same-sex marriages in
    Massachusetts, 194
Daughters of Bilitis (DOB), 17, 146–47,
    149, 231, 233
David (Biblical), 12
D.C. Madam, 66
Deason, Claire B., 259–60
Death, as punishment for same-sex
    relationships, 85
"Debate: Should Same Sex Marriage
    Be Legal?" (La Pook), 266
De facto couples, 98
De facto relationship, 97
De facto unions, 98
Defending a Higher Law (TFP
    Committee on American Issues),
    242–43
Defense of Marriage Act (DOMA), 3,
    55, 65, 117, 157–58, 168, 208
    Barr and, 135–36
    IRS and, 135
"Defense of Marriage Act" (GAO), 267
Defense of marriage acts, in states, 25,
    57, 117
Defoe, Daniel, 43
"Delegates Endorse Same-Sex
    Adoption" (Brunk), 239
D'Emilio, John, 147, 231
Democracy Project, 204
Democratic Republic of Congo, 87
Denmark
    number of same-sex couples in
        legally recognized relationships,
        195, 196
    public opinion on same-sex
        marriage, 101
    registered partnerships in,
        87–88, 115
    same-sex couple rights, 114
De Santa v. Barnsley, 114
DeSanto, John, 114
Deseret News, 151
Di Bello, José María, 130, 131, 132
*Different Daughters: A History of the
    Daughters of Bilitis . . .* (Gallo), 233
Dishonorable Passions (Eskridge), 232

District of Columbia
    antidiscrimination law, 21
    domestic partnership law, 70
    same-sex marriage in, 68–69, 131
    sodomy law, 15
Divorce
    recognition of same-sex marriage
      and right to, 192–94
    trends, 53–54
Divorce rate
    correlation to same-sex/opposite-
      sex marriage laws, 53–54, 267
    Denmark, 196
    U.S., by state, 197–98
"Divorce Rates Higher in States with
    Gay Marriage Bans" (Silver), 267
DOB. *See* Daughters of Bilitis (DOB)
Dobson, James, 142–43, 241, 260, 263
Documents and data, 157–98
    court cases, 174–94
    data and statistics, 195–98
    legislation, 157–68
    reports, 168–73
DOMA. *See* Defense of Marriage Act
    (DOMA)
DOMA Section 3 Challenge program,
    204
DOMA Watch, 215
Domestic partnerships
    in Australia, 97–98
    Berkeley and, 114
    chronology of, 127, 130
    constitutional amendments
      to ban, 87
    public opinion on, 71
    in United States, 70–71. *See also* Civil
      unions; Registered partnerships
Domestic Relations Act (Australia), 97
Domestic Relationship Act, 116
Dominican Republic, 87
"Don't ask, don't tell" policy, 208, 213
Doskow, Emily, 246–47
Douglas, Jim, 68
Duberman, Martin, 231
Dugan, Kimberly B., 232
Duncan, William C., 243
Dunlap, Victoria, 122
Dunne, Bruce, 257
Dupree, Melvin, 223
Dvorak, Petula, 265

East Coast Homophile Organizations
    (ECHO), 18
Eastern Orthodox Church, same-sex
    unions in Middle Ages and, 37,
    40–41
East Lansing (Michigan), 20
E. B. v. France, 174–76
ECHO. *See* East Coast Homophile
    Organizations (ECHO)
"An Economic Assessment of Same-
    Sex Marriage Laws" (Allen), 248
Economic benefits, of marriage, 63
Ecuador
    ban on same-sex marriage in, 87
    same-sex marriage in, 102
    same-sex unions in, 96, 128
Edelman, Murray S., 236
"Editors' Symposium: The Meaning
    of Marriage," 249
EF. *See* Equality Federation (EF)
"Effects of Same-Sex Unions"
    (O'Grair), 266
Egale Canada, 201
Egan, Patrick J., 236
Eisenbach, David, 232
Elizabeth I, 14
Elizabeth II, 122, 124
El Salvador, 87
Employment, antidiscrimination in, 20
Employment benefits for same-sex
    couples, 116, 123, 126, 127
Employment Non-Discrimination
    Act (ENDA), 202
ENDA. *See* Employment Non-
    Discrimination Act (ENDA)
Endean, Steve, 232
Enfraternization, 40
England
    number of same-sex couples in legally
      recognized relationships, 195
    sodomy laws, 14. *See also* United
      Kingdom
Equality Federation (EF), 201–202
Equality for Same-Sex Couples (Merin), 229
Equality from State to State (Human Rights
    Campaign Foundation), 236
Equality under the law provisions, 61
ERLC. *See* Ethics & Religious Liberty
    Commission (ERLC) of the
    Southern Baptist Convention

Eskridge, William N., Jr., 53–54, 144, 229–30, 232, 256, 265
Ethics & Religious Liberty Commission (ERLC) of the Southern Baptist Convention, 218–19
Ethnographic Atlas Codebook, 81
Ethnology, 81
Eurobarometer program, 101
European Commission, 101
European Convention on Human Rights, same-sex adoption and, 174
European Court of Human Rights, *E. B. v. France*, 174–76
European Parliament, Resolution . . . on the Situation of Fundamental Rights in the European Union, 172–73
European Union
  legal status of same-sex relationships and, 92–93
  resolution on situation of fundamental rights in, 172–73
  support for same-sex marriage, 103
"An Evaluation of Professor Michael Seidman's . . . Testimony Regarding the Proposed Federal Marriage Amendment," 264–65 (Ventrella)
Evans, Anthony, 223
Everything-but-marriage bill, 70, 129, 130
Extremadura (Spain), 98

Falwell, Jerry, 221
Families Like Ours (FLO), 202
Family
  same-sex couple defined as, 115
  same-sex marriage and, 51–54, 64–65
Family, Unvalued Discrimination, Denial and the Fate of Binational Same-Sex Couples under U.S. Law (Human Rights Watch), 236
Family Equality Council, 201, 202–203
Family in Transition (Skolnick & Skolnick), 82
"Family Law in the Secular State and Restriction on Same-Sex Marriage" (Becker), 239

"Family Portrait: Continuity and Change in Canadian Families and Households in 2006," 267
Family Protection Act, 20
Family Research Council (FRC), 66, 132, 143, 219, 263
Faucette, Judith, 260
Fauntroy, Walter, 223
Fawcett, Henry, 43
Fawcett, Millicent Garrett, 43
Federal Marriage Amendment, 151, 159–60, 216, 217, 260–61, 264–65
Fejes, Fred, 232–33
Feldblum, Chai, 235
"Female husband," 84
Fenty, Adrian, 68
Fetner, Tina, 233
Fight Repression of Erotic Expression (FREE), 134–35
Findings from the Hunter College Poll of Lesbians, Gays and Bisexuals (Egan et al.), 236
Fine, Dakota, 203
Finland, 89, 120
Fitzpatrick, Brian, 257
"Five Myths about Same Sex Marriage" (Crouse), 263
Flaubert, Gustave, 6
FLO. *See* Families Like Ours (FLO)
Florenskij, Pavel, 40
Florida
  divorce rate, 53
  In re: Gill, 185–87
  restriction of marriage to man and woman, 128
  same-sex adoption ban, 113, 185–87
Focus on the Family, 52, 142–43, 219–20
Foley, Mark, 66
Forbes, Jack D., 7, 48, 230, 266
Ford, Clellan S., 3
"Foreword: The Next Normal" (Weiser), 252–53
"Forging Gay Identities" (Freeman), 235
"Four Reasons to Support Gay Marriage and Oppose the Federal Marriage Amendment" (Head), 260–61
Frakes, Robert, 254

France
  civil pact of solidarity in, 89, 119
  E. B. v. France, 174–76
  rights of same-sex couples in, 52
Frank, Barney, 213
Franke, Katherine M., 249–50
FRC. *See* Family Research Council (FRC)
FREE. *See* Fight Repression of Erotic
  Expression (FREE)
Freedom to Marry, 203
Freeman, Susan Kathleen, 235
Freyre, Alex, 130, 131, 132
Friedan, Betty, 44, 310
Frist, Bill, 168
Fujian province, same-sex marriages
  in, 5, 83, 112, 255
Full faith and credit clause, recogni-
  tion of same-sex marriage
  and, 25
Fundamentalist Church of Jesus Christ
  of Latter Day Saints, 48
Fundamentalist Mormonism, 48
Futuna, 95

GAA. *See* Gay Activists Alliance
  (GAA)
Gallagher, Maggie, 144–45
Gallo, Marcia M., 233
Gandy, Kim, 203
Gates, Gary J., 254
Gay Activists Alliance (GAA), 20
"The Gay Adoption Mailing List," 259
Gay American History (Katz), 6
Gay American: Struggle for Equality
  (Alsenas), 230–31
"Gay and Lesbian Adoptive and Foster
  Care Placements" (Brooks &
  Goldberg)
Gay and Lesbian Advocates and
  Defenders (GLAD), 204
Gay and lesbian civil rights issues,
  resources on
  articles, 234–36
  books, 230–34
  Internet sources, 256–59
  reports, 236–37
Gay and lesbian civil rights movement,
  16–22
  antidiscrimination laws, 20–22
  early organizations, 17–18

gay liberation movement, 19–20
Stonewall riots, 18–19
Gay and Lesbian Parents Coalition
  International, 201, 202–203
*Gay and Lesbian Rights in the United
  States* (Retter), 234
"Gay and Lesbian Rights/Sexual
  Orientation Discrimination," 257
Gay Christian Network, 260
Gay Families and the Courts (Mezey), 247
Gay father, custody rights of, 115
Gay Fathers Coalition, 202
Gay & Lesbian Advocates & Defenders
  (GLAD), 137, 146
Gay, Lesbian & Straight Education
  Network (GLSEN), 146
Gay liberation movement, 19–20
"Gay Life," 256
"A Gay Man Decries 'Gay Rights'"
  (Raimondo), 235–36
Gay Marriage: For Better or for Worse?
  (Eskridge & Spedale), 53–54, 144
"Gay Marriage: The Arguments and
  the Motives" (Bistrup), 259
Gay Marriage (Rauch), 238
Gay Parent Magazine, 240
Gay parents, 59–60
Gay Power (Eisenbach), 232
"Gay Rights," 258–59
Gay Rights and American Law (Pinello),
  258
Gay Rights and Moral Panic (Fejes),
  232–33
"Gay Rights and the Rehnquist Court"
  (Feldblum), 235
General Accounting Office
  federal benefits available to married
  couples, 63, 168–69, 267
Germany, 89, 119–20
Gerstmann, Evan, 237
Gibbon, Edward, 9
Gibbons, Jim, 130
Gikuyu women, same-sex marriage
  and, 84
Gilgamesh, 4
Gill, Martin, 185
Gill, Tim, 204
Gill Foundation, 204–205
GLAD. *See* Gay & Lesbian Advocates
  & Defenders (GLAD)

GLSEN. *See* Gay, Lesbian & Straight
   Education Network (GLSEN)
"Gods and Gays" (Schuman), 252
Goldberg, Sheryl, 249
Goldberg, Suzanne B., 230, 250
Goodridge, Hillary, 145
Goodridge, Julie, 145–46
Goodridge v. Department of Public Health,
   121–22, 137, 145, 146, 176–80
Gozemba, Patricia A., 228
Greece
   public opinion on same-sex
      marriage, 101
   same-sex relationships in ancient, 7–9
Greenland, 88, 117
Greenwood, David Valdes, 237

Hadrian, 9
Halpern v. Canada, 58
Hanson, Robert B., 128, 129
Hara, Lloyd, 113
"The Harm of Same-Sex Marriage"
   (Lipkin), 251
Haspisperch, Lord, 14
Hatred in the Hallways (Human Rights
   Watch), 236–37
Hawaii
   antidiscrimination law, 21
   court on restriction of marriage to
      opposite-sex couples, 117
   domestic partnership law, 70
   restriction of marriage to man and
      woman, 116, 118
   same-sex marriage in, 23–24
Hay, Bob, 255
Hays, Harry, 17
Head, Tom, 260
Hennepin County (Minnesota), 1–2,
   112, 134
Henry VIII, 14
Herdt, Gilbert H., 228
"Here's Your 'Traditional Marriage' "
   (Ryan), 251
Heritage Foundation, 220
Herskovits, Melville J., 84
Hertz, Frederick, 246–47
Hess, Cheryl, 191
*Hidden from History: Reclaiming the Gay
   and Lesbian Past* (Duberman et al.),
   231–32

Hide or Seek (Dobson), 143
Hinckley, Gordon B., 151
Hinsch, Bret, 5, 83, 228
"A Historical Guide to the Future of
   Marriage for Same-Sex Couples"
   (Goldberg), 230, 250
"History of Chinese Homosexuality,"
   255
"A History of Same-Sex Marriage"
   (Eskridge), 144, 229–30
History of same-sex unions, 8–11,
   82–84
   articles, 229–30
   books, 227–29
   Internet sources, 254–56
   in Judeo-Christian history, 33–36
   in Native American cultures, 48–49
   in Rome and the Middle Ages,
      36–42
   in Western culture, 45–49
Hitchens, Donna, 209
Hitchings, Emma, 250
HIV/AIDS epidemic, 22–23
   same-sex marriage and, 64
Homer, 8
Homo Domesticus (Greenwood), 237
Homosexual activity, Supreme Court
   on legality of, 114
"Homosexuality and Bisexuality"
   (Robinson), 258
"Homosexuality in India" (Vanita), 256
Honduras, ban on same-sex marriage
   and adoption in, 86
Horvat, Marian Therese, 41
"How Does Legalizing 'Same-Sex
   Marriage' Deny the True Nature
   of Marriage?," 264
Howerton, Joseph D., 113
*How the Religous Right Shaped Lesbian
   and Gay Activism* (Fetner), 233
HRC. *See* Human Rights Campaign
   (HRC)
HRW. *See* Human Rights Watch (HRW)
Hudson Valley Magazine, 156
Human Rights Campaign Founda-
   tion, 236
Human Rights Campaign (HRC),
   20, 205
Human Rights Watch (HRW), 205–206,
   236–37

Hungary
  common-law marriage rights
    for same-sex couples, 117
  registered partnerships in, 89,
    129, 130
Hyde, Henry, 65, 168

Iceland, registered partnerships
    in, 89, 117
Idaho
  divorce rate, 53
  repeal of sodomy law, 15
IE. *See* Immigration Equality (IE)
Igarzabal, Felix Gustavo de, 132
IGLHRC. *See* International Gay
    and Lesbian Human Rights
    Commission (IGLHRC)
Igwe, Leo, 255
ILGA. *See* International Lesbian
    and Gay Association (ILGA)
Iliad (Homer), 8
Illinois, repeal of sodomy law, 15
IMAPP. *See* Institute for Marriage
    and Public Policy (IMAPP)
Immigration and Naturalization
    Service (INS), 113
Immigration Equality (IE), 206
Immigration laws, Uniting American
    Families Act, 164–66
Independent Mormon
    fundamentalists, 48
India
  attitude toward same-sex
    relationships in, 85
  homosexuality in, 256
Indian Penal Code, section 377, 85
"InFocus" Web page, 263
Inheritance rights for same-sex
    couples, 115–16, 127
Initiative petition, 67–68
Innocent IV, 36
In re: Gill, 185–87
In re: Marriage Cases, 62, 127, 200
Institute for Advanced Study
    of Human Sexuality, 147
Institute for Gay and Lesbian Strategic
    Studies, 214
Institute for Marriage and Public
    Policy (IMAPP), 145, 220–21, 222
Internal Revenue Service, 115, 135

International Gay and Lesbian
    Human Rights Commission
    (IGLHRC), 207
International Lesbian and Gay
    Association (ILGA), 207
Internet sources
  arguments in favor of same-sex
    marriage, 259–61
  arguments opposed to same-sex
    marriage, 262–65
  gay and lesbian civil rights issues,
    256–59
  general reviews of same-sex
    marriage, 265–67
  on history of same-sex unions,
    254–56
"Interstate Recognition of Same-Sex
    Marriages and Civil Unions"
    (Koppelman), 250–51
Iowa
  same-sex marriage in, 67, 69, 128, 129
  Varnum v. Brien, 69, 188–190
Iowa State Supreme Court, 69, 188–90
Iran, 85
Ireland, registered partnership, 89, 130
"Is Gay Rights a Civil Rights Issue?"
    (Bond), 234
Islam
  homosexual relationships and, 257
  opposition to same-sex
    relationships, 5–6, 84–85
Israel
  court ruling on benefits for same-sex
    couples, 116–17
  public opinion on same-sex
    marriage, 102
  recognition of same-sex marriage, 125
  rights of same-sex couples in, 100
Israelites, attitudes toward same-sex
    relationships among early, 11–12
"Issue Guide: Gay Rights," 258
Italy
  court ruling on rights of same-sex
    couples, 100
  rights and duties of stable
    co-habitants, 126
  same-sex unions in, 120

Jackson, Glenda, 140
Jackson, Harry, 223

Jackson, Robert H., 188
Jamaica, 87
Jefferson County (Kentucky), 2, 112
Jersey (UK), 99
John XI, 38
Jonathan (Biblical), 12
Jones, Marjorie, 2, 22, 112
Jordan, Mark D., 228–29, 247
Juan Carlos, 89
Judeo-Christian history, same-sex
    marriage in, 33–36. *See also*
    Christianity
"Judicial Redefinition of Marriage"
    (Stewart), 252
Jurand, Sara Hoffman, 243
Just for Us, 201
Justinian, 37

Kahn, Karen, 228
Katz, Jonathan, 6, 16
Katz, Pamela S., 240
Kavanagh, Michael, 155
Kennedy, Anthony M., 121
Kennedy, D. James, 241
Kentucky, divorce rate, 53
Kenya, same-sex marriage guidelines,
    82–83
Keyes, Alan, 222
Kidwai, Saleem, 229
King, Robert, 223
Kirk, Marshall, 52
Klaus, Václav, 124
Knauer, Nancy J., 250
Knight, Tracy, 2, 22, 112
Koppelman, Andrew, 250–51
Kotulski, Davina, 237–38
Krige, Eileen Jensen, 84
Kurtz, Stanley, 244
Kutil, Kathryn, 191
Kutil and Hess v. Blake, 190–92

The Ladder, 149
Lafitau, Joseph François, 6
Lagon, Pat, 23
LaHaye, Beverly, 44, 218
LaHaye, Timothy, 218
Lambda Legal, 208
La Pook, Jon, 266
Latin America, future of same-sex
    marriage in, 102

Latter Day Church of Christ (Kingston
    clan), 48
Latvia
    public opinion on same-sex
        marriage, 101
    restriction of marriage to man
        and woman, 87, 124
Laudonnière, René Goulaine de, 6
Lavender Law conferences, 210
"Law and Civil Rights" Web site, 266
Lawrence v. Texas, 16, 232, 249–50
Laws
    antidiscrimination, 20–22
    antimiscegenation, 51, 112, 269
    canon, 14, 37
    defining marriage as between man
        and woman, 2–3, 68
    prohibition of same-sex
        relationships, 14–16
    sodomy, 14–16, 20. *See also*
        Constitutional amendments;
        individual laws
Laycock, Douglas, 247
Leahy, Patrick, 164
Lederman, Cindy, 185
Legislation, 157–68
    Alabama Marriage Protection Act,
        158–59
    An Act to End Discrimination in
        Civil Marriage and Affirm
        Religious Freedom, 166–67
    Arkansas Same-Sex Adoption Law,
        162–64
    banning same-sex marriage, 24–25
    Federal Defense of Marriage Act,
        157–58
    Federal Marriage Amendment,
        159–60
    Oregon Family Fairness Act,
        160–62
    Uniting American Families Act,
        164–66
Legislative Assembly of the Federal
    District (Mexico), 99
Leland, John, 235
Lesbian. *See* Gay and lesbian civil
    rights issues
Lesbian and Gay Studies Center, 139
Lesbian Gay Bisexual Transgender
    Project, 200

Lesbian mothers, custody rights, 112, 113
Lesbian Rights Project, 115
Lesbian/Woman (Lyon & Martin), 147, 149
Lester, Arthur, 91
Levi Strauss & Company, 116
Leviticus, passages regarding same-sex relationships, 11, 13, 15, 33, 261
Levy, Donna, 113
Lewis, John, 203
Lewis v. Harris, 133, 180–185
Liberty Counsel, 221
Liechtenstein, 89
Liette, Pierre, 6
Life partnerships, 89
Lincoln, Abraham, 50
Lipkin, Robert Justin, 251
Livingstone, Ken, 91
Li Yinhe, 5
LLEGO. *See* National Latina/o Gay, Bisexual, and Transgender Organization (LLEGO)
Log Cabin Republicans, 208
London Partnerships Register, 91
Louisiana, ban against civil unions, 70–71
Louÿs, Pierre, 17
"Love, Marriage, Romance & Women . . . in Medieval and Celtic Culture," 255
Love's Rite: Same-Sex Marriage in India and the West (Vanita), 229
Loving, Jeter, 51
Loving v. Virginia, 51, 112
Lutzer, Erwin W., 59, 241–42
Luxembourg, 89, 122, 126
Lynch, Jim, 68
Lynch, John, 130
Lynn, Roger, 135
Lyon, Phyllis, 146–47

MacLeod, Adam J., 244
Macomber, Jennifer Ehrle, 254
Madrid (Spain), 88, 98
Madsen, Hunter, 52
Maier, Bill, 242
Maine
    An Act to End Discrimination in Civil Marriage and Affirm Religious Freedom, 166–67

domestic partnership law, 70
same-sex marriage in, 68, 129, 130
Making Babies (Shanley), 248
Making Gay History (Marcus), 233
Making It Legal (Hertz & Doskow), 246–47
Malone, Richard, 147–48
The Manifesto, 47
Marcus, Eric, 233
Marino-Thomas, Cathy, 266
Marjorie Jones et al., Appellants v. James Hallahan, Clerk of the Jefferson County Court, Appellee, 2
Marquette, Jacques, 6
Marriage
    Boston, 44
    Christian model of, 35–36
    complex, 46
    DOMA definition of, 158
    as economic transaction, 42
    inequality of sexes in traditional, 43–44
    laws defining as between man and woman, 2–3
    nontraditional, in Western culture, 45–49
    polygynous, 81
    same-sex marriage and procreation as goal of, 55–58
    "traditional," 42–45
    trends in, 53–54. *See also* Same-sex marriage
Marriage, a History (Coontz), 228
Marriage Affirmation and Protection Amendment, 262–63
Marriage Equality New York, 266
Marriage Equality USA (MEUSA), 208–209
Marriage (Gender Clarification) Amendment Bill, 95
Marriage Law Project (MLP), 221–22
Marriage on Trial (Stanton & Maier), 242
Marriage Protection Sunday, 219
Marriage rate, Denmark, 196
Marriage Under Fire (Dobson), 241, 260
"Marriage Under Fire" (Dobson), 263
Married couples, federal benefits available to, 63, 168–69, 267
Martin, Del, 146, 148–49
Martin, James, 149

Martin, Kendra, 149
Maryland
    ban on same-sex marriage, 112, 128
    domestic partnerships in, 127
    recognition of same-sex marriages
        from other states, 67
Maryland Supreme Court, on same-sex
    marriage, 62
Mary (Queen), 14
Massachusetts
    antidiscrimination law, 21
    court ruling on same-sex marriage,
        121–22, 137, 145, 146, 176–180, 246
    divorce rate, 53, 197–98
    same-sex marriage and divorce rate
        in, 53
    same-sex marriage in, 67, 69, 122,
        123, 124–25, 126, 194
Massachusetts Bay Colony, sodomy
    law, 15
Massachusetts Supreme Judicial Court,
    69, 176–80
Mass Equality, 146
Matrimonial Causes Act, 91
Mattachine Foundation (Mattachine
    Society), 17, 231
Matter of Cooper, 115–16
Mauritania, 85
McCambley, Kirk, 66
McConnell, James, 112
McConnell, Michael, 1–2, 22, 134, 135
    biographical sketch, 149–50
McCord, David, 2, 22
McFarlane, J. D., 2
McGreevey, James E., 134
McLachlin, Beverly, 94
Meciar, Vladimir, 118
"Media Ignore Impending Collision"
    (Fitzpatrick), 257
Melillo, Joseph, 23
Merin, Yuval, 229
Mesopotamia, same-sex relationships
    in, 4
MEUSA. *See* Marriage Equality USA
    (MEUSA)
Mexico, same-sex unions in, 99
Mexico City
    civil unions in, 125
    same-sex marriage and adoption
        in, 131

Mezey, Susan, 247
Michalski, Peter A., 118
Michigan
    civil rights granted to lesbians
        and gay men, 20
    custody rights of lesbian mothers, 113
    employment benefits for same-sex
        couples, 127
Middle Ages
    prohibition of same-sex
        relationships in, 14
    same-sex marriage in, 38–42
Miike, Lawrence, 23
Military, "don't ask, don't tell" policy,
    20, 208, 213
Military Freedom Project, 20
Miller, Marshall, 225
Ming Dynasty, 112
Miscegenation, 51
Mitchell, Camille, 112
Mlamblo-Ngcuka, Phumzile, 93
MLP. *See* Marriage Law Project (MLP)
Model Penal Code, 15
Mohammed, 5
Monserrate, Hiram, 66
Monson, Thomas S., 150–51
Montana, employment benefits
    for same-sex couples, 123
Moody Church, 59
*Moral Argument, Religion and Same-Sex
    Marriage* (Babst et al.), 237
Mormon church. *See* Church of Jesus
    Christ of Latter-day Saints
    (Mormons)
Mormon fundamentalism, 48
Mother Ann Lee, 45
Moyne de Morgues, Jacques le, 6
Mucciaroni, Gary, 233–34
Museveni, Yoweri, 124
Musgrave, Marilyn, 151–52, 159
Myers, David G., 238

NACHO. *See* North American
    Conference of Homophile
    Organizations (NACHO)
Nadler, Jerry, 152–53, 164
Naomi (Biblical), 12
Nashville Declaration, 219
National Center for Lesbian Rights
    (NCLR), 115, 209, 257

National Conference of State
Legislatures, 267
National Defense of Marriage Act, 25
National Family Legal Foundation, 215
National Freedom to Marry Day, 208
National Front, 56
National Gay and Lesbian Task Force
(NGLTF), 20, 209–10
National Gay Task Force, 20
National Latina/o Gay, Bisexual, and
Transgender Organization
(LLEGO), 214
National Law Journal, 141
National Lesbian and Gay Law
Association (NLGLA), 210
National Marriage Project (NMP),
225–26
National Organization for Marriage
(NOM), 145, 222
National Organization for Women
(NOW), 210–11, 218
National Planning Conference of
Homophile Organizations
(NPCHO), 18
Native Americans. *See* American
Indians
"Naturalized Virtue Ethics and Same-
Sex Love" (Brown), 239
Natural law, 240, 244
"Natural Law, Same-Sex Marriage,
and the Politics of Virtue"
(Chartier), 240
Navarre (Spain), 88, 98
NCLR. *See* National Center for Lesbian
Rights (NCLR)
Nebraska, constitutional amendment
banning legal recognition of
same-sex unions, 119
Neill, James, 229
Nelson, Gerald R., 1
Nepal
rights of same-sex couples in, 100
same-sex marriage in, 128
Nero, 8–9, 111
Netherlands
number of same-sex couples in
legally recognized relation-
ships, 195
public opinion on same-sex
marriage, 101

registered partnerships in, 87, 118
same-sex and opposite-sex marriage
data, 195–96
same-sex common-law marriage
in, 113–14
same-sex marriage in, 120, 246
Netherlands Antilles, 99
Nevada, domestic partnerships in,
70, 130
New Caledonia, 95
Newcombe, Jerry, 241
New England Marriage Campaign, 204
New Family Social (NFS), 211
New Hampshire
civil unions in, 70, 127
same-sex adoption in, 119
same-sex marriage in, 67, 68, 130
New Jersey
antidiscrimination law, 21
civil union law, 70
court on same-sex adoption, 118
court on same-sex unions, 125
Lewis v. Harris, 180–85
same-sex marriage in, 131
New natural law, 240
Newsom, Gavin, 147
New South Wales, same-sex adoption
report, 169–72
New York
debate over same-sex marriage
in Senate, 261
recognition of same-sex marriage
by, 67
same-sex marriage in, 125, 252–53
New York City, recognition of same-sex
marriage, 123
New York Court of Appeals, 115
"New York's Heroes," 261
New York Supreme Court, 115
New York Times, 145
New Zealand
civil unions in, 95, 123
common-law marriage rights
for same-sex couples, 119
number of same-sex couples in
legally recognized relationships,
195
NFS. *See* New Family Social (NFS)
NGLTF. *See* National Gay and Lesbian
Task Force (NGLTF)

Nielsen/Naylor Group, 48
Nigeria
    penalty for same-sex relationships,
        85, 129
    restriction of marriage to opposite-
        sex couples, 87, 129
    same-sex marriage in, 255
Njambi, Wairimu, 84
NLGLA. *See* National Lesbian and Gay
    Law Association (NLGLA)
NMP. *See* National Marriage Project
    (NMP)
Nobel, Elaine, 20–21
NOM. *See* National Organization for
    Marriage (NOM)
Nonmarital births, same-sex
    partnerships and trends in, 54
"Nordic Bliss? Scandinavian
    Registered Partnerships and the
    Same-Sex Marriage Debate"
    (Eskridge et al.), 265
North American Conference of
    Homophile Organizations
    (NACHO), 18
Northern Ireland
    number of same-sex couples
        in legally recognized
        relationships, 195
    same-sex marriage in, 91
Northstar Asset Management, Inc., 146
Northwest Territories (Canada), 94
Norway
    common-law marriage rights
        for same-sex couples, 115
    marriage laws, 122
    number of same-sex couples in legally
        recognized relationships, 195
    registered partnerships in, 116
    same-sex marriage in, 88, 127
NOW. *See* National Organization
    for Women (NOW)
Noyes, John Humphrey, 45–46
NPCHO. *See* National Planning
    Conference of Homophile
    Organizations (NPCHO)
Nullity of Marriage Act 1971, 90–91
Nunavut (Canada), 94

Obama, Barack, 208
O'Brien, William, 84

OFC. *See* Our Family Coalition (OFC)
Offences Against the Person Act, 14
"Office for Same-Gender Union,"
    39–40
O'Grair, Scot, 54, 266
Oklahoma, divorce rate in, 53
Olson, Theodore B., 136, 153–54, 261
Oneida community, 45–46
Order on Intervenor's Plea to the
    Jurisdiction, 192–94
Oregon, domestic partnerships in,
    70, 127
Oregon Family Fairness Act, 160–62
Organizations
    in favor of same-sex marriage,
        199–215
    with interest in marriage, who are
        neutral about same-sex marriage,
        224–26
    opposed to same-sex marriage,
        215–24
*The Origins and Role of Same-Sex
    Relations in Human Societies*
    (Neill), 229
Our Family Coalition (OFC), 211–12
OutGiving, 204
*Outrage: How Gay Activists and Liberal
    Judges Are Trashing Democracy to
    Redefine Marriage* (Sprigg), 242
Outrage (film), 67
"Overruling *Dred Scott*" (Burt), 239

Pakistan, 85
Palin, Sarah, 126
Pareja, Francisco de, 6
Parents, Families & Friends of Lesbians
    & Gays (PFLAG), 212
Passions of the Cut Sleeve (Hinsch), 5,
    83, 228
Paterson, David, 154–55
Patroclus, 8
Pennsylvania, refusal of divorce for
    two men in common-law
    marriage, 114
"Pennsylvania Nixes Second-Parent
    Adoptions for Same-Sex
    Couples" (Jurand), 243
Perfectionism, 46
Perry v. Schwarzenegger, 136, 140, 261
Peterson, C. Donald, 36

PFLAG. *See* Parents, Families &
Friends of Lesbians & Gays
(PFLAG)
Pierceson, Jason, 237
Pinello, Daniel R., 247, 257–58
Poland
court rulings and same-sex
unions, 100
public opinion on same-sex
marriage, 101, 102
Polikoff, Nancy D., 238, 247–48
*Political Institutions and Lesbian and Gay
Rights in the United States and
Canada* (Smith), 234
"The Politics of Same-Sex Marriage
Politics" (Franke), 249–50
Polyandry, 81
legalization of same-sex marriage
and, 54, 55
Polygamy, 81
legalization of same-sex marriage
and, 54–55
Mormons and, 46–48
Polygyny, 81–82
Poritz, Deborah T., 184
Portugal
court rulings and same-sex
unions, 100
public opinion on same-sex
marriage, 101
registered partnerships in, 120
same-sex marriage in, 89, 90, 128,
131, 132
"Power and Sexuality in the Middle
East" (Dunne), 257
Pratt, Orson, 47
Pregil, Antoinette, 23
Prejean, Carrie, 66
Prince Edward Island, 94
Print resources, 227–54
arguments in favor of same-sex
marriage, 237–41
arguments opposed to same-sex
marriage, 241–45
gay and lesbian civil rights issues,
230–37
general reviews of same-sex
marriage and adoption, 245–54
history of same-sex unions, 227–30
Privacy Project, 20

Procreation
marriage and, 42
same-sex marriage and, 55–58
Prodi, Romano, 126
Proposition 8, 31, 128, 129, 136, 140, 153
court case on, 71–72
Mormon church and, 150–51, 217–18
"Protecting Marriage to Protect
Children" (Blankenhorn), 262
Public Agenda, 258
Public opinion
on civil unions and domestic
partnerships, 71
on same-sex marriage, 32, 71,
100–102, 266
Publisher's Weekly, 147
Punishments, for homosexual
behavior, 3–4

Quayle, Dan, 145
"Queer Resources Directory," 258

Raimondo, Justin, 235–36
Rational basis standard, 62–63
Rauch, Jonathan, 238, 248–49
Razú, David, 99
"Reaffirming Marriage" (Coolidge &
Duncan), 243
Reagan, Ronald, 136
"Reality Makes Gay Marriage Debate
Obsolete" (Dvorak), 265
Reciprocal beneficiaries, 24
"A Reconciliation on Gay Marriage"
(Blankenhorn & Rauch), 248–49
"Reconsidering Homosexuality and
the Bible," 256
Referendum, 67–68
Registered life partnerships, 119–20
Registered partnerships, 87–88, 89,
130, 265
chronology of, 115, 116, 117, 118, 119,
120, 123, 124, 129. *See also* Civil
unions; Domestic partnerships
Rehnquist, William H., 140, 235
Reid, Eric, 244
Rekers, George Alan, 66, 132
Religious ceremonies, marriage
and, 61, 62
Renew America, 222
Rent control, same-sex couples and, 115

Reports, 168–73
  adoption by same-sex couples,
    169–72
  European Parliament Resolution of
    14 January 2009 on the Situation
    of Fundamental Rights in the
    European Union, 172–73
  gay and lesbian civil rights issues,
    236–37
  reviews of same-sex marriage and
    adoption, 253–54
  U.S. General Accounting Office,
    168–69
Research Fund for Lesbian and Gay
    Studies, 139
Resources
  nonprint, 254–67
  print, 227–54
Respect for Marriage Act, 136, 152
Responsible Wealth, 146
Retter, Yolanda, 234
Reuniting Families Act, 202
Rhode Island, recognition of same-sex
    marriages, 67, 126
Righteous Branch of the Church of Jesus
    Christ of Latter-day Saints, 48
Rights and duties of stable
    co-habitants, 126
Riley, Bob C., 154
The Rise of a Gay and Lesbian Movement
    (Adam), 230
Ritualized Homosexuality in Melanesia
    (Herdt), 228
Robinson, Bruce A., 258
Robinson, Iris, 66
Rodrigues, Tammy, 23
Roman Catholic Church
  marriage as sacrament in, 36
  same-sex marriage guidelines in
    Kenya, 82–83
  same-sex relationships among
    clergy, 38–40
  same-sex unions in Middle Ages
    and, 37–40, 41–42
  sex scandal, 67
Rome, same-sex marriage in ancient,
    7–9, 36–37, 111, 254
Romney, Mitt, 69
Roney, Paul, 140
Rorex, Clela, 2, 254

Rosenbaum, Stuart E., 246
Roste, Vaughn, 261
Rudolph I, 14
Russia, 100, 131
Rutgers University, 225
Ruth (Biblical), 12
Ryan, Patrick J., 251

Sagar, Tracey, 250
Saint Paul, 36
Samar, Vincent J., 251
Same Sex, Different Politics
    (Mucciaroni), 233–34
Same-sex adoption, 114, 157
  in Alaska, 114
  in Arkansas, 162–64
  ban in Florida, 113, 185–87
  in Belgium, 125
  Bottoms v. Bottoms, 117
  constitutional amendments to ban,
    86–87
  E .B. v. France, 174–76
  general reviews of, 245–254
  Kutil and Hess v. Blake, 190–192
  in Mexico City, 131
  in New Hampshire, 119
  New Jersey ruling on, 118
  In re: Gill, 185–87
  studies of, 169–72, 240
  in Sweden, 120
Same-sex couples
  defined as family, 115
  legal rights of, 100
  numbers in legally recognized
    relationships, 195
"Same-Sex Couples: Defining Marriage
    in the Twenty-first Century,"
    251–52
Same-Sex Love in India (Vanita &
    Kidwai), 229
Same-sex marriage
  alternatives to, 70–71, 87–88, 89–89
  arguments in favor of, 61–67,
    237–41, 259–61
  arguments opposed to, 49–61,
    241–45, 262–65
  child rearing and, 58–60
  chronology, 111–32
  early attempts to obtain marriage
    licenses in United States, 1–2

equality under the law provisions and, 61
future of, 102–103
future of, in United States, 71–72
general reviews of, 245–54, 265–67
in Hawaii, 23–24
historical and cross-cultural existence of, 8–11
historical perspective on, 82–84
in Judeo-Christian history, 33–36
legalization process, 67–68
in Native American cultures, 48–49
opposition to, 84–87
organizations in favor, 199–215
organizations opposed, 215–24
organizations with interest in marriage, but neutrality on same-sex marriage, 224–26
proponents' argument for, 31–32
public opinion on, 100–102
recognition of, 113
in Rome and the Middle Ages, 36–42
status in United States, 67–69
support for, 87–100
as threat to traditional family, 51–54
in United States, 22–25
"Same-Sex Marriage: A Selective Bibliography of the Legal Literature" (Axel-Lute), 265
"Same-Sex Marriage: A Timeline," 255–56
"Same-Sex Marriage, Civil Unions and Domestic Partnerships," 267
"Same-Sex Marriage and Federalism" (Knauer), 250
Same-Sex Marriage and Religious Liberty (Laycock), 247
Same-Sex Marriage (Andryszewski), 245
"Same-Sex Marriage and Slippery Slopes" (Volokh), 241
Same-Sex Marriage and the Constitution (Gerstmann), 237
Same-Sex Marriage (Baird & Rosenbaum), 246
Same-sex marriage data
Belgium, 196, 197
Massachusetts, 194
Netherlands, 195–96
Same-Sex Marriages Pros and Cons, 266

Same-Sex Marriage (Staver), 242
Same-Sex Marriage (Sullivan), 248
Same-sex relationships
attitudes toward in Western culture, 11–14
historical and cross-cultural existence of, 3–11
in history, 3–4
Islam and, 84–85
Same-Sex Unions in Premodern Europe (Boswell), 39, 41, 138, 227–28
San Bernardino (California), 115
Sandoval County (New Mexico), 122
Sanford, Mark, 65
Saudi Arabia, 85
Save Our Children, 56
Scanzoni, Letha Dawson, 238
"Scholars' Conference on Same-Sex Marriage and Religious Liberty," 253
School of the Prophets, 48
Schuler, Marilyn Neoma. *See* Musgrave, Marilyn
Schuman, Ben, 252
Scotland
number of same-sex couples in legally recognized relationships, 195
same-sex marriage in, 91
"The Search for Moral Neutrality in Same-Sex Marriage Decisions" (MacLeod), 244
Second-parent adoptions, 115, 243
Secular law, prohibition of same-sex relationships in, 14
Sekulow, Jay Alan, 49–50, 264
Serbia, 87
Sergius III, 38
"Serious Study of Leviticus," 261
Sexual inequality, in traditional marriage, 43–44
Sexual Offences Act, 14
Sexual orientation, European Parliament resolution on fundamental rights and, 172–73
Sexual Politics, Sexual Communities (D'Emilio), 231
"Shade of Gay" (Leland), 235
Shakers, 45
Shanley, Mary L., 248
Sheldon, Louis P., 223

Sherrill, Kenneth, 236
Shows, Ronnie, 151
Silva, Anibal Cavaco, 90, 132
Silver, James, 223
Silver, Nate, 267
Silverman, Jennifer, 240–41
Singer, John F., 113
Singer v. Hara, 113
Sinkford, William G., 203
Skolnick, Arlene S., 82
Skolnick, Jerome H., 82
Slavery, 50–51
Slippery-slope argument, 54
Slovakia, 118
Slovenia
  court rulings and same-sex
    unions, 100
  family code, 131
  registered partnerships in, 89, 123
  same-sex marriage in, 125
Smith, Joseph, 46–47
Smith, Miriam, 234
Smith, Rebecca, 114
Social Investment Forum, 146
Society for Human Rights, 17
Socrates, Jose, 90
Sodom and Gomorrah story, 11, 13
Sodomy laws
  repeal of, 15–16, 20
  in United States, 14–16, 232
Solot, Dorian, 225
Somerville, Margaret A., 56, 263–64
Sommerville, Margaret, 244–45
The Songs of Bilitis, 17
Sosman, Martha B., 179–80
Souder, Mark, 66, 132
South Africa
  common-law marriage rights for
    same-sex couples, 119
  court rulings and same-sex
    unions, 100
  same-sex marriage in, 93, 125–26
South America, same-sex unions in,
  95–96
Southern Baptist Convention, Ethics &
  Religious Liberty Commission,
  218–19
Spain
  same-sex marriage in, 88–89, 123–24
  same-sex unions in, 98

Spedale, Darren R., 53–54, 265
Spina, Francis X., 179
Spiritual brotherhood, 40
Spitzer, Eliot, 154, 155
Spontaneous Celebrations, 146
Spotlight (television program), 66
Spouse, defined, 158
Sprigg, Peter, 242
Srivastav, Raman, 145
Stable union, 98
Stable union of a couple, 89
Stamper, Jacqueline, 113
Stand4Marriage, 223
Stanton, Glenn T., 242
States
  antidiscrimination law, 21
  defense of marriage acts, 25, 57, 117
  equality under the law provisions
    and same-sex marriage, 61–62
  individual marriage requirements,
    61–62
  legalization of same-sex marriage,
    67–68
  legislation banning same-sex
    marriage, 24–25, 68
Statute Law Amendment
  (Relationships) Act 2001, 97
Statute Law Further Amendment
  (Relationships) Act 2001, 97
Staver, Mathew D., 242
Stewart, Monte Neil, 252
Stonewall Democrats, 213
Stonewall (Duberman), 231
Stonewall (organization), 212–13
Stonewall riots, 18–19
Strict scrutiny standard, 62–63
*The Struggle over Gay, Lesbian, and
  Bisexual Rights* (Dugan), 232
Subnational entities, same-sex unions
  and, 96–98
Sudan, 85
Sullivan, Andrew, 248
Sullivan, Anthony, 113
Supreme Court
  decline of case on same-sex
    marriage, 123
  on legality of homosexual activity,
    16, 114
  Loving v. Virginia, 112
Susan B. Anthony List, 152

Sweden
common-law marriage rights and
same-sex couples, 115
public opinion on same-sex
marriage, 101
registered partnerships, 117
same-sex adoption in, 120
same-sex marriage in, 88, 129
Swedish Lutheran Church, same-sex
marriage and, 130
Switzerland, 89, 123

Taliaferro, Dorothy L., 149
Tasmania (Australia), 97–98
Tasmanian Domestic Partnerships 2003
Act, 97
"Ten Really Bad Arguments against
Same-Sex Marriage" (Head), 260
"Ten Reasons Why Christians Should
Support Same-Sex Marriage"
(Roste), 261
"Testimony of Jay Alan Sekulow ...,"
264
Texas, divorce and recognition of
same-sex marriage, 192–94
*Their World: A Study of Homosexuality in
China* (Li Yinhe), 5
Theodosian Code, 13–14, 37, 111
Theodosius II, 13
Third gender, among American
Indians, 7
"The Threat to Marriage from the
Courts" (Republican Policy
Committee), 244
"Throwing Down the International
Gauntlet" (Samar), 251
Thurmond, Strom, 65
"The Tide in Favour of Equality"
(Wright), 253
Tierra del Fuego (Argentina), 131
Time magazine, 137
"Top 10 Reasons to Support the
Marriage Affirmation and
Protection Amendment," 262–63
"Traditional" marriage, 31, 42–45
Traditional Values Coalition, 223
"Tradition of Same Gender Marriage
in Igboland" (Leo), 255
True and Living Church of Jesus Christ
of Saints of the Last Days, 48

"The Truth about Same-Sex
'Marriage,'" 262
The Truth about Same-Sex Marriage
(Lutzer), 59, 241–42

Uganda
ban on same-sex marriage/
domestic partnerships, 87, 124
penalties for same-sex behavior,
85–86
Unid@s, the National Latina/o
Lesbian, Gay, Bisexual &
Transgender Human Rights
Organization, 214
United Arab Emirates, 85
United for a Fair Economy, 146
United Kingdom
civil partnerships in, 89, 122, 124
court rulings and same-sex
unions, 100
legality of same-sex relationships in,
90–93
number of civil partnerships formed
in, 92–93
number of same-sex couples in
legally recognized relationships,
195
public opinion on same-sex
marriage, 102. *See also* England
United States
divorce rates, by state, 197–98
future of same-sex marriage in,
71–72
public opinion on same-sex
relationships/marriage, 32, 102
same-sex marriage in, 22–25, 67–69
sodomy laws, 14–16, 20
United States Conference of Catholic
Bishops (USCCB), 223–24
United States Conference of Catholics
Bishops (USCCB), 264
Uniting American Families Act, 152,
164–66, 206
University of Virginia, 226
Unregistered cohabitation, 87
Uranga, Enoé, 99
Uruguay
civil unions in, 95–96
cohabitation union in, 127
same-sex marriage in, 102

U.S. Civil Service Commission, 20
U.S. Constitution, equality under the
    law provisions and same-sex
    marriage, 61
USCCB. *See* United States Conference
    of Catholic Bishops (USCCB)
Utah, ban on same-sex marriage, 11, 25

Valencia (Spain), 88, 98
Valentinian III, 13
Vanita, Ruth, 229, 256
Varnell, Joe, 120
Varnum v. Brien, 188–90
Vautour, Anne, 120
Vautour, Elaine, 120
Venezuela, 103
Vermont
    antidiscrimination law, 21
    civil unions in, 70, 119
    court ruling on same-sex marriage,
        119
    same-sex marriage in, 67, 68, 129
Vetrella, Jeffrey J., 264–65
Victoria (Australia), domestic
    partnerships, 97–98
Vike-Freiberga, Vaira, 124
Vincus, Martha, 231
Virginia
    ban on same-sex marriage, 113
    sodomy law, 15
Vitter, David, 65
Voices of Equality program, 203
Volokh, Eugene, 55, 241

Wafer, Dale, 223
Wales, number of same-sex couples
    in legally recognized relation-
    ships, 195
Walker, Jonathan P., 256
Walker, Vaughn, 72
Wallace, Artie, 115
Wallace, Shawn, 115
Wallis, 95
Wardle, Lynn D., 252
Washington State
    domestic partnerships in, 70, 127
    everything-but-marriage bill, 129, 130
    same-sex marriage in, 113
Washington State Supreme Court, on
    state defense of marriage act, 57

Weekly Standard, 145
Weeks, Jeffrey, 234
Weinfeld, Edward, 144
Weiser, Jay, 252–53
West, Jason, 155–56
Western culture
    attitudes toward same-sex
        relationships, 11–14
    nontraditional marriage in, 45–49
Western Europe, support for same-sex
    marriage in, 87–93
What God Has Joined Together? (Myers &
    Scanzoni), 238
"What I Believe," 260
"What Is Marriage?" (Forbes), 230
"What Is Marriage? A Native
    American View" (Forbes), 266
"What Made Stonewall Different"
    (Carter), 234–35
"What Same-Sex 'Marriage' Has
    Done to Massachusetts"
    (Camenker), 262
What's Wrong with Same-Sex Marriage?
    (Kennedy & Newcombe), 241
When Gay People Get Married (Badgett),
    245–46
Why Marriage? (Chauncey), 246
Why Marriage Matters (Wolfson),
    238–39
"Why the Romans Are Important
    in the Debate about Gay
    Marriage," 254
*Why You Should Give a Damn about Gay
    Marriage* (Kotulski), 237–38
Wilkins, Richard G., 245
William of Adam, 6
Williams, Walter L., 234
Williams Institute at the University of
    California at Los Angeles School
    of Law, 214–15
Winn, Peter, 52
Wisconsin
    antidiscrimination law, 21
    domestic partnerships in, 70, 130
Wolfson, Evan, 203, 238–39
Women, in same-sex marriage
    in Africa, 83–84
Woodruff, Wilford, 47
Woolley, Lorin C., 48
World Congress of Families IV, 52

"A World History of Homosexuality"
    (Hay), 255
Wrecking amendment, 92
Wriggins, Jennifer, 137
Wright, Wade K., 253

Yale Human Relations Files, 3

Yemen, 85
Young, Brigham, 47
Ytterberg, Hans, 265

Zambia, 87
Zamora, David, 2, 22
Zapatero, José Luis Rodrìguez, 89

About the Author

David E. Newton holds an associate's degree in science from Grand Rapids (Michigan) Junior College, a BA in chemistry (with high distinction), an MA in education from the University of Michigan, and an EdD in science education from Harvard University. He is the author of more than 400 textbooks, encyclopedias, resource books, research manuals, laboratory manuals, trade books, and other educational materials. He taught mathematics, chemistry, and physical science in Grand Rapids, Michigan, for 13 years; was professor of chemistry and physics at Salem State College in Massachusetts for 15 years; and was adjunct professor in the College of Professional Studies at the University of San Francisco for 10 years. Previous books for ABC-CLIO include *Global Warming* (1993), *Gay and Lesbian Rights—A Resource Handbook* (1994, 2009), *The Ozone Dilemma* (1995), *Violence and the Mass Media* (1996), *Environmental Justice* (1996, 2009), *Encyclopedia of Cryptology* (1997), *Social Issues in Science and Technology: An Encyclopedia* (1999), *DNA Technology* (2009), and *Sexual Health* (2010). Other recent books include *Physics: Oryx Frontiers of Science Series* (2000), *Sick!* (4 volumes; 2000), *Science, Technology, and Society: The Impact of Science in the 19th Century* (2 volumes; 2001), *Encyclopedia of Fire* (2002), *Molecular Nanotechnology: Oryx Frontiers of Science Series* (2002), *Encyclopedia of Water* (2003), *Encyclopedia of Air* (2004), *The New Chemistry* (6 volumes; 2007), *Nuclear Power* (2005), *Stem Cell Research* (2006), *Latinos in the Sciences, Math, and Professions* (2007), and *DNA Evidence and Forensic Science* (2008). He has also been an updating and consulting editor on a number of books and reference works for Gale/Cengage, including *Chemical Compounds* (2005), *Chemical Elements* (2006), *Encyclopedia of Endangered Species* (2006), *World of Mathematics* (2006), *World of Chemistry* (2006), *World of Health* (2006),

UXL Encyclopedia of Science (2007), *Alternative Medicine* (2008), *Grzimek's Animal Life Encyclopedia* (2009), *Community Health* (2009), *Genetic Medicine* (2009), and Gale Online Science Resource Center (2010).